Applied Data
Analytic Techniques for
Turning Points Research

Multivariate Applications Series

Sponsored by the Society of Multivariate Psychology, the goal of this series is to apply complex statistical methods to significant social or behavioral issues, in such a way so as to be accessible to a nontechnical-oriented readership (e.g., nonmethodological researchers, teachers, students, government personnel, practitioners, and other professionals). Applications from a variety of disciplines such as psychology, public health, sociology, education, and business are welcome. Books can be single- or multiple-authored or edited volumes that (1) demonstrate the application of a variety of multivariate methods to a single, major area of research; (2) describe a multivariate procedure or framework that could be applied to a number of research areas; or (3) present a variety of perspectives on a controversial topic of interest to applied multivariate researchers.

There are currently 13 books in the series:

- *What if there were no significance tests?* co-edited by Lisa L. Harlow, Stanley A. Mulaik, and James H. Steiger (1997).
- *Structural Equation Modeling with LISREL, PRELIS, and SIMPLIS: Basic Concepts, Applications, and Programming,* written by Barbara M. Byrne (1998).
- *Multivariate Applications in Substance Use Research: New Methods for New Questions,* co-edited by Jennifer S. Rose, Laurie Chassin, Clark C. Presson, and Steven J. Sherman (2000).
- *Item Response Theory for Psychologists,* co-authored by Susan E. Embretson and Steven P. Reise (2000).
- *Structural Equation Modeling with AMOS: Basic Concepts, Applications, and Programming,* written by Barbara M. Byrne (2001).
- *Conducting Meta-Analysis Using SAS,* written by Winfred Arthur, Jr., Winston Bennett, Jr., and Allen I. Huffcutt (2001).
- *Modeling Intraindividual Variability with Repeated Measures Data: Methods and Applications,* co-edited by D. S. Moskowitz and Scott L. Hershberger (2002).
- *Multilevel Modeling: Methodological Advances, Issues, and Applications,* co-edited by Steven P. Reise and Naihua Duan (2003).
- *The Essence of Multivariate Thinking: Basic Themes and Methods,* written by Lisa Harlow (2005).
- *Contemporary Psychometrics: A Festschrift for Roderick P. McDonald,* co-edited by Albert Maydeu-Olivares and John J. McArdle (2005).
- *Structural Equation Modeling with EQS: Basic Concepts, Applications, and Programming, Second Edition,* written by Barbara M. Byrne (2006).
- *Introduction to Statistical Mediation Analysis,* written by David P. MacKinnon (2008).
- *Applied Data Analytic Techniques for Turning Points Research,* edited by Patricia Cohen (2008).

Anyone wishing to submit a book proposal should send the following; (1) author/title; (2) timeline including completion date; (3) brief overview of the book's focus, including table of contents, and, ideally, a sample chapter (or more); (4) a brief description competing publications; and (5) targeted audiences.

For more information, please contact the series editor, Lisa Harlow, at Department of Psychology, University of Rhode Island, 10 Chafee Road, Suite 8, Kingston, RI 02881–0808; Phone (401) 874–4242; Fax (401) 874–5562; or e-mail LHarlow@uri.edu. Information may also be obtained from members of the advisory board: Leona Aiken (Arizona State University), Gwyneth Boodoo (Educational Testing Services), Barbara M. Byrne (University of Ottawa), Patrick Curran (University of North Carolina), Scott E. Maxwell (University of Notre Dame), David Rindskopf (City University of New York), Liora Schmelkin (Hofstra University), and Stephen West (Arizona State University).

Applied Data Analytic Techniques for Turning Points Research

Edited by
Patricia Cohen

Routledge
Taylor & Francis Group
New York   London

For more information about this book, please visit: www.researchmethodsarena.com <http://www.researchmethodsarena.com/>

Routledge
Taylor & Francis Group
270 Madison Avenue
New York, NY 10016

Routledge
Taylor & Francis Group
2 Park Square
Milton Park, Abingdon
Oxon OX14 4RN

© 2008 by Taylor & Francis Group, LLC
Routledge is an imprint of Taylor & Francis Group, an Informa business

Printed in the United States of America on acid-free paper
10 9 8 7 6 5 4 3 2 1

International Standard Book Number-13: 978-0-8058-5452-7 (Softcover) 978-0-8058-5451-0 (Hardcover)

Library of Congress Cataloging-in-Publication Data

Applied data analytic techniques for turning points research / editor, Patricia Cohen.
    p. cm. -- (Multivariate applications series)
    Includes bibliographical references and index.
    ISBN 978-0-8058-5452-7 (alk. paper) -- ISBN 978-0-8058-5451-0 (alk. paper) 1.
    Change (Psychology)--Statistical methods. 2. Psychology--Statistical methods. 3.
    Longitudinal method. I. Cohen, Patricia.

BF637.C4A67 2008
155.2'50727--dc22   2007049963

Visit the Taylor & Francis Web site at
http://www.taylorandfrancis.com

and the Psychology Press Web site at
http://www.psypress.com

Contents

Preface vii

Chapter 1   The origins of this book 1
Patricia Cohen

Chapter 2   The interrelationship of temporally distinct risk
             markers and the transition from childhood physical
             aggression to adolescent violent delinquency 17
Daniel S. Nagin, Ted Barker, Eric Lacourse, and Richard E. Tremblay

Chapter 3   Estimating time-varying causes and outcomes, with
             application to incarceration and crime 37
Christopher Wimer, Robert J. Sampson, and John H. Laub

Chapter 4   Turning points in family contact during emerging
             adulthood 61
David Rindskopf and Joel R. Sneed

Chapter 5   Testing turning points using latest growth curve
             models: *Competing models of substance abuse
             and desistance in young adulthood* 81
Andrea M. Hussong, Patrick J. Curran, Terrie E. Moffitt, and Avshalom Caspi

Chapter 6   Modeling age-based turning points in longitudinal
             life-span growth curves of cognition 105
John J. McArdle and Lijuan Wang

Chapter 7   Bereavement as a potential turning point: *Modeling between-person variability in adjustment to conjugal loss*...129
Christopher T. Burke, Patrick E. Shrout, and Niall Bolger

Chapter 8   Application of change point theory to modeling state-related activity in fMRI...............................149
Martin A. Lindquist and Tor D. Wager

Chapter 9   Using an econometric model of change points to locate turning points in individual time series.............183
Henian Chen, Patricia Cohen, and Kathy Gordon

Chapter 10   Developmental structural change in the maturity of role assumption..195
Patricia Cohen, Kathy Gordon, Stephanie Kasen, and Henian Chen

Appendix 1   Computer programs for change-point analysis 215

Appendix 2   Equivalent forms of the Level 1 equation for the bereavement model in Chapter 7....................................219

Appendix 3A   The variance of the EWMA statistic assuming ARMA (1,1) noise...221

Appendix 3B   Maximum likelihood estimation of change point 227

Appendix 3C   EM algorithm for Gaussian mixture model...............231

Appendix 3D   Estimating variance components using restricted maximum likelihood 233

Author Index 235

Subject Index 241

Preface

This innovative volume demonstrates the use of a range of statistical approaches to help researchers identify "turning points" in real data. Turning points are defined as a change in direction and/or magnitude of one or more variables in long- or short-term studies. The hope is that statistically identifying "turning points" will help researchers more easily identify another variable or event that tends to precede such a point, increasing one's chance of predicting the future. A variety of research design and data analysis techniques are reviewed including some new approaches and others that are adaptations of techniques used in a variety of fields. As such, the book will appeal to a variety of researchers including:

- Developmental researchers interested in identifying factors precipitating turning points at various life span stages
- Medical or substance abuse researchers looking for turning points in disease or recovery
- Social researchers interested in finding individual or collective behavior "triggers" that lead to behavioral changes
- Interpersonal behavior researchers looking for turning points in relationships
- Public opinion and/or political researchers looking for turning points in aggregate data
- Economists looking for "leading indicators" for which a change in one variable may precede a change in more general economic conditions

The book opens with the goals and theoretical definitions of turning-points data to help researchers determine how to best apply these methods to their own studies. An overview of the various methods presented in subsequent chapters is then provided. Some chapters focus on potentiators of change, while others identify new patterns that may occur at varying time points. Highlights of the methods reviewed include structural equation latent variable methods, methods of exploring successive trajectory links, latent growth curve models using multilevel modeling techniques, inverse propensity analysis, time series methods, coping with extreme variable distributions, identifying change points in fMRI data, and alternative investigations of structural change. From an applied perspective, the book explores such things as influence on trajectory change in antisocial/aggressive behavior in boys, the impact of imprisonment on subsequent criminal behavior, how predictors of changes in the frequency of family contact affects individuals over time, alternative models of the effects of substance abuse on antisocial behavior in men in transition from adolescence to adulthood, the changing trajectories of intelligence over the life span, different ways of assessing and understanding the effects of spousal death on depression, and linking risky behavior to later outcomes. Each chapter is based on analyses of real longitudinal data assessed at multiple time points.

Ideal for advanced students and researchers interested in identifying a point of sudden or significant change in data in a variety of fields including psychology, medicine and health related disciplines, education, political science, criminology, and sociology, this innovative reference will be invaluable in advanced research methods and/or statistics courses in a variety of disciplines.

chapter one

The origins of this book

Patricia Cohen
New York State Psychiatric Institute and Columbia University

Contents

Introduction 1
What is a turning point? 3
Why might turning points be worth identifying? 3
How turning point analyses may differ
from other longitudinal analyses 4
Historical turning point approaches 5
    Comparison with norms 5
    Self-identified turning points 5
    Developmental turning points and life stages 6
    Disease course and turning points 6
    Turning points in aggregate analysis 6
    Events or experiences that may precipitate a turning point 7
Defining turning points 7
How turning points are addressed in the following chapters 8
    Causal models of turning points 8
    Normative turning points 10
    Individual risks and turning point outcomes 11
    Structural change as a potential turning point 11
Conclusion 12
References 14

Introduction

At the very end of the 20th century, as part of an ongoing longitudinal study of a cohort from the general U.S. population, we collected detailed data on the period of transition from adolescence to adulthood. Narratives from 240 of our Children in the Community study participants described their own role behavior and associated variables in extended telephone interviews and thus created a unique data set describing 120 continuous months covering the years between their 17th and 27th birthdays. For each month, we employed the narrated behavioral descriptions to rate and score approximately a dozen categorical variables and 40 scaled variables. Our primary motivation was to gain knowledge about the connection between growing maturity and the course of mental illness. An additional interest, motivated in part by Sir Michael Rutter's excellent 1996 paper on turning points, was to identify events or time points that represented a distinct break between past and future behavior.

Probably as a reflection of real life in this developmental period, the resulting role-level ratings for the individual narrators were overwhelmingly jagged, with most respondents going back and forth between often-dramatically more and less adult role assumption (Cohen, Kasen, Chen, Hartmark, & Gordon, 2003). When averaged across the narrators, of course, the trajectories looked like a smooth progression to adult roles, reminding us again of how careful we must be not to think that mean values actually characterize the individuals making up those means.

These jagged profiles presented a considerable challenge to our goal of identifying "turning points" in these data: There seemed to be just too many. We turned to our professional friends and experts, Jack McArdle and his right-hand algorithm development and implementing colleague Aki Hamigami for help. Our first article picked a relatively simple problem, what precipitated getting in trouble with the law, and identified financial problems in the previous 2 months as a powerful predictor (Cohen, Chen, Hamigami, Gordon, & McArdle, 2000). Since then, we have used these data to explore a range of questions related to our goals of understanding life and its challenges in this period (Chen, Cohen, Johnson, Kasen, Sneed, & Crawford, 2004; Cohen et al., 2003; Cohen, Chen, et al., 2005; Johnson, Chen, & Cohen, 2004; Sneed et al., 2006; Sneed, Hamigami, McArdle, Cohen, & Chen, 2007).

My talented team of researchers, aided by our consultants, reviewed and tried out some of the available statistical methods, including those devised by economists, particularly the trajectory grouping methods of Daniel Nagin (1999). Clearly, there is a connection to the literature on "change points," but the distinction we wanted to maintain was between potentially many change points over time in a single measured unit and those that represented a relatively lasting "new stage" of function, development, or problem. In searching for statistical methods to identify turning points in this specific data set, we became interested in the larger question of turning points in any dynamic system and methods of identification and analysis.

What is a turning point?

The *Oxford English Dictionary* defines a *turning point* as a change in direction, especially as a low point or high point on a graph or a point of decisive change of any kind. Its associated quotation is, "One of those turning points in the evolution of thought which mark the end of the old epoch." This quotation particularly indicates the kinds of turning points to which this book is addressed, namely, nontrivial change in some variable, variable trajectory, or variable relationships that are relatively stable over time. These may be quantitative changes in direction or magnitude of some ongoing process of growth or disease or change in level of one or more variables. Or, turning points may reflect qualitative change, as when some resource, event, or idea is attributed as the cause (or opportunity) for a new class of behavior, institution, contract, or ontogenetic or philosophical system. In the developmental literature, certain status changes have often been used as demographic markers of potential turning points in the lives of individuals — graduation, first employment, job loss, retirement, marriage, birth of offspring, or home ownership — indicating that whole new behavior systems may develop in response to the opportunities and demands of the new status. In Rutter's comprehensive review of definitions of turning points (1996), such normative status changes are viewed as transitions, and *turning point* is reserved for less-normative and more theoretically motivated investigations of changes in behavior, functional level, or psychopathology. In this book, we accept a broad definition with the goal of demonstrating a range of statistical approaches to identification of turning points in real data.

Why might turning points be worth identifying?

A number of motivations may lie behind an interest in identifying a point at which the initiation, level, or frequency of a variable markedly changes. In many cases, the goal is identification of another variable or event that tends to precede such a point, making it possible to predict the future. In economic analyses of aggregate data, for example, the goal may be to find "leading indicators" for which a change in one variable may precede a substantial or long-term change in more general indicators of economic conditions. In medicine, the goal may be to determine the level or rate of change in some health or illness indicators that predict subsequent organ or system recovery or failure. In analyses of individual or collective behavior of humans or other animals, the goal may be to identify "triggers" of certain changes, motivated by the awareness that one of the basic requirements of causal inference is temporal priority.

How turning point analyses may differ from other longitudinal analyses

Longitudinal data are often used to bolster inferences about causal processes.[1] Thus, when a putative influence X on some variable Y is of interest, stronger inferences about the potential causal meaning can be achieved by 1) assessing X at an earlier time point[1] and 2) assessing the association of X_1 with Y_2 partialing the association of Y_1 with Y_2. (Here, we ignore for the present any consideration of other potential influences on both X and Y as well as issues of the theoretical timing required for such influences to take place, discussed below.) This is because any influence of Y or its correlates on X that may have taken place prior to Time 1 has been taken into account. In some more complex regression models, a third time point may be added, and the potential mediation or moderation of the effects of X_1 on Y_3 by W_2 also assessed, further elaborating the potential process leading to changes in Y.

Does such an analysis tell us about turning points in Y? Usually not. First, by partialing Y_1 from Y_2 we are not examining changes in Y but rather the differences between the observed value of Y at the later time point and the expected or predicted value of Y based on the correlation between the measures of Y at the two time points. Given the often relatively modest correlation over time, Y_{21} may reflect a minimally changed value: An ordinary regression model leaves the researcher to distinguish between small changes and changes that would be clearly seen as representing a turning point. There is no simple ordinary least squares (OLS) regression method for determining changes that are persistent over time, although multiple assessments employing hierarchical linear analyses can do so.

As can be intuited, some of these problems are aided by the employment of difference scores in Y ($Y_2 - Y_1$ rather than Y_{21}) and possibly in X as well, although this is still a relatively unconventional and disputed approach. Disputed disadvantages include the lower reliability of difference scores according to classical measurement theory assumptions. That is, the variance of difference scores reflects a smaller true score component because of the differencing plus a sum of uncorrelated error variance from the two assessments. A clear advantage of difference scores is that common influences on the dependent and independent variables present in the measures at the earlier point in time are removed from both variables when time 1 values are subtracted from time 2 values, without requiring their explicit inclusion in the analytic model. Thus, the effects

---

[1] In what follows, numerical subscripts indicate the time of measurement.

of confounders on the estimated influence of some potential turning point trigger will be minimized.

Historical turning point approaches

Comparison with norms

Elder (1986) noted the World War II armed services as representing a turning point for some young men from lower-class backgrounds. The entrance of the United States into World War II led to draft and enlistment for these men, necessitating a delay in marriage and family formation. The armed services also provided a substantial increase in educational and training opportunities. For some of these young men, this training took place under the "G.I. bill," which funded postwar education and train-ing. These experiences led to increases in their vocational expectations and economic opportunities. Interestingly, Elder's work was not based on examination of a long-term trajectory but rather on differences from expected and normative attainments: The associated trajectory change did not characterize men entering the service at older ages or from higher socioeconomic status (SES) backgrounds.

Self-identified turning points

Several of the efforts to identify major turning points have asked study participants to identify whether they had such and, if so, to describe and account for them. Major investigations covering many years have inter-viewed participants about turning points, asking these individuals to identify major changes in their behavior or in the emotional "tone" of their lives (see, e.g., Clauson, 1995; Laub & Sampson, 1993; Sampson & Laub, 1993, 1996; Werner & Smith, 1992, 2001). Such procedures are impor-tant starting points for theory development but rely heavily on the partici-pants' insight, recall, verbal expressiveness, and cooperation. As theory advances in any given area, it is obviously best to have a more empirical and objective means of identifying whether a turning point has occurred and what putative prior influences predict such points.

When general population samples are asked whether they have expe-rienced a turning point in their life in the recent past, many will say yes. Although we may argue, as does Rutter (1996), that a significant change in people's lives cannot happen that frequently, an alternative view is that such changes really do happen fairly often from the perspective of the respondent. A person may fairly often make what feels like a signifi-cant change in allocation of time or resources, in work or leisure activi-ties, or in how they will approach an important problem in their lives, in their relationship with a very significant other, or in their plans for the future. Over time, such change points, defined as decisions or the first step in execution of a resolve, may be forgotten as specific time points, especially if the behavioral change, setting, activity, or relationship that followed took some time to carry out. For this reason, the studies in this book do not investigate self-identified turning points but focus rather on empirical evidence of a significant change, either in selected or identified individuals or "on the average," as associated with particular experiences or with age.

Developmental turning points and life stages

Traditional developmental psychology focused particularly on ages at which the emergence of certain behaviors or major changes in behaviors are normative (Scarr, 1992). Often, these norms were developed by observing or testing children of different ages using an analysis-of-variance framework to determine the age groups for whom some significant change in level or frequency of a behavior or skill occurred. Developmental investigations of turning points and life stages in persons at older ages are more likely to have employed longitudinal designs.

Other longitudinal investigators have used event–history or other categorical or regression methods to identify previous experiences that discriminate between investigator-defined turning point outcomes, such as desistance in antisocial or criminal behavior (e.g., latent class models; Pickles & Rutter, 1991).

Disease course and turning points

As noted, turning point models of the course of disease could be an important adjunct to medical knowledge and decision making. Although such disease-specific models are a reasonable goal, we did not succeed in finding many examples of this approach (but see Hall et al., 2001). Informal knowledge of the typical course of an infection or other disease is an important part of clinical wisdom, and formal efforts to empirically validate turning point indicators in medical research would seem an important goal. Change point analyses of medical laboratory/experimental data are more common in the literature (e.g., Ya & Shishkin, 2000).

Another reasonable application of the search for turning points is in addiction research. A period may be characterized by specific behaviors or by specific physiological reactions to the addictive substance that represents a turning point into addiction (see Schulenberg, Wadsworth, O'Malley, Bachman, & Johnston, 1997). Similarly, such a phenomenon may be generalizable to other habitual behaviors by which a set of specifiable reactions to settings, frustrations, or opportunities may characterize a definable turning point by becoming relatively automatic.

Turning points in aggregate analysis

We have noted that students of aggregate economic behavior are often interested in the predictors of change because of the implications for economic policy as well as investment. Because economic indicators have been routinely collected over fixed intervals (daily, monthly, quarterly, annually), the analyses often employ time series regression analysis. Lagged predictors may be tested for their utility in forecasting subsequent changes in a given economic measure. Public opinion is another area in which there is long-term interest in turning points, for example, as applied to polls of potential voters. In this volume, one such method of identifying a change point is employed as a potential start for a turning point analysis, not in aggregated data but for data from each study participant (see Chapter 9, this volume).

Events or experiences that may precipitate a turning point

When a theory has hypothesized variables that may initiate subsequent turning points in another variable, the research design may start with participants who have and have not experienced such factors. In such designs, the weakness is likely to be in ascertaining the participants' status regarding the variable in which the turning point occurs prior to the hypothesized influential experience. When Y represents a transitional change of status (e.g., marriage), that is, a qualitative variable, such a prior status may be easily and reliably determined and event–history models may be employed to analyze predictors and other correlated variables. When Y is a quantitative variable, determining Y status prior to the putative trigger is more likely to be problematic.

There are several questions regarding the domain of potential triggers or theory-predicted explanatory contributors to turning points that may be usefully addressed. How much time is required or expected between these factors and turning points? Are their effects conditional on proximal or resilience person or setting variables? These questions will need to be considered in advance of study design to enable reasonable answers.

Defining turning points

Suppose that one begins with a data set having at least several time points with the relevant data for each of a number of study participants or other study units. To investigate turning points in scaled variables, it will be necessary to define what will be considered a turning point and what will not. These definitions are not only data analytic considerations but also important components of the theory under formulation. These defining questions include the following:

> *Does everyone have one?* For some developmental variables (e.g., aspects of language development), the answer for a particular sample studied over a sufficient number of data points may be yes, and the goal may be determining influences on the timing or age of the change.
>
> *May study participants or other units have more than one turning point?* Again, it depends on the study domain: For developmental phenomena typically, the answer is perhaps, no; for others (e.g., think of recovery from an addiction), the answer may be yes.
>
> *How much change is required to define a turning point?* This decision will ordinarily require some sense of normal or routine variation and measurement error to be discounted in the turning point definition. Some changes may be considered "disturbances" and others turning points.
>
> *Are turning point changes gradual or abrupt?* Are changes in slope over time, changes in subsequent level, or both, included?
>
> *How long does the change have to persist to be considered a turning point?*
>
> *Does a meaningful turning point require change in several distinct constructs, or will a single measure suffice?*

All of these issues are likely to influence both the research design and the selected analytic method.

How turning points are addressed in the following chapters

The two basic requirements for each of the following chapters are a data set with at least several consecutive time point measures of a theoretically relevant variable on a sample of units such as people and a theory that links a turning point in this series with some other variable or variables of interest. My colleagues well fulfill these requirements in their presentations of novel approaches and the rationales for managing the data problems that inevitably appear.

Causal models of turning points

Chapters 2 through 5 use a range of methods to determine empirically whether a potential causal experience accounts for differential subsequent longitudinal trajectories. The first of these chapters, by Nagin, Barker, LaCourse, and Tremblay, examines experiences that may alter the link between two consecutive trajectories (Nagin, Pagnai, Tremblay, & Vitaro, 2003). The trajectories involve the 1987 data of Tremblay, Desmarais-Gervais, Gagnon, and Charlebois on antisocial/aggressive behavior in boys from first grade to age 18, divided into the years prior to early adolescence (age 13) and the adolescent years. It begins by applying a previously published method of linking trajectories (Nagin & Tremblay, 2001). Subsequent analyses examine the influence of two experiences in the interval between these trajectories on the connection between individual trajectories, net of vulnerabilities common to these trajectories. These influences are the first experience of school grade retention and joining an antisocial gang.

The following chapter by Wimer, Sampson, and Laub employs data covering ages 17 to 70 from a sample originating from the Glueck and Glueck 1950 study. The motivating question is whether imprisonment constitutes a turning point event, lowering (or increasing) the probability of subsequent criminal behavior (Laub & Sampson, 1993). Analyses were conducted both on intensive data between ages 17 and 32 and on a selected surviving sample of 52 participants followed with interviews and crime records covering the ages from 32 to 70. These analyses adapted a method based on the "counterfactual" model of accounting for differential likelihood of receiving a "treatment" (here, imprisonment) in the absence of the ability to randomly assign the treatment (Robins, 1986; Robins, Hernan, & Brumback, 2000; Rosenbaum & Rubin, 1983). The logic motivating this model began with acknowledgment that, in the evaluation of the effect of a treatment on symptoms or behavior, observations contribute usefully to the conclusions about its effects only to the extent that the treatment actually experienced is unbiased regarding these outcomes (here, criminal behavior). Obviously, people are generally imprisoned for criminal behavior (although also for "offenses" like parole violation). Consequently, one would expect more criminal behavior postprison based on the likely continuity of behavior over time.

In analyses of these longitudinal data, each participant's data on criminal behavior for each year out of prison was weighted inversely to the propensity of imprisonment in the previous year, if the person was imprisoned, and directly to the propensity of imprisonment in the previous year if not. Such weights were based on a range of time-varying variables previously shown to be related to crime. These weighted data, then, more closely approximate the expected effects of a random assignment of prison to a population with a prison history. We leave it to the reader to turn to the chapter to find the answer to the question of how imprisonment affected criminal behavior in this population.

In Chapter 4, Rindskopf and Sneed use the narrative transition data that motivated this book to examine the trajectory of an ordinal measure of frequency of family contact. Treatment of this "scaled" variable in this way led to managing its otherwise extremely skewed distribution across participants at every point in time. The first question was determining who changed in level of family contract and who did not over this decade. The following analyses then focused on those for whom such changes took place. To determine these predictors, the investigators used demographic data, data on previous history, and time-changing variables within this decade of monthly data.

The sequence of analyses illustrates the advantages of addressing questions that cross the boundaries of substantive and statistical decisions. For example, those participants showing no change in the frequency category of family contact over this decade were virtually all in the highest (most frequent) category. Thus, we cannot expect to find within-period predictors of change in this group: There was a confound between level and within-period variability. Treating the prediction of membership in this group separately from the prediction of those with time-varying change also removed the otherwise severe distributional problem in the data. Another feature of these analyses is a focus on accounting for age-based changes rather than accepting age as an explanatory variable.

In Chapter 5, Hussong, Curran, Moffit, and Caspi employ structural equation latent variable methods to test alternative models of desistance or failure to desist in antisocial behavior in the transition to adulthood. Data came from the Dunedin, New Zealand, birth cohort study (Silva & Stanton, 1996) and examined effects of substance abuse on normatively declining antisocial trajectories of antisocial men in the transition from adolescence to adulthood. The first of the two alternative models tested is the "launch" hypothesis, in which substance abuse at the beginning of this transition period predicts a lesser decline in the subsequent trajectory of antisocial behavior. The other model is the "snare" hypothesis, in which substance abuse at any point has a temporally "local" effect of elevating antisocial behavior (but is not a turning point generator).

Normative turning points

In Chapter 6, we turn to analyses of "normative" turning points. McArdle and Wang examine average trajectories in fluid and crystallized intelligence over much of the life span, using data from the Bradway-McArdle study, with measures previously adapted to a common frame using Rasch analyses. Theory hypothesized three different trajectories, one in the childhood period, another over much of middle adulthood, and a third in later adulthood, and the "onset" points for these changing trajectories can be seen as turning points. The authors demonstrate and discuss the advantages and disadvantages of each of several alternative analytic models and programs in determining these normative trajectories.

In Chapter 7, Burke, Shrout, and Bolger look at normative and individual trajectories following spousal death; they used data from the Changing Lives of Older Couples (CLOC) study from Institute for Social Research at the University of Michigan. All analyses used a multilevel model of individual differences in model parameters to expand the negative exponential model of time to recovery from spousal death. A critical contribution of this chapter is the demonstration that many different combinations of parameters can be used to examine the same data, addressing different theoretical issues. For example, a preloss assessment of depression can be viewed as representing the person's normative level; alternatively, the difference between the preloss and the postloss assessment of depression can be viewed as the loss magnitude for the person.

In Chapter 8, Lindquist and Wager provide a method of coping with a very different turning point problem. They examine a "longitudinal" data set over a vastly different timescale, with the goal of identifying a turning point for every study participant. The model for identifying such a point in functional magnetic resonance imaging (fMRI) data employs an adaptation taken from quality control monitoring and analytic methods. The central problem is one of identifying "start points" for an analysis of cortical brain responses to stimuli when such timing varies across individuals.

In this application, necessarily, such data present problems of multidimensionality and sheer volume. And, the goal in the identification of such turning points is not substantive but methodological. Nevertheless, such an analysis may usefully expand our perspective from the currently popular and widely available methods to potential future alternative analytic frames.

Individual risks and turning point outcomes

Chapter 9 again uses data from the Children in the Community Transitions study (Cohen, Kasen, Bifulco, Andrews, & Gordon, 2005) that originally motivated this book. Chen, Cohen, and Gordon address the problem of identifying individuals who have a turning point to link these identifications with earlier risks and later outcomes. To do so, they use an econometric method of identifying change points in trajectories and subsequently define which change points may be considered, based on magnitude and duration, to be turning points in financial difficulty. Data from this long-term longitudinal study are then examined to determine predictors of such turning points reflected in links with significant variables assessed in adolescence.

Structural change as a potential turning point

The final chapter addresses a kind of turning point not addressed in other chapters: structural change in the relationships among variables as a developmental turning point in the period of transition to adulthood. Again, these issues are addressed using the narrative data that motivated this volume and covering the 10 years beginning with the 17th birthday. The first set of analyses examines this structural change as a change in the factor structure of narrative-based measures when assessed in the 19th year in comparison to assessments in the 27th year. It is shown that these "structures" and the nature of the structural change associated with age differ substantially by SES of young women's family of origin.

The second analysis examines the changing magnitude over this entire decade in the correlation between age-related change in two variables. Each of these variables is aggregated over four of the study's role domains: residential, financial, career (combining advanced education and occupation), and romantic partner commitment. One variable is *agency*, indicating the time-varying extent to which the assumed roles (over these domains) were the consequence of the narrator's own choices and initiative. The second variable, *satisfaction*, indicated the extent to which, at the time, the narrator had been satisfied with and identified with the assumed role. The basic hypothesis was that early independence would relatively frequently lead to assumption of roles that had unanticipated difficulties and disadvantages (and thus less satisfaction), producing a low or even negative correlation between the consecutive monthly values of these two variables. Nevertheless, it was hypothesized, over the decade of this transition to adulthood the magnitude of the relationship between monthly values of agency and satisfaction would become increasingly positive.

This section begins with a multilevel look at the change in the relationship between these variables for the sample as a whole, showing the hypothesized interaction between age and agency in predicting role satisfaction. Subsequent analyses examined the data from selected individuals whose changes in the relationship between these variables with age were the most extreme and potentially consistent with a turning point. The chapter concludes with a discussion of aspects of supplementing a confirmation of an "average" structural turning point with the identification of individuals showing a dramatic manifestation of such a turning point.

Conclusion

No matter where in the scheme of sampling design and measurement choices planned research fits, there will be a range of choices and decisions that will need to be made to clarify the meaning — and threats to the meaning — of study findings. Of course, these choices and decisions will have to be made in the context of the available data or data that can be practically collected. In our experience, the richer the data set is, the more critical and difficult these decisions may be. Such decisions involve the spacing, range, and number of time points to be included in the analysis and the choices of comparison groups, if any, in addition to selection and adaptation of available statistical approaches.

An important thing we learned from the transitions data is that, unlike the annual or other widely spaced assessments often shown in the illustrations of individual turning points or transitions, people do make major changes in role "level" in both directions and over long (e.g., more than a year) or short (e.g., 1 month) periods of time. For the sample as a whole, these measures rose relatively linearly over age. The high individual variance in these measures raised some serious questions for future research. Do these frequent changes mean that our monthly interval was too short to produce valid assessments of real turning points? How can we use ratings of descriptions of actual behavior to maximize the reliability and probable validity of the narratives if we ask narrators to generalize over long periods? How should we decide what an appropriate time unit is? Should we produce more stable estimates by averaging over the months to produce quarterly, annual, or semiannual estimates? Or, should we measure role function only at a fixed larger interval (e.g., annually)? How do these decisions relate to the theoretically interesting influences that we expect may precipitate these changes? These choices can be critical in terms of their effects on the study conclusions.

We also learned a useful lesson from our investigation of a small subgroup who underwent a "high risk." We investigated potential turning points in role function following rape experienced during this transition decade as reported by 12 of the 140 women narrators. (We omitted 1 woman whose experience was too close to her 27th birthday to permit valid investigation of the duration of effects). We explored the utility of hierarchical regression analyses of the developmental trajectories of these women prior to and following this experience in comparison to matched "control" women over matched ages. Although there were significant differences, we found these analyses to be less useful than simple inspection of these women's trajectories using the raw data. Doing so, we identified immediate role function decline in nearly all of these women (as did the multilevel analyses). Nevertheless, most women showed a recovery reflected in a minimal "deficit" by 1 year later and generally not detectable in these overt role behaviors after 2 years. Only 1 woman showed very impaired function, which lasted about 4 years, after which her overall role function became approximately normative. We conclude from these data that, in contrast to the potentially more lasting negative emotional impact of such an experience, normal role function is more readily reassumed. We also believe that for these data, no more elaborate analyses could compete with simple inspection of the raw data. Ultimately, we concluded that even with a larger sample of persons experiencing a potential instigator of a turning point, it may often be the case that no analyses will be more useful in identifying individuals who actually display a consequent turning point than visual examination of graphed data covering the period prior to and following the experience. In our examination of individual structural change in the final book chapter, we illustrate some such data.

Finally, we regret that a new analytic technique arising from a very different substantive field was called to our attention too late to permit its inclusion in this book. The method is jump regression analysis (Qiu, 2005), and it could potentially be used to identify such "skips" in a sequence as might be characterized as turning points.

References

Chen, H., Cohen, P., Johnson, J. G., Kasen, S., Sneed, J., & Crawford, T. (2004). Adolescent personality disorders and conflict with romantic partners during the transition to adulthood. *Journal of Personality Disorders, 18*, 507–525.

Clausen, J. A. (1995). Gender, context, and turning points in adult lives. In P. Moen, G. H. Elder, Jr., & K. Luscher (Eds.), *Examining lives in context: Perspectives on the ecology of human development* (pp. 365–389). Washington, DC: American Psychological Association.

Cohen, P., Chen, H., Hamigami, F., Gordon, K., & McArdle, J. J. (2000). Multilevel analyses for predicting sequence effects of financial and employment problems on the probability of arrest. *Journal of Quantitative Criminology, 16*, 223–236.

Cohen, P., Chen, H., Kasen, S., Johnson, J. G., Crawford, T., & Gordon, K. (2005). Adolescent cluster A personality symptoms, role assumption in the transition to adulthood, and resolution or persistence of symptoms. *Development and Psychopathology, 17*, 549–568.

Cohen, P., Kasen, S., Bifulco, A., Andrews, H., & Gordon, K. (2005). The accuracy of retrospective narrative reports of developmental trajectories. *International Journal of Behavior Development, 29*, 345–355.

Cohen, P., Kasen, S., Chen, H., Hartmark, C., & Gordon, K. (2003). Variations in patterns of developmental transitions in the emerging adulthood period. *Developmental Psychology, 39*, 657–669.

Elder, G. H., Jr. (1986). Military times and turning points in men's lives. *Developmental Psychology, 22*, 233–245.

Glueck, S., & Glueck, E. (1950). *Unraveling juvenile delinquency*. New York: Commonwealth Fund.

Hall, C. B., Ying, J., Kuo, L., Sliwinski, M., Buschke, H., Katz, M., et al. (2001). Estimation of bivariate measurements having different change points, with application to cognitive ageing. *Statistics in Medicine, 20*, 3695–3714.

Johnson, J. G., Chen, H., & Cohen, P. (2004). Personality disorder traits during adolescence and relationships with family members during the transition to adulthood. *Journal of Consulting and Clinical Psychology, 72*, 923–932.

Laub, J. H., & Sampson, R. J. (1993). Turning points in the life course: Why change matters to the study of crime. *Criminology, 31*, 301–325.

Nagin, D. S. (1999). Analyzing developmental trajectories: A semiparametric, group based approach. *Psychological Methods, 4*, 139–57.

Nagin, D. S., Pagani, L., Tremblay, R. E., & Vitaro, F. (2003). Life course turning points: The effect of grade retention on physical aggression. *Development and Psychopathology, 15*, 343–361.

Nagin, D. S., & Tremblay, R. E. (2001). Analyzing developmental trajectories of distinct but related behaviors: A group-based method. *Psychological Methods, 6*, 18–34.

Pickles, A., & Rutter, M. (1991). Statistical and conceptual models of "turning points" in developmental processes. In D. Magnusson, L. R. Bergmann, G. Rudinger, & B. Torestad (Eds.), *Problems and methods in longitudinal research: Stability and change* (pp. 133–165). Cambridge, UK: Cambridge University Press.

Qui, P. (2005). *Image processing and jump regression analysis*. New York: Wiley Interscience.

Robins, J. (1986). A new approach to causal inference in mortality studies with a sustained exposure period: Application to the healthy worker survival effect. *Mathematical Modeling, 7*, 1393–1512.

Robins, J. M., Hernan, M. A., & Brumback, B. (2000). Marginal structural models and causal inference in epidemiology. *Epidemiology, 11*, 550–560.

Rosenbaum, P., & Rubin, D. (1983). The central role of the propensity score in observational studies for causal effects. *Biometrika, 70*, 41–55.

Rutter, M. (1996). Transitions and turning points in developmental psychopathology as applied to the age span between childhood and mid-adulthood. *International Journal of Behavioral Development, 19*, 603–626.

Sampson, R. J., & Laub, J. H. (1993). *Crime in the making: Pathways and turning points through life*. Cambridge: Harvard University Press.

Sampson, R. J., & Laub, J. H. (1996). Socioeconomic achievement in the life course of disadvantaged men: Military service as a turning point, circa 1940–1965. *American Sociological Review, 61*, 347–367.

Scarr, S. (1992). Developmental theories for the 1990s: Development and individual differences. *Child Development, 63*, 1–19.

Schulenberg, J., Wadsworth, K. N., O'Malley, P. M., Bachman, J. G., & Johnston, L. D. (1997). Adolescent risk factors for binge drinking during the transition to young adulthood: Variable-and pattern-centered approaches to change. In G. A. Marlatt & G. R. VandenBos (Eds.), *Addictive behaviors: Readings on etiology, prevention, and treatment* (pp. 129–165). Washington, DC: American Psychological Association.

Silva, P. A., & Stanton, W. R. (1996). *From child to adult: The Dunedin Multidisciplinary Health and Development Study*. Auckland: Oxford University Press.

Sneed, J., Hamigami, F., McArdle, J. J., Cohen, P., & Chen, H. (2007). The dynamic interdependence of developmental domains across emerging adulthood. *Journal of Youth and Adolescence, 36*, 351–363.

Sneed, J., Johnson, J. G., Cohen, P., Chen, H., Crawford, T. N., Kasen, S., et al. (2006). Gender differences in the developmental trajectories of family contact and agency in distinct domains of psychosocial functioning during emerging adulthood. *Developmental Psychology, 42,* 787–797.

Tremblay, R. E., Desmarais-Gervais, L., Gagnon, C., & Charlebois, P. (1987). The Preschool Behaviour Questionnaire: Stability of its factor structure between cultures, sexes, ages and socioeconomic classes. *International Journal of Behavioral Development, 10,* 467–484.

Werner, E. E., & Smith, R. S. (1992). *Overcoming the odds: High risk children from birth to adulthood.* Ithaca, NY: Cornell University Press.

Werner, E. E., & Smith, R. S. (2001). *Journeys from childhood to midlife: Risk, resilience, and recovery.* Ithaca, NY: Cornell University Press.

Ya, A., Shishkin, S. L. (2000). Application of the change-point analysis to the investigation of the brain electrical activity. In B. E. Brodsky & B. S. Darkhovsky (Eds.), *Nonparametric statistical diagnosis: Problems and methods* (pp. 333–388). Dordrecht, Netherlands: Kluwer Academic.

chapter two

The interrelationship of temporally distinct risk markers and the transition from childhood physical aggression to adolescent violent delinquency

Daniel S. Nagin
Carnegie Mellon University

Ted Barker
Kings College London

Eric Lacourse
University of Montreal

Richard E. Tremblay
University of Montreal

Contents

Introduction 18
The dual-trajectory model 19
    The basic dual-trajectory model 20
    Generalizing the basic model to include covariates
    in the probabilities linking Y^1 and Y^2 22
Transitions and turning points 25
Data: The Montreal Experimental Study of Boys 26

Results... 27
   The basic dual model 27
   Dual model extended to include predictors of probability
   of trajectory group membership 29
Conclusion.. 33
References 34

Introduction

A key aim of life course research is identification of whether turning point events such as marriage, entry into the work force or the military, grade retention, or joining a gang affect behavioral trajectories (Farrington & West, 1985; Hagan, MacMillan, & Wheaton, 1996; Lacourse, Nagin, Tremblay, Vitaro, & Claes, 2003; Nagin, Pagani, Tremblay, & Vitaro, 2003; Rutter, 1989; Sampson & Laub, 1993, 1996; Wheaton, 1990). The purpose of this chapter is to demonstrate an analytical strategy laid out by Nagin (2005) for analyzing such impacts in the context of the dual group-based trajectory model. The dual model was designed to analyze the developmental course of two distinct but related outcomes (Nagin & Tremblay, 2001). The model can be used to analyze connections between the developmental trajectories of two outcomes that are evolving contemporaneously (e.g., depression and alcohol use) or over different time periods (e.g., prosocial behavior in childhood and school achievement in adolescence). The latter type of application is the focus of this chapter.

The three key outputs of the dual model are (1) the trajectory groups for both measurement series; (2) the probability of membership in each identified trajectory group; and (3) conditional probabilities linking membership across the trajectory groups of the two respective behaviors. The extension we demonstrate allows the conditional probabilities to vary as a function of individual-level variables such as the individual's experience with turning point events.

The specific application used to demonstrate the model extension examines the linkage between childhood physical aggression from ages 6 to 13 and adolescent violent delinquency from ages 13 to 17. Specifically, we examine how the probabilities of transition from each of the childhood physical aggression trajectories to each of adolescent trajectories varies as a function of the individual having experienced three potential turning point events at the time of the transition: joining a gang at age 12, using drugs at age 12, and retention in school for the first time at age 11, 12, or 13.

We also illustrate how the model extension can be used to analyze a broadened conception of a turning point event motivated by the interactional theory of Thornberry and Krohn (2001) that allows for the possibility that the response to the event may depend on preexisting vulnerabilities. In the context of the illustrative example, this broadened conception is designed to illuminate such fundamental questions as: What factors, if any, explain the differences in adolescent violence of individuals who followed the same trajectory of childhood physical aggression? Is the divergence attributable to long-standing individual differences that first manifest themselves at the important developmental transition from childhood to adolescence? Alternatively, is the divergence attributable to experiences during the transition to adolescence that trigger a separation of theretofore similar trajectories of development? Still another possibility is that the divergence is attributable to an interaction of the preexisting vulnerabilities and the experience of one or more of the turning point events. A comparable set of explanations could be posed about most behaviors or outcomes that evolve over time. Thus, this model generalization has many important applications.

The next section lays out the form of the likelihood function used to estimate the basic dual-trajectory model. It also describes the extension of that model that allows investigation of how turning points as well as other variables may affect the probabilities that link trajectories across the two groups of behavioral trajectories. The third section provides substantive background on our modeling strategy for measuring the impact of turning points and preexisting vulnerabilities on the probabilistic linkage between trajectories of physical aggression in childhood and trajectories of violent delinquency in adolescence. The fourth section describes the data used in the illustrative application. The fifth section reports the results of the illustrative analysis, and this is followed by the concluding section.

The dual-trajectory model

Group-based trajectory modeling is a specialized application of finite-mixture modeling. The models are estimated by the method of maximum likelihood. The rationale for and technical underpinnings of group-based trajectory modeling have previously been elaborated (Muthen, 2001; Nagin, 1999). We attempt only to provide a technical overview of the application of the group-based trajectory model framework to modeling the trajectories of two distinct but related outcomes. We begin with a discussion of the basic dual-trajectory model described in detail by Nagin and Tremblay (2001) and Nagin (2005). We then move on to a summary of the model extension, first laid out by Nagin (2005), that forms the basis for the demonstration reported in this chapter.

The basic dual-trajectory model

Because the dual model is an elaboration of the group-based trajectory model for a single outcome or behavior, we begin with a brief summary of the form of the likelihood function for the single-outcome model. A developmental trajectory describes the course of behavior over age or time. Let

$$Y_i = \{y_{i1}, y_{i2}, y_{i3} \cdots y_{1T}\}$$

denote a longitudinal sequence of measurements of individual i over T periods. Let $P(Y_i)$ denote the probability of Y_i.

The group-based trajectory model assumes that the population is composed of a mixture of J underlying trajectory groups by which

$$P(Y_i) = \sum_j \pi^j P^j(Y_i)$$

where $P^j(Y_i)$ is the probability of Y_i given membership in group j, and π^j is the probability of group j. The form of $P^j(Y_i)$ is selected to conform to the type of data under analysis.

The basic model also assumes that, conditional on membership in group j, the random variables y_{it} $t = 1, 2, \ldots, T$ are independent. Thus,

$$P^j(Y_i) = \prod^T P^{jt}(y_{it})$$

The censored normal distribution is used to model trajectories of an outcome measured on a psychometric scale having a scale minimum or maximum or both. The model is intended to account explicitly for such censoring (Nagin & Tremblay, 1999). For the censored normal model, the linkage between age and behavior is established via a latent variable y_{it}^{*j} that varies as a function of a polynomial function of a specified order in age or time. The appropriate order of the polynomial is specified a priori or in the model selection phase of analysis. This latent variable can be thought of as measuring individual i's potential for engaging in the behavior of interest, say physical aggression, at time t given membership in group j. The latent variable y_{it}^{*j} is linked to its observed but censored counterpart y_{it} as follows: Let $S_{\min}$ and $S_{\max}$, respectively, denote the minimum and maximum possible score on the measurement scale. The model assumes

$$y_{it} = S_{\min} \text{ if } y_{it}^{*j} < S_{\min}$$

$$y_{it} = y_{it}^{*j} \text{ if } S_{\min} \leq y_{it}^{*j} \leq S_{\max}$$

and

$$y_{it} = S_{\max} \text{ if } y_{it}^{*j} > S_{\max}$$

In words, if the latent variable y_{it}^{*j} is less than $S_{\min}$, it is assumed that the observed behavior equals this minimum. Likewise, if the latent variable y_{it}^{*j} is greater than $S_{\max}$, it is assumed that observed behavior equals this maximum. Only if y_{it}^{*j} is within the scale minimum and maximum does $y_{it} = y_{it}^{*j}$.

For the Poisson-based version of the model, which is used to model count data, the conceptual setup is similar. Here, the trajectory is defined in terms of a trajectory group-specific path of the Poisson rate parameter λ over age or time. Like the censored normal model, this path is defined by a polynomial function of age or time, but in the Poisson-based model the path describes the course of the natural log of λ for each trajectory group.

The joint trajectory model builds from the univariate model as follows: Let Y^1 and Y^2 denote the two longitudinal series to be modeled in a joint trajectory format where Y^1 is measured over T^1 periods, Y^2 is measured over T^2 periods, and the index i has been suppressed for notational convenience. The maintained assumption of conditional independence given group membership is continued. Thus,

$$f^j(Y^1) = \prod^{T_1} f^{jt}\left(y_t^1\right)$$

and

$$h^j(Y^2) = \prod^{T_2} h^{jt}\left(y_t^2\right)$$

where $f(*)$ and $h(*)$ are suitably defined probability distributions given the form of the data.

A new layer to the conditional independence assumption is added with the assumption that conditional on j and k, Y^1 and Y^2 are independently distributed,

$$P^{jk}(Y^1, Y^2) = f^j(Y^1)h^j(Y^2)$$

Thus, the unconditional likelihood function of Y^1 and Y^2 sums across $P^{jk}(Y^1, Y^2)$ with each such conditional distribution weighted by the joint probability of membership in trajectory group j for Y^1 and trajectory group k for Y^2, π^{jk}:

$$P(Y^1, Y^2) = \sum_j \sum_k \pi^{jk} f^j(Y^1)h^j(Y^2)$$

An alternative and equivalent form of the likelihood function builds from the result that $\pi^{jk} = \pi^{k|j}\pi^j$. Thus,

$$P(Y^1, Y^2) = \sum_j \sum_k \pi^{k|j}\pi^j f^j(Y^1)h^k(Y^2) = \sum_j \pi^j f^j(Y^1) \sum_k \pi^{k|j}h^k(Y^2)$$

Observe that this second likelihood function has a sequential construction: Each group j of Y^1 (e.g., childhood physical aggression) is linked to each group k of Y^2 (e.g., adolescent violence) via a conditional probability $\pi^{k|j}$. For problems in which Y^1 temporally precedes Y^2, this formulation is natural. This form of the likelihood function is adopted for this analysis because our aim is to describe a framework that is suitable for analyzing the factors that may affect the linkage between two distinct outcomes or behaviors that evolve sequentially over time or age. Specifically, the generalization of the basic dual model allows $\pi^{k|j}$ to vary as a function of covariates measuring individual-level characteristics and circumstances, including whether an individual experienced a potential turning point event at the time of the transition (e.g., began using drugs).

Generalizing the basic model to include covariates in the probabilities linking Y^1 and Y^2

As a prelude to the description of this generalization, the estimation of π^j and $\pi^{k|j}$ without covariates is first discussed. Both sets of probabilities are estimated using multinomial logit functions without covariates:

$$\pi_j = e^{\theta_j^0} \bigg/ \sum_j e^{\theta_j^0}$$

(2.1)

and

$$\pi_{k|j} = e^{\gamma^0_{k|j}} \Big/ \sum_k e^{\gamma^0_{k|j}} \qquad j = 1,...J \tag{2.2}$$

While Equations 2.1 and 2.2 follow the same functional form, they differ in one very important respect: Estimation of the former requires the estimation of many fewer parameters than the latter. Estimation of Equation 2.1 requires the estimation of $J - 1$ parameters. By contrast, Equation 2.2 specifies $J*K$ probabilities. For each of Y^1's J trajectory groups there are a total of K transition probabilities, one for each of Y^2's K groups. Thus, for *each* group j a total of $K - 1$ parameters must be estimated, each corresponding to one of the $K - 1$ trajectory groups of Y^{2*}. Thus, in total, estimation of the transition probabilities described by Equation 2.2 requires the estimation of $J*(K - 1)$ parameters — one set of $K - 1$ parameters for each of the J groups of Y^1.

The difference in number of model parameters required to specify π_j and $\pi_{k|j}$ without covariates has important implications for the specification of a model that allows π_j and $\pi_{k|j}$ to vary as a function of covariates. Let x_i and w_i denote sets of potential predictors of π_j and $\pi_{k|j}$, respectively. The two sets may be comprised of variables that are identical, partially overlapping, or nonoverlapping. This generalization of the dual model assumes that π_j follows the multinomial logit function:

$$\pi_j(x_i) = \frac{e^{x_i\theta_j}}{\sum_j e^{x_i\theta_j}} \tag{2.3}$$

To help to make clear a point about the specification of $\pi_{k|j}(w_i)$, Equation 2.3 can be rewritten in a form that more obviously ties it to Equation 2.1:

$$\pi_j(x_i) = e^{\theta^0_j + \theta'_j x_i} \Big/ \sum_j e^{\theta^0_j + \theta'_j x_i} \tag{2.3'}$$

This alternative format makes it clear that for each group j, θ_j includes two components — an intercept θ^0_j and a set of parameters θ_j — that measure the impact of each variable included in x_i on the probability of group j relative to the reference group. Thus, if x_i included seven predictors of trajectory

---

* The transition probability to the Kth group can be calculated as 1 minus the sum of the probabilities for the other $K - 1$ groups.

group membership and $J = 4$, a total of 24 parameters would be estimated. The total includes 3 estimates of θ_j^0 plus 21 estimates of θ_j' comprised of a set of seven parameters for each of the three nonreference groups.

This example illustrates an important feature of logit models: Because θ_j' is group specific, one set of parameters must be estimated for each trajectory group. As a result, there is a risk that the number of parameters in the model may outstrip the information in the data that is required for their estimation.

The risk of parameter proliferation is particularly acute if the equivalent generalization is applied to Equation 2.2 by which

$$\pi_{k|j}(w_i) = e^{\gamma_{k|j}^0 + \gamma_{k|j}'w_i} \Big/ \sum_k e^{\gamma_{k|j}^0 + \gamma_{k|j}'w_i} \qquad j = 1,\ldots,J \qquad (2.4)$$

This risk is most easily illustrated with an example. The model of childhood physical aggression and adolescent violence described in the results section includes three trajectories of childhood physical aggression ($J = 3$) and five trajectories of adolescent violent delinquency ($K = 5$). In this application, w_i includes seven characteristics that might affect the probability of transitioning from a given trajectory j of physical aggression (Y^1) to each trajectory k of violent delinquency (Y^2). For each of Y^1's J trajectory groups, this specification requires the estimation of a total of 32 logit parameters — four estimates of $\gamma_{k|j}^0$ plus a set of 7 parameters that comprise $\gamma_{k|j}'$ for each of the four noncontrast delinquency groups. Thus, across the three childhood physical aggression groups, Equation 2.4 requires the estimation of a total of 96 parameters. This is more parameters than can be feasibly estimated in most longitudinal data sets.

One way to streamline the model is to assume that effects of the variables included in w_i do not depend on the trajectory group membership for Y^1. Under this assumption, the various values of $\gamma_{k|j}$ are equal across the J trajectory groups in Y^1, and therefore they can be denoted by γ_k. Conceptually, this modification amounts to assuming that the influence of a particular variable on the probability of transition to a specific trajectory group k of Y^2 as measured by γ_k' does not interact with trajectory membership for Y^1. For the above example, this reduces the number of required parameters from 96 to 40. With the introduction of the no-interaction constraint, Equation 2.4 can be restated as

$$\pi_{k|j}(w_i) = e^{\gamma_{k|j}^0 + \gamma_k'w_i} \Big/ \sum_k e^{\gamma_{k|jk}^0 + \gamma_k'w_i} \qquad j = 1,\ldots,J \qquad (2.5)$$

Note that the no-interaction model continues to allow the intercepts $\gamma'_{k|j}$ to vary freely across Y^1's J trajectories. Consequently, the transition probabilities $\pi^{k|j}$ will be different for two individuals with identical characteristics w_i but who had followed different trajectories for behavior Y^1. Thus, the no-interaction model still allows the trajectory that is followed for Y^1 to influence the probability of trajectory group membership for Y^2 even controlling for the variables in w_i.

Indeed, in the special circumstance in which the factors included in w_i have no impact on the transition probabilities (i.e., $\gamma'_k = 0$), Equation 2.5 reduces to its original form without covariates, Equation 2.2. This circumstance has special substantive implications. It implies that the transition across trajectories for the behaviors Y^1 and Y^2 is wholly determined by the developmental trajectory that is followed for the earlier behavior Y^1 and not by turning point events experienced at the time of the transition.

Transitions and turning points

Our conception of turning points and long-standing vulnerabilities discussed in the introduction is heavily influenced by the literature on the development of problem behaviors such as conduct disorder and delinquency. Much research has shown that chronically aggressive males, compared to their counterparts who desist in postadolescence, suffer from a disproportionate number of vulnerabilities established early in life (e.g., Moffitt, 1993; Moffitt, Caspi, Dickson, Silva, & Stanton, 1996; Patterson, Forgatch, Yoerger, & Stoolmiller, 1998). A nonexhaustive list of such vulnerabilities includes low IQ (Moffitt, 1993), adolescent single mothers (Fagot, Pears, Capaldi, Crosby, & Leve, 1998; Nagin, Pogarsky, & Farrington, 1997; Pagani, Boulerice, & Tremblay, 1997), disadvantaged neighborhoods (Gottfredson et al., 1990; Thornberry et al., 2003), and disrupted family processes (Patterson et al., 1998). Adolescent limited males, on the other hand, are believed to be more normative than chronically aggressive boys and experience fewer personal and environmental disadvantages in early childhood (Moffitt et al., 1996).

Further, the chronically aggressive males are more likely to engage in behaviors in adolescence, such as gang membership, that may exacerbate their already aggressive behavior (Thornberry et al., 2003). For instance, living in a structurally disadvantaged neighborhood or having a young single mother is thought to lower the quality of parenting and supervision and to afford greater opportunities to affiliate with deviant peers at early ages (Dishion, Poulin, & Medici-Skaggs, 2000; Gottfredson & Hirschi, 1990; Patterson et al., 1998; Thornberry et al., 2003). Affiliation with deviant peers has also been conceptualized as a training process (Poulin,

Dishion, & Haas, 1999) in which these boys tend to engage in high rates of many different problem behaviors, such as sexual activity, smoking, and use of alcohol and drugs (Farrington, 1998). Not surprisingly, these boys have also been identified as highly physically aggressive, perhaps the most robust predictor of subsequent violence (Brame, Nagin, & Tremblay, 2001; Broidy et al., 2003; Lacourse et al., 2003; Lipsey & Derzon, 1998; Loeber & Hay, 1997; Nagin et al., 1999). Conversely, adolescent limited boys tend to associate with deviant peers at later ages, and therefore the onset of delinquent behaviors is believed to be a delayed process (Moffitt et al., 1996).

Data: The Montreal Experimental Study of Boys

The Montreal Experimental Study of Boys was started in the spring 1984. Teachers of kindergarten classes in 53 schools located in low socioeconomic areas of Montreal, Canada, rated the behavior of each boy in their respective classes ($N = 1,161$). To maintain a homogeneous sample and to control for cultural effects, boys were included in the study only if their biological parents were born in Canada and the mother's native language was French. The resulting sample was comprised of 1,037 white, French-speaking boys. The boys parents' average score on the Blishen, Carroll, and Moore (1987) scale for occupational prestige was 38.29 ($SD = 12.10$) for the mothers and 39.44 ($SD = 12.86$) for the fathers. These scores represent low-to-average socioeconomic levels. Informed consent was regularly obtained from the mothers and the youths throughout the span of the study. Assessments were made at age 6 and annually from ages 10 to 17. Wide-ranging measurements of social and psychological functioning were taken from multiple sources (i.e., parents, teachers, peers, self-reports) as well as administrative records from schools and courts. See Tremblay et al. (1987) for further details.

Measurements that are central to our analysis are those of childhood physical aggression and adolescent violent delinquency. Childhood physical aggression was measured by teacher-based assessments of three items: fights with other children; kicks, bites, or hits other children; and bullies or intimidates other children. Violent delinquency in adolescence was measured by self-reports of the frequency of fistfighting; carrying/using a deadly weapon; threatening and attacking someone; and throwing an object at someone.

The factor representing long-standing vulnerabilities consists of a summed index of binary indicators of whether the subject's mother had less than a 10th grade education, whether she began childbearing as a teenager, whether the subject's parents separated by age 6, and whether the subject was in the lower quartile of the IQ distribution. Factors contemporaneous to the transition from childhood to adolescence included binary indicators of gang affiliation at 12 years of age, the use of alcohol or illicit drugs at 12 years of age, and first-time grade retention at age 11, 12, or 13.

Results

The results of the analysis are reported in two stages. We first describe the results of application of the basic dual-trajectory model to the data on childhood physical aggression from ages 6 to 13 and adolescent violent delinquency from ages 13 to 17. In the second stage, we report the results of an analysis that demonstrated the model extension in which the conditional probabilities linking the trajectories of childhood physical aggression from 6 to 13 and adolescent violence from 13 to 17, $\pi_{k|j}$, are specified to vary as a function of long-standing vulnerabilities and contemporaneous events and behaviors.

The basic dual model

An important first step in group-based trajectory modeling is determining the number of trajectory groups that best characterizes the data for the outcome variable of interest. A related issue is specification of the appropriate order of the polynomial that specifies the course of each trajectory group over age or time. This step involves the use of appropriate model selection statistics such as the Bayesian information criterion or the Aikaike information criterion and domain knowledge. The issues involved in the model selection process are complex and discussion is beyond the scope of this chapter. See Nagin (2005) for elaboration.

For our purposes, we simply note that the trajectories for childhood physical aggression, which derive from application of the censored normal model, and the trajectories of adolescent violent delinquency, which derive from application of the Poisson model, are the outcome of a model selection process based in part on the Bayesian information criterion and in part on an effort to identify models that best represented the distinctive features of the data.

The size and shapes of the trajectory groups for childhood aggression and adolescent delinquency are shown in Figure 2.1. Model selection resulted in a three-group model for childhood physical aggression. Two of the trajectories were of nearly equal size. One, which was estimated to involve 40.4% of the population, consisted of boys who were always low in their use of aggression. Another group, involving an estimated 36.9% of the population, was composed of boys who were moderate in their use of physical aggression at 6 years of age, but thereafter declined. Finally, there was a group, estimated to make up about 20% of the population, who were consistently highly physically aggressive. For adolescent violent delinquency,

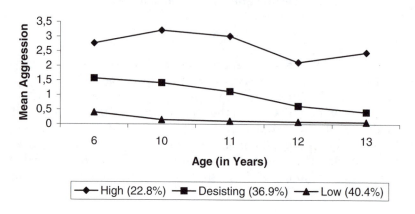

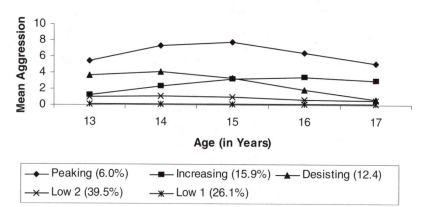

Figure 2.1 Independent trajectory models.

an estimated 66% of the boys followed one of two trajectories of low violence, labeled the Low 1 and Low 2 trajectories. The remaining one-third of the boys engaged in violent delinquency much more frequently at least at some ages. These boys were split among three trajectories, a declining group (12.4%), an increasing group (15.9%), and a small minority who were high and peaking (7.0%).

Consider next the estimates of $\pi_{k|j}$ that link the childhood and adolescent trajectories. Estimates of these probabilities are reported in Table 2.1A. The estimates overwhelmingly indicate that an individual in the low childhood physical aggression group is very likely to transition to the Low 1 or Low 2 adolescent groups (.85). Also, there is virtually no chance of their transiting to the high and peaking adolescent trajectory. Conversely, as might be expected, a sizable proportion of the boys who followed the high childhood group transitioned to the high and peaking adolescent group (.20). However, the modal transition for even the high childhood aggression group was either to the Low 1 or Low 2 adolescent group (.59 = .36 + .23). In between the transition probabilities for the high and low childhood physical aggression trajectories are the probabilities for the boys following the desisting childhood trajectory. Like the boys in the low and chronic trajectories, the modal transition was to the Low 1 and Low 2 trajectories (.79 = .58 + .21). However, unlike the boys in the low childhood physical aggression trajectory, boys following the desisting trajectory through age 13 still had a small probability of transitioning to the high and peaking adolescent trajectory.

With the estimates of $\pi_{k|j}$ and π_j in hand, it is also possible to calculate

$$\pi_{j|k} = \pi_{k|j} \frac{\pi_j}{\pi_k}$$

These probabilities provide the basis for describing the composition of each adolescent violent trajectory group in terms of the representation of each childhood trajectory group and are reported in Table 2.1B. These probability estimates are also revealing. They show, for example, that while the peaking trajectory of adolescent violence is entirely composed of individuals from the desisting and chronic childhood trajectories, the increasing adolescent trajectory is composed of a sizable minority of boys from the low childhood physical aggression trajectory.

Dual model extended to include predictors of probability of trajectory group membership

The conditional probabilities reported in Table 2.1 make clear that there is continuity in physical aggression between childhood and adolescent — a finding long ago established in the developmental literature on aggression (Heusmann, Eron, Lefkowitz, & Walter, 1986; Olweus, 1979). However, the transition probabilities also make clear that the continuity of aggression is only an *average* tendency and that at the level of the individual is far from immutable. Even among the boys following the chronic childhood trajectory, an estimated 60% went on to follow either the Low 1 or Low 2 adolescent trajectory. On the other hand, a sizable proportion of the boys following a seeming path of declining childhood physical aggression went on to follow one of the three trajectories of elevated violent delinquency

Table 2.1 Estimates of $\pi_{k|j}$ and $\pi_{j|k}$ in Dual Model of Childhood Physical Aggression and Adolescent Violence

A. Probability of Delinquency Group k Conditional on Childhood Aggression Group j ($\pi_{k|j}$)

	Low 1 and 2	Desisting	Increasing	Peaking
Low	.85	.06	.09	.00
Desisting	.58	.21	.15	.06
High	.36	.23	.21	.20

B. Probability of Childhood Aggression Group j Conditional on k Delinquency Group ($\pi_{j|k}$)

	Low	Desisting	High
Low 1	.63	.33	.04
Low 2	.39	.45	.17
Desisting	.13	.57	.30
Increasing	.23	.46	.31
Peaking	.00	.40	.60

in adolescence. In this section, we examine the extent that turning point events and preexisting vulnerabilities may explain these individual differences in developmental path.

Recall from the data description in the data section that the variable measuring long-standing vulnerabilities consists of a summed index of binary indicators of maternal teenage onset of childbearing, low maternal educational level, whether the subject's family was intact at 6 years of age, and low IQ. Variables measuring turning point events contemporaneous to the transition from childhood to adolescence are gang affiliation at age 12, the use of drugs at age 12, and first-time grade retention at age 11, 12, or 13.

Results of the extended model that allow $\pi_{k|j}$ to vary as a function of these vulnerabilities and the turning point events are reported in Table 2.2. Table 2.2A reports coefficient estimates of the impact of the vulnerability index on probability of membership in the desisting and chronic childhood physical aggression trajectories relative to the low childhood trajectory. The impact is positive and highly significant for both trajectory groups. This implies that the vulnerabilities measured in the index are associated with elevated levels of childhood physical aggression, a finding that is consistent with much prior research on risk factors for aggression in childhood and beyond (Borge, Rutter, Cote, & Tremblay, 2004;

Table 2.2

A. Probabilities of Long-Standing Probabilities and Childhood Physical Aggression Trajectory Membership

Group	Parameter	Estimate	Standard error	T for H0: Parameter = 0
Moderate	Constant	− 0.292	.40	− 1.22
	Vulnerabilities	0.519	.120	4.33
High	Constant	− 1.766	.282	− 6.26
	Vulnerabilities	1.025	.126	8.12

B. Relative Impact of Temporally Distinct Covariates and Interactions (Low 1 Adolescent Trajectory Is Reference)

Group	Parameter	Estimate	Standard error	T value
Low 2	Vulnerabilities	0.051	.173	0.29
	Drugs at 12	0.690	.281	2.46
	Fail School (11–13)	0.016	.521	0.03
	Gang at 12	0.230	.700	0.39
	Vuln*Drugs	−0.234	.275	−0.85
	Vuln*Fail	−0.007	.412	−0.02
	Vuln*Gang	0.981	.929	1.06
Desisting	Vulnerabilities	−0.149	.260	−0.57
	Drugs at 12	1.540	.290	5.32
	Fail School (11–13)	0.109	.684	0.16
	Gang at 12	1.150	.703	1.64
	Vuln*Drugs	−0.067	.250	−0.27
	Vuln*Fail	−0.158	.521	−0.30
	Vuln*Gang	1.841	.914	2.01
Increasing	Vulnerabilities	−0.017	.212	−0.08
	Drugs at 12	0.793	.290	2.74
	Fail School (11–13)	1.113	.535	2.08
	Gang at 12	0.788	.695	1.13
	Vuln*Drugs	0.078	.244	0.32
	Vuln*Fail	−0.485	.438	−1.11
	Vuln*Gang	1.084	.932	1.16
Peaking	Vulnerabilities	0.239	.347	0.69
	Drugs at 12	1.475	.315	4.69
	Fail School (11–13)	0.605	.787	0.77
	Gang at 12	2.980	.844	3.53
	Vuln*Drugs	0.069	.257	0.27
	Vuln*Fail	−0.179	.574	−0.31
	Vuln*Gang	1.261	.953	1.32

Tremblay et al., 2004). The estimates imply that the magnitude of the impact is quite large. For example, an increase in the index from its minimum of 0 to its maximum of 4 implies an increase in probability of membership in the chronic trajectory from .09 to .60.

Table 2.2B reports coefficient estimates of the risk index, turning point events, and the interaction of the risk index and turning point events on $\pi_{k|j}$. Note that none of the risk index coefficient estimates are even remotely close to statistical significance. This implies that these early risks do not predict violent delinquency trajectory group *controlling* for childhood physical aggression trajectory.

Consider now the variables measuring events occurring contemporaneously with the transition point between the childhood and adolescent trajectories. Controlling for childhood physical aggression trajectory, drug use at age 12 significantly increased the risk of transition to all four adolescent trajectories relative to the lowest adolescent trajectory of virtually no violence (Low 1). The drug use estimates are not only statistically significant but large in magnitude. For the Low 2 and increasing trajectories, the drug use coefficient estimates imply about a twofold increase in the odds of these trajectories compared to the Low 1 trajectory. For the declining and peaking trajectories, drug use implies more than a fourfold increase. By contrast, the impacts of gang membership at age 12 and first-time grade retention at ages 11 to 13 are specific to certain trajectories. Gang membership is only associated with increased risk of transition to the most violence prone trajectory in adolescence — the peaking trajectory. First-time grade retention's impact was limited to heightened risk of transitioning to the increasing group. This suggests that grade retention may trigger aggression in previously nonaggressive boys. Last, consider the interactions between the turning point variables and the risk index. With one exception, these impact estimates are insignificant. That exception involves the interaction of the vulnerability index and gang membership at age 12 in the transition to the decreasing trajectory.

The key findings of this illustrative analysis were (1) preexisting vulnerabilities did not seem to influence the transition from childhood physical trajectory to the adolescent violence trajectory; (2) drug use at age 12 was associated with a generalized increase in the risk of transition to an elevated trajectory of adolescent violence; (3) the impacts of first-time grade retentions and gang membership seemed to be more limited, the former to increase the risk of following the trajectory of increasing adolescent violence and the latter to heightened risk of following the peaking trajectory; and (4) there was no systematic evidence of an interaction between vulnerabilities and contemporaneous turning point events.

These findings illustrate several useful features of group-based trajectory modeling in analyzing the impact of potential turning point events.

One is that the framework lends itself to describing population heterogeneity in behavioral trajectories across life stages. This is a valuable first step in setting the stage for an investigation into potential explanations for the divergence of trajectories of individuals who had previously been following similar trajectories. A second is that the group-based framework lends itself to analyzing whether the impact of potential turning point events is contingent on an individual's prior behavioral trajectory. Such contingencies are a key premise of life course research (Elder, 1998).

Conclusion

This chapter has demonstrated an approach to analyzing factors that may affect the transition between trajectories of distinct but related behaviors that unfold sequentially over age or time. Such factors might measure events that occur at the point in time when one behavioral trajectory ends and the other begins. Such events can be thought of as turning points. Other variables might measure long-standing characteristics of an individual. Such characteristics might measure preexisting vulnerabilities (or preexisting indicators of resilience) that might also be associated with the transition. The objective of this extension of the dual group-based trajectory model was to provide an analytical framework within the context of the group-based trajectory model to explore the role of potential turning point events and long-standing vulnerabilities in influencing connections of behavioral trajectories across distinct life stages.

As with all statistical methods that attempt to identify the impact of turning point events and other variables on behavioral transitions from observational data, the caveat emptor that association does not demonstrate causality applies here. The discussion has used terms like *influence* and *impact* to describe the association of variables with $\pi_{k|j}$. It is important to keep in mind that these terms only describe an association.

There are inherent limits to the degree to which observational data can be used to draw causal inference. Still, all methods do not have an equal capacity for drawing such inferences, however fragile they may be. Further development of the method described in this chapter is required to allow for more confident causal interpretation. Haviland and Nagin (2005) described out an approach that draws on work on propensity scores (Rosenbaum, 2002; Rosenbaum & Rubin, 1983) for the purpose of creating a more confident basis for drawing causal inferences within the context of the group-based trajectory model. The method uses trajectory groups as a statistical device for creating balance on the values of the outcome variable defining the trajectory as well as on other variables measured up to the last period of the trajectory. Thus, the trajectory is playing the role of a propensity score. Assuming there is balance, the method compares the outcome variable for periods after the end of the trajectory for individuals who do and do not experience a turning point event. A natural extension of this approach involves a generalization to the dual trajectory format. This would involve a comparison of the entire trajectories of an individual experiencing and not experiencing the turning point event.

References

Blishen, B. R., Carroll, W. K., & Moore, C. (1987). The 1981 socioeconomic index for occupations in Canada. *Canadian Review of Sociology and Anthropology, 24*, 465–488.

Borge, A., Rutter, M., Cote, S., & Tremblay, R. E. (2004). Early childcare and physical aggression: Differentiating social selection and social causation. *Journal of Child Psychology and Psychiatry and Allied Disciplines, 45*, 367–376.

Brame, R., Nagin, D. S., & Tremblay, R. (2001). Developmental trajectories of aggression. *Journal of Child Psychology and Psychiatry, 52*, 503–512.

Broidy, L. M., Nagin, D. S., Tremblay, R. E., Brame, B., Dodge. K., Fergusson, D. M., et al. (2003). Developmental trajectories of childhood disruptive behaviors and adolescent delinquency: A six site, cross national study. *Developmental Psychology, 39*, 222–245.

Dishion, T. J., Poulin, F., & Medici-Skaggs, N. (2000). The ecology of premature autonomy in adolescence: Biological and social influences. In K. A. Kerns, J. M. Contreras, & A. M. Neal-Barnett (Eds.), Family and peers: Linking two social worlds (pp. 27–45). Westport, CT: Praeger.

Elder, G. H., Jr. (1998). The life course and human development. In R. M. Lerner (Ed.) & W. Damon (General Ed.), *Handbook of child psychology: Vol. 1. Theoretical models of human development* (pp. 939–991). New York: Wiley.

Fagot, B. I., Pears, K. C., Capaldi, D. M., Crosby, L., & Leve, C. S. (1998). Becoming an adolescent father: Precursors and parenting. *Developmental Psychology, 34*, 1209–1212.

Farrington, D. P. (1998). Predictors, causes and correlates of male youth violence. In M. Tonry & M. Moore (Eds.), *Youth violence* (pp. 317–371). Chicago: University of Chicago Press.

Farrington, D. P., & West, D. J. (1985). The Cambridge study in delinquent development: A prospective longitudinal study of 411 males. In H. Kerner & G. Kaiser (Eds.), *Criminality: Personality, behavior, and life history*, (pp. 115–138), New York: Springer-Verlag.

Gottfredson, M. R., & Hirschi, T. (1990). *A general theory of crime.* Stanford, CA: Stanford University Press.

Hagan, J., MacMillan, R., & Wheaton, B. (1996). *American Sociological Review, 61*, 368–385.

Haviland, D.M., & Nagin, D.S. (2005). Casual inferences with group-based trajectory models. *Psychometrika 70*, 557–578.

Heusmann, L. R., Eron, L. D., Lefkowitz, M. M., & Walder, L. O. (1984). Stability of aggression over time and generations. *Developmental Psychology, 20*, 1120–1134.

Lacourse, E., Nagin, D., Tremblay, R. E., Vitaro, F., & Claes, M. (2003). Developmental trajectories of boys' delinquent group membership and facilitation of violent behaviors during adolescence. *Development and Psychopathology, 15*, 183–197.

Lipsey, M. W., & Derzon , J. H. (1998). Predictors of violent or serious delinquency in adolescence and early adulthood. In R. Loeber & D. P. Farrington (Eds.), *Serious and violent juvenile offenders. Risk factors and successful interventions* (pp. 86–105). Thousand Oaks, CA: Sage.

Loeber, R., & Hay, D. (1997). Key issues in the development of aggression and violence from childhood to early adulthood. *Annual Review of Psychology, 48*, 371–410.

Moffitt, T. E. (1993). Adolescence-limited and life-course-persistent antisocial behavior: A developmental taxonomy. *Psychological Review, 100*, 674–701.

Moffitt, T. E., Caspi, A., Dickson, N., Silva, P., & Stanton, W. (1996). Childhood-onset versus adolescent-onset antisocial conduct problems in males: Natural history from ages 3 to 18 years. *Development and Psychopathology, 8*, 399–424.

Muthen, B. O. (2001). Latent variable mixture modeling. In G. A. Marcoulides & R. E. Schumacker (Eds.), *New developments and techniques in structural equation modeling* (pp. 1–33). Hillsdale, NJ: Erlbaum.

Nagin, D. S. (1999) Analyzing developmental trajectories: A semiparametric, group-based approach. *Psychological Methods, 4*, 139–57.

Nagin, D.S. (2005). *Group-based modeling of development.* Cambridge: Harvard University Press.

Nagin, D., Pagani, L., Tremblay, R., & Vitaro, F. (2003). Life course turning points: A case study of the effect of school failure on interpersonal violence. *Development and Psychopathology, 15*, 343–361.

Nagin, D. S., Pogarsky, G., & Farrington, D. P. (1997). Adolescent mothers and the criminal behavior of their children. Law and Society Review, *31*, 137–162.

Nagin, D. S. & Tremblay, R. E. (1999). Trajectories of boys' physical aggression, opposition, and hyperactivity on the path to physically violent and nonviolent juvenile delinquency. *Child Development, 70*, 1181–1196.

Nagin, D. S., & Tremblay, R. E. (2001). Parental and early childhood predictors of persistent physical aggression in boys from kindergarten to high school. *Archives of General Psychiatry, 58*, 389–394.

Olweus, D. (1979). Stability of aggressive reaction patterns in males: A review. *Psychological Bulletin, 86*, 852–875.

Pagani, L. S., Boulerice, B., & Tremblay, R. E. (1997). The influence of poverty on children's classroom placement and behavior problems during elementary school: A change model approach. In G. Duncan & J. Brooks-Gunn (Eds.), *Consequences of growing up poor* (pp. 311–339). New York: Sage.

Patterson, G. R., Forgatch, M. S., Yoerger, K. L., & Stoolmiller, M. (1998). Variables that initiate and maintain an early-onset trajectory for juvenile offending. *Development and Psychopathology, 10*, 531–547.

Poulin, F., Dishion, T. J., & Haas, E. (1999). The peer influence paradox: Friendship quality and deviancy training within male adolescent friendships. *Merrill-Palmer Quarterly, 45*, 42–61.

Rosenbaum, P. R. (2002). *Observational Studies* (2nd ed.). New York: Springer-Verlag.
Rosenbaum, P., & Rubin, D. (1983). The central role of the propensity score in observational studies for causal effects. *Biometrika, 70,* 41–55.
Rutter, M. (1989). Pathways from childhood to adult life. *Journal of Child Psychology and Psychiatry, 30,* 25–31.
Sampson, R. J., & Laub, J. H. (1993). *Crime in the making: Pathways and turning points through life.* Cambridge: Harvard University Press.
Sampson, R. J., & Laub, J. H. (1990). Crime and deviance over the life course: The salience of adult social bonds. *American Sociological Review, 55,* 609–627.
Thornberry, T. P., & Krohn, M. D. (2001). The development of delinquency: An interactional perspective. In S. O. White (Ed.), *Handbook of youth and justice,* (pp. 289–305), New York: Plenum.
Thornberry, T. P., Freeman-Gallant, A., Lizotte, A. J., Krohn, M. D., & Smith, C. A. (2003). Linked lives: The intergenerational transmission of antisocial behavior. *Journal of Abnormal Child Psychology, 31,* 171–184.
Thornberry, T. P., Krohn, M. D., Lizotte, A. J., Smith, C. A., & Tobin, K. (2003) *Gangs and delinquency in developmental perspective.* New York: Cambridge University Press.
Tremblay, R. E., Nagin, D. S., Seguin, J. R., Zoccolillo, M., Zelazo, P., Boivin, M., et al. (2004). Physical aggression during early childhood: Trajectories and predictors. *Pediatrics, 114*(1), e43–e50.
Wheaton, B. (1990). Life transitions, role histories, and mental health. *American Sociological Review, 55,* 209–224.

chapter three

Estimating time-varying causes and outcomes, with application to incarceration and crime

Christopher Wimer
Stanford University

Robert J. Sampson
Harvard University

John H. Laub
University of Maryland

Contents

Introduction 38
The counterfactual approach 39
Inverse probability-of-treatment weighting 41
Study design 43
Measures 44
IPTW models of within-individual change 47
Hierarchical IPTW models of criminal propensity 49
Causal estimates 50
Conclusion 55
Acknowledgment 56
References 56
Endnotes 58

Introduction

Many, if not most, questions in the social sciences involve causal processes that unfold over time. Researchers often wonder whether events happening at some initial point in time lead to changes in other events happening in the future. For instance, does getting assigned to a small class size in first grade lead to improvements in student performance in second grade and beyond? Does attending an Ivy League college increase adult earnings? Does getting married lead to improvements in men's psychological or physical health? The potential questions of interest are endless. As such, finding and employing rigorous empirical methods able to address causal processes unfolding over time — sometimes referred to as *turning points* — is critical to the accumulation of social scientific knowledge. This chapter employs and illustrates one such method, inverse probability-of-treatment weighting (IPTW), to help understand our potential for estimating time-varying causes and outcomes.

A major debate in the criminological literature involves the effects of incarceration on criminal offending and recidivism among ex-offenders. Extant theory suggests widely varying potential effects of incarceration on the likelihood of reoffending over the life course. On the one hand, incarceration could lead to decreases in offending subsequent to release if incarceration had a *deterrent* effect by dissuading ex-offenders from recidivating because of negative reactions to incarceration or a desire to avoid future incarceration spells (see, e.g., Nagin, 1998). Furthermore, a period of confinement in prison may expose offenders to educational and vocational programs; thus, incarceration may have a *rehabilitative* effect (see, e.g., MacKenzie, 2006). On the other hand, incarceration could lead to increases in offending subsequent to release if *differential association* with criminals behind bars led to the calcification of criminal tendencies or an increased predisposition toward willingness to commit crime (see, e.g., Matsueda & Heimer, 1997). Similarly, if *blocked opportunities* stemming from criminal records impeded access to legitimate opportunities in the mainstream economy, incarceration might result in an increased propensity for additional offenses (see, e.g., Pettit & Western 2004). The available literature, using varying methods, finds discrepant findings when trying to determine the effect of incarceration on subsequent offending.

This chapter addresses the challenge of causality in a long-term study of incarceration and crime over the life course, utilizing recently pioneered empirical strategies to more adequately estimate time-varying causal effects. Specifically, our approach builds on a contribution by Sampson, Laub, and Wimer (2006) that proposed an extension of "counterfactual" methods for time-varying covariates to a within-individual analysis of the causal role of marriage on changes in crime in the lives of 500 men who entered the transition to adulthood at high risk for continued involvement in crime. Committed to reform schools in Massachusetts during their adolescence in the 1940s, these men were the original subjects of a classic study of juvenile delinquency and its aftermath (Glueck & Glueck, 1950, 1968). Followed to age 32 by the Gluecks, the early and young adult lives of these men were later investigated by Sampson and Laub (1993).

The analysis in this chapter is based on three sets of additional data. As described in the chapter, we first launched a 35-year follow-up study to age 70 in which we conducted state and national searches of both crime and death records for the original 500 delinquent men. Second, we tracked and conducted in-depth interviews with a targeted subsample of 52 of the men who varied in patterns of criminality in adulthood. During these interviews, we administered a life history calendar to assess yearly changes in key life events (e.g., incarceration, marriage, and crime). Finally, we coded yearly data on key time-varying covariates for the full sample of 500 over the ages 17 to 32 from the original study's data archives (for more details on the follow-up study, see Laub & Sampson, 2003).

Unlike research that contrasts the outcomes of incarcerated with never-incarcerated individuals, our strategy is to capitalize on variations within individuals over time, separating the effects of stable characteristics from change. We capitalize on recent advances in counterfactual analysis for longitudinal data, comparing the average causal effect of incarceration to no incarceration for the same person. By weighting for time-varying propensities to incarceration over each year of the life course, our counterfactual strategy "thinks" like an experiment and provides an alternative to the static between-individual comparisons that dominate the incarceration and crime literature. We do not claim to identify the causal influence of incarceration with the rigor possible if offenders were randomly assigned to prison in a true social experiment. But, by modeling within-individual changes in the propensity to be incarcerated, we can at least come closer to the goal of explaining consequences for crime by bringing what is typically viewed as a nuisance — selection into and out of incarceration — explicitly into the investigation.

The counterfactual approach

One of the major threats to any analysis claiming causal effects of an experience like incarceration is accounting for the nonrandom selection of individuals into that experience. For instance, those who become incarcerated could be those with more serious or extensive criminal records, which could also reflect a preexisting proclivity to commit crime subsequent to any incarceration spells. To the extent that incarceration is influenced by individual self-selection, its relationship to crime is therefore potentially spurious.

Whereas causal claims proliferate in the criminological literature, albeit often ambiguously stated or rendered implicit, the strategies that are used to support them often fall well short (see the review by Moffitt, 2005). To illustrate, take the ubiquitous "control variable" approach. Because incarceration cannot be randomized in practice, the canonical solution to date has been to control a host of potentially confounding factors, most notably lagged states of crime itself and other factors that may cause both incarceration and crime, such as unemployment, marriage, and the like. But, controlling past values of the treatment or outcome can easily lead to null or biased estimates because they control for the very developmental pathways that are hypothesized to lead to crime. Controlling for endogenous time-varying confounders can also induce a correlation between the treatment and response even when no causal association exists (Robins, 1999).

We address this problem with a multiprong approach that combines a longitudinal fixed-effects analysis of changes in incarceration and crime over the life course with recently pioneered methods for identifying causal effects using observational data — what are typically called *counterfactual methods* of causal inference. Drawing from the language of randomized experiments, counterfactual methods conceptualize causality in terms of the effect of a definable treatment (e.g., incarceration) on some outcome (e.g., likelihood of committing a crime). In this case, one divides the sample population into a treatment group (those who are incarcerated) and a control group (those who are not incarcerated). When examining the causal effect of the treatment, counterfactual methods assume that each individual has two potential outcomes, at least theoretically. The first is the outcome that the individual demonstrates under the treatment condition, which we call Y_i^t. The second is the outcome that the individual demonstrates under the control condition, which we call Y_i^c. For each individual, however, only one of these outcomes can be actually observed at the same time. We can thus recast questions of causality as a "missing data problem" of the unobserved counterfactual (Winship & Morgan, 1999), one that is solved in experimentation through randomization. Assuming equivalence of controls and treatments, in other words, permits the estimation of the causal effect $\bar{Y}_t - \bar{Y}_c$.

When dealing with a treatment at one point in time, an increasingly common statistical approach is to use propensity score matching (for a formal discussion, see Rosenbaum & Rubin, 1983; for empirical examples in the social sciences, see Harding, 2003; Morgan, 2001). With this technique, one can model the propensity that each individual receives the treatment and then create two groups by matching those who did or did not receive the treatment on this propensity score. This strategy has been shown to yield consistent and unbiased estimates of causal effects as long as all potential confounding factors are included in the model used to create the propensity score. In essence, the surprising outcome is that matching on the propensity score fully balances the treatment and control groups on all of the covariates used in modeling the propensity of receiving the treatment, allowing the researcher to identify the causal effect by estimating $\bar{Y}_t - \bar{Y}_c$. But, propensity score matching is an inappropriate method for dealing with time-varying treatments and outcomes. When later treatments are endogenous to intermediate outcomes of prior treatments, both linear adjustments and propensity score matching can produce biased estimates (Rosenbaum, 1984; Raudenbush, Hong, & Rowan). Instead, we rely on a recently pioneered method for longitudinal data, IPTW.

Inverse probability-of-treatment weighting

Epidemiologist James Robins and colleagues (Hernán, Brumback, & Robins, 2000, 2002; Robins, 1986, 1987, 1999; Robins, Hernán, & Brumback, 2000) have shown that estimates of causal effects may be biased when time-dependent covariates predict both the outcome of interest and subsequent exposure to the treatment and when past exposure history of the treatment predicts the time-varying confounder. Figure 3.1 depicts the simple example of one time-varying treatment (such as incarceration) over two years, X_1 and X_2; one outcome (such as crime) at Time 3 (Y_3); and one time-varying confounder (such as income), Z_1 and Z_2. Assume we want to identify the causal effect of X_2 on Y_3. If we do not control for Z_1 and Z_2

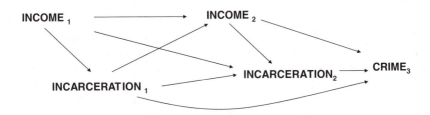

• Not including Income$_2$ and Incarceration$_1$ will cause bias since both are confounded with Incarceration$_2$ and Crime$_3$.

• But, including both Income$_2$ and Incarceration$_1$ will also cause bias since Income$_2$ can be affected by Incarceration$_1$.

Figure 3.1 Three time-point example of confounding in lagged methods.

as covariates, using either traditional regression techniques or propensity score methods, we will bias our treatment effect estimates because Z_1 and Z_2 are likely to predict both X_2 (getting the treatment in Year 2) and Y_3 (the outcome). Yet, we also have a problem if we control for Z_2 because Z_2 is an outcome of the original treatment X_1. In other words, the Year 2 treatment is endogenous to outcomes of prior treatments, and it can thus be seen that typical panel models that simply control for time-varying covariates are inherently flawed. The problem becomes worse when we introduce time-varying outcomes: Although not graphed in Figure 3.1 to maintain parsimony, prior crime can influence later states of both incarceration and income, again biasing estimates when using lagged controls.

Robins and colleagues (see Hernán et al., 2000; Robins et al., 2000) have pioneered the innovative IPTW method for dealing with this problem. They show that bias and the inducement of artificial correlations between treatment and outcome can be appropriately dealt with by fitting a model that weights each subject i at time k by a weight consisting of the inverse of the predicted probability that the subject received the treatment *that they actually received* at time k given prior treatment history, time-varying covariate history, and baseline (time-invariant) covariates. More formally,

$$W_i(t) = \frac{1}{\prod_{k=0}^{t} f[A_i(k) \mid \bar{A}_i(k-1), \bar{L}_i(k)]}$$

where $A_i(k)$ is subject i's treatment status at time k, $\bar{A}_i(k-1)$ is subject i's treatment history up to time $k - 1$, and $\bar{L}_i(k)$ is a vector of both time-varying and time-invariant covariates, which depending on the nature of the treatment and the outcome, can also include subject i's outcome history up to time $k - 1$.[1] In using IPTW weights, we borrow more information from cases with smaller probabilities of receiving the treatment at any given period given selection factors such as treatment and covariate history. Barber, Murphy, and Verbitsky (2004) provided an excellent and more detailed description of the IPTW logic for time-varying confounders in survival analysis.

Simply using the weights defined thus far, however, can lead to highly inefficient and unstable estimates when some subjects have very low probabilities of receiving the treatment that they received (that is, they would be assigned exceedingly high IPTW weights, and these small numbers of observations would dominate the analysis). Robins et al. (2000) proposed the use of an alternative set of "stabilized weights," which (in words) consist of a denominator — the probability that the subject received the subject's observed treatment at time k given past treatment and covariate history — and a numerator, the probability that the subject received the subject's observed treatment given past treatment history but not further adjusting for covariate history. More formally,

$$SW_i(t) = \prod_{k=0}^{t} \frac{f[A_i(k) \mid \bar{A}_i(k-1)]}{f[A_i(k) \mid \bar{A}_i(k-1), \bar{L}_i(k)]}$$

In short, IPTW models address fundamental problems associated with estimating causal effects of time-varying treatments on outcomes. Rather than creating potential biases by including endogenous confounders, either as control variables or as part of a model creating a propensity score, IPTW methods weight each person-period by the inverse of the predicted probability of receiving the treatment status that they actually received in that period. Analogous to survey weights, IPTW models create a "pseudopopulation" of weighted replicates, allowing one to compare times when one does and does not experience a "treatment" without making distributional assumptions about counterfactuals. IPTW models thus also provide a strategy to properly deal with potentially complex parametric causal pathways among time-varying treatments, time-varying covariates, and time-varying responses (Ko, Hogan, & Mayer, 2003). In the following section, we describe our data and measures, followed by a tailored implementation of the IPTW model.

Study design

Our main source of data was a long-term follow-up of the original subjects studied by Glueck and Glueck in *Unraveling Juvenile Delinquency* (1950). The Gluecks' study of juvenile and adult criminal behavior involved a sample of 500 male delinquents aged 10 to 17 and 500 male nondelinquents aged 10 to 17 matched on age, ethnicity, IQ, and low-income residence. Over a 25-year period from 1940 to 1965, a wealth of information was collected in childhood, adolescence, and adulthood (Glueck & Glueck, 1950, 1968). Subjects were originally interviewed at an average age of 14, at age 25, and again at age 32, with only 8% attrition. Data reconstruction and an analysis of continuity and change in crime for the Glueck men up to age 32 were described in *Crime in the Making: Pathways and Turning Points Through Life* (Sampson & Laub, 1993).[2]

The men were born between 1924 and 1932 and grew up in central Boston. When we launched a follow-up study in 1994, the oldest subject was nearing 70, and the youngest was 61. We collected three sets of data on the men: criminal records, both at the state and national levels; death records, also at the state and national levels; and interviews with a targeted subset of original delinquent subjects. Additional details on all aspects of the research design and data collection can be found in Laub and Sampson (2003) and Sampson et al. (2006). A key part of our follow-up study involved tracking and conducting detailed interviews with a targeted subset of the original delinquent subjects. After setting aside those men who had died (N = 245), we conducted a comprehensive search to locate the living original subjects. Of the 230 members of the study who were alive and thus eligible for an interview at the time of the follow-up study, we located reliable information on 181 men, yielding a location rate of 79%. Of these, we were able to contact 88 men, 52 (59%) of whom were interviewed; 36 (41%) refused or were unable for health reasons to be interviewed. The analysis in this chapter relies on both the original sample of 500 men as well as the long-term follow-up sample of 52 men.

Analyses not presented in tabular form demonstrated that our stratified sampling strategy in the follow-up captured variability in crime while maintaining representativeness relative to the larger group. Namely, when we compared the 52 men to the rest of the delinquent group on a wide range of variables, including risk factors in childhood, measures of delinquency in adolescence, and numerous adult outcomes, the differences were surprisingly nil. Of 23 comparisons and formal tests, there was only one significant difference, almost exactly what one would expect by chance at the .05 level (results available on request). These results allow us to conclude that neither our sampling stratification scheme nor interview-based attrition (including death) served to create a sample of interviewed men distinct from the pool from which they were drawn.

Measures

For the IPTW estimation techniques to properly eliminate confounding and provide a robust estimate of causal effects, we first need to specify a proper model of nonrandom selection into incarceration. Because the purpose of this chapter is primarily one of application, we draw heavily on the work of Sampson et al. (2006) and specify the same set of time-varying and time-invariant covariates that cover factors from early childhood to each year of adult life.

At the person level, we examined 10 individual-specific differences and 10 family and parental background factors exogenous to age 17. Individual differences are comprised of five measures:

1. Intelligence assessed using the Wechsler-Bellevue Full-Score IQ test (mean IQ = 92)
2. A composite scale (ranging from 1 to 26) based on parent-, like self- and teacher reports of delinquent behavior (such as stealing, vandalism)

and other misconduct (such as truancy, running away) not necessarily known to the police (mean number of offenses = 14.21)
3.   Age of first arrest (mean = 11.92)
4.   Total number of days incarcerated up to age 17 (mean = 553 or 1.52 years)
5.   A multi-item scale of adolescent competence (ranging from 0 to 6) that includes ambitions, planfulness, conscientiousness, attitudes toward school, and actual school grades (mean = 1.24)

From a detailed and independent psychiatric assessment of each boy, five dichotomous indicators tapping personality are examined:

6.   *Extroversion*, defined as "uninhibited in regard to motor responses to stimuli" (56% of the delinquent sample)
7.   *Adventurousness*, defined as "desirous of change, excitement, or risk" (55% of the delinquent sample)
8.   *Egocentricity*, defined as "self-centered, inclined not to make allowances for others, selfishly narrow in viewpoint" (14% of the delinquent sample)
9.   *Aggressiveness*, defined as "inclined to impose one's will on others" (15% of the delinquent sample)
10. *Stubbornness*, defined as "resistive or persistent" (41% of the delinquent sample)

For more details on all of these measures, see Glueck and Glueck (1950, pp. 245–247), Laub and Sampson (1998), and Sampson and Laub (1993).
     The 10 indicators of family and parental background are derived from home interviews and supplemental records:

1.   Family poverty status: a standardized scale drawing on information on the family's average weekly income and the family's reliance on public assistance (mean = .00)
2.   Parental education: 27% of the parents of delinquents attended or completed high school
3.   Residential mobility: the number of times the boy's family moved during his childhood (ranged from 1 to 16 with a mean of 8.67)
4.   Mother's supervision: defined as suitable, fair, or unsuitable depending on whether the mother monitored the boy's activities in the home and in the neighborhood (mean = 1.43)
5.   Immigrant status: whether one or both parents were born outside the United States (58% of the parents of delinquents were born outside of United States)

6. Family size: defined as the number of children in the boy's family (mean = 5.44 children)
7. Erratic–threatening discipline measures: the degree to which parents used inconsistent disciplinary measures in conjunction with harsh, physical punishment or threatening or scolding behavior (mean of standardized scale = −.08)
8. Family disruption: coded one when the boy was reared in a home with one or both parents absent because of divorce, separation, desertion, or death (61% of the delinquents)
9. Criminality–alcoholism of parent or parents (ranged from 0 to 4): determined by official records of arrest or conviction along with reports from interviews of frequent, regular, or chronic addiction to alcohol (mean = 1.97)
10. Mental disorder of parent or parents (ranged from 0 to 2): draws on medical reports to capture whether the boy's parents were diagnosed with "severe mental disease or distortion," including "marked emotional instability," "pronounced temperamental deviation," or "extreme impulsiveness" (mean = .87)

For more details on all of these measures, see the work Glueck and Glueck (1950), Sampson and Laub (1993, pp. 71–77), and Sampson and Laub (1994). Overall, the 20 measures cover a comprehensive multimethod and multiscore inventory of between-individual predictors that might lead individuals to have different propensities toward incarceration, including child and adolescent behavior, ability, personality, social background, parental personality-criminality, and family processes.

Finally, we exploited the prospective longitudinal nature of the yearly data and coded the time-varying treatment, confounders, and crime. Because of our focus on the life course, we chose age-years as the unit of within-individual change. We coded person-year observations for each of the men beginning at age 17, marking the transition to young adulthood and potentially a first adult incarceration spell. Based on the combination of Massachusetts criminal histories, national Federal Bureau of Investigation data, and death records, we coded the number of criminal events for each year at ages 17 to 32 in the full delinquent group and at ages 17 to 70 in the interviewed follow-up sample, in both cases adjusting for mortality. From official records and interviews, we coded the number of days free from incarceration each year for both samples. More precisely, using incarceration dates from the Glueck archives up to age 32 and from the life history calendars from age 32 onward, we coded whether each man was incarcerated (1 = yes, 0 = no) during each year from ages 17 to 70. For the full delinquent group, we also coded yearly episodes of military service, stable employment, marriage, and the number of subject's biological children in the household.[3] Each of these factors could increase one's probability of both becoming incarcerated and committing crimes, and hence each is a potential confounder for estimating the effect of incarceration on crime. For the long-term follow-up (ages 32 to 70), we were unable to reliably measure age-specific employment.

IPTW models of within-individual change

To calculate both the nonstabilized and stabilized IPTW weights, we first arranged the data longitudinally by person-years. We then estimated a series of pooled logistic regression models with time-dependent intercepts to determine the predicted probability of receiving the treatment status that the subject actually received in year k. To account for the nonindependence of observations over time within persons, we used the Huber-White adjustment for standard errors (StataCorp, 2003, pp. 270–275) clustered on the person. For the calculation of the weights' denominator, these pooled (or yearly specific) logit models took the form:

Logit pr

$$[A_k = 1 | A_{k-1} = a_{k-1}, \quad L_k = l_k] = \alpha_0 + \alpha_1(age) + \alpha_2(age^2) + \alpha_3(a_{k-1}) + \bar{\alpha}_j(\bar{l}_{k-1})$$

where age is modeled as a quadratic function, a_{k-1} represents the respondent's treatment history, and l_{k-1} is the vector of time-varying and time-invariant covariates as specified above. That is, we entered the vector of both lagged (i.e., stable employment in the prior year) and cumulative (i.e., number of years prior with stable employment) history measures for time-varying covariates, with the result that we generated two predictors for each time-varying confounder. It is important to note that the predicted probabilities used in the construction of the weights should be the predicted probability of receiving the treatment status that the subject *actually received*. Statistical programs such as Stata typically produce predicted probabilities that binary variables equal "1," so for subjects not receiving the treatment, the analyst needs to calculate the predicted probability that their treatment status equals "0" when in that state.

To derive the numerator of the stabilized weights, we estimated a pooled (or yearly specific) logistic regression model of the form:

$$\text{Logit pr } [A_k = 1 | A_{k-1} = a_{k-1}, \quad L_k = l_k] = \alpha_0 + \alpha_1(age) + \alpha_2(age^2) + \alpha_3(a_{k-1})$$

We modeled the treatment history as a cumulative history of the number of years up to time $k - 1$ in which the respondent had been incarcerated, along with a "recency" parameter for whether the respondent was incarcerated in the previous person-year. The cumulative history and lagged state of incarceration independently predicted the present state of incarceration in the multivariate estimation of the IPTW weights. After deriving these "raw" numerator and denominator values in each person-period, we then calculated the cross-product of these raw weights through time to arrive at the final stabilized IPTW weights. So, for example, for a subject aged 22, we would calculate the subject's final stabilized IPTW weight as the subject's raw weight at age 22 multiplied by the individual's raw weights at ages 21, 20, 19, 18, and 17.

To give an example, men who have a high probability of incarceration at any given age based on their criminal, employment, military, marital, and childbearing history would effectively be "downweighted" in the IPTW analysis for that year. Such person-periods reflect a higher degree of "selection" into the observed treatment status given values on confounding covariate histories that make them especially likely to be incarcerated (or not). As a result, we do not want them to contribute as much information to the estimation of the causal effect of incarceration on crime. On the other hand, men with low probabilities of incarceration (but who actually were incarcerated) at a given age provide more useful information and are therefore "upweighted" when estimating the final causal effect. An examination of the calculated IPTW weights confirmed that those person-periods with high degrees of selection on the observed covariates were appropriately downweighted, whereas those with lower degrees of selection present on the observed covariates were appropriately upweighted.[4]

To ensure the robustness of results, we created an additional set of weights: We split our sample into person-periods when the respondent was incarcerated in the prior person-year and when the respondent was not incarcerated in the prior person-year. We then reestimated the full pooled logistic regression models on each subsample and recalculated the predicted probabilities for the weight construction from the results of the appropriate model (J. Robins, 2005, personal communication). So, for example, a man who was not incarcerated in the previous year would get his weight values from the predicted probabilities that he was incarcerated in the current year from logistic regression models predicting incarceration only among person-periods when men were not incarcerated in the previous year. This last procedure thus allowed us to treat the covariates in our selection model as fully interactive with the incarceration history of respondents as the predicted probabilities generated by the covariates varied depending on the respondent's treatment history status. We report the results from both IPTW weighting procedures below.

Hierarchical IPTW models of criminal propensity

As in Sampson et al. (2006), we merged the IPTW model with an extended generalized hierarchical model for longitudinal data (see also Raudenbush et al., forthcoming). Time periods are nested within individuals, so that Level 1 of the hierarchical model becomes the change analysis, and Level 2 yields between-individual parameters. The interdependence of observations over time was explicitly modeled, and the IPTW weights were applied to the Level 1 analysis of within-individual change.

The hierarchical model addressed three important features of the data. The first is a conception of crime as a rare event in any 1 year, especially in the older ages. The second is unexplained variation (heterogeneity) between individuals in the underlying or latent propensity to offend (Bushway, Piquero, Broidy, Cauffman, & Mazerolle, 2001). The third is that there is variation across time and individuals in incarceration, yielding a varying "street time" during which one has the opportunity to commit crime (Blumstein, Cohen, Roth, & Visher, 1986). To accommodate these three features, our model viewed the count of crime Y_{ij} for a given person i at time j as sampled from a Poisson distribution with mean $n_{ij} \lambda_{ij}$, where n_{ij} is the number of days free on the street for person i at time j, and λ_{ij} is the latent or "true" offending rate for person i per day free in year j. We viewed the resulting log-event rates of crime as normally distributed across persons; using a hierarchical generalized linear model (Raudenbush & Bryk, 2002), we set the natural log link $\eta_{ij} = \log (\lambda_{ij})$ equal to a mixed linear model that includes relevant covariates, a random effect for each person to account for heterogeneity, and an overdispersion parameter.[5] The individual offending rate thus conformed to a Poisson distribution, allowing for overdispersion, which incorporated the skewed nature of crime with its many values of zero in any given year, while at the same time creating a metric to define meaningful effect sizes. Our approach also incorporated unique unobserved differences between persons via random effects (Horney, Osgood, & Marshall, 1995, 661). If individuals have stable features that affect crime, random effects can be important in accounting for variation not explainable by the structural model.

We specified the log of a person's total crime rate per day free[6] as a function of our causal "treatment" of incarceration lagged 1 year, weighted at Level 1 (time) with IPTW also lagged 1 year to match the temporal effect of incarceration. We used a lag model to avoid the possibility of reverse causation in any single year, in which committing a crime could lead to incarcerating. Note also that incarceration was used as the exposure variable (days free) in the Poisson models for each person-year crime rate. Because of the time-varying nature of the outcome and our interest in the average *within-individual* change estimates, we did not further condition in the crime models presented on baseline covariates. Using the above notation, the final elements of interest in the within-person model thus became:

$$E(\text{Crime}_{ij}|\beta_i) = n_i *\lambda_{ij}$$

$$\text{Log }(\lambda_{ij}) = \beta_{0,i} + \beta_{1,i}\text{ Incarceration}_{ij-1} + r_{ij}$$

where i is the index for individuals, j is for longitudinal observations, and n_{ij} is the number of days free on the street for person i at time j. Incarceration is a time-varying covariate that can take on values of 0 (not incarcerated) or 1 (incarcerated) during each year of observation. The intercept $\beta_{0,i}$ is the estimated log event-rate of crime while free during nonincarcerated person-years. Each observation at Level 1 was weighted via the IPTW methodology, yielding the causal effect interpretation for the incarceration parameter.

The between-person model takes the following general form:

$$\beta_{0,i} = \gamma_{0,0} + u_{0,i}$$

$$\beta_{1,i} = \gamma_{1,0} (+ u_{1,i})$$

As indicated by the presence of an error term, persistent heterogeneity was modeled by allowing the latent rate of offending to vary randomly across persons. We also estimated models in which the incarceration effect was allowed to vary, but the random effects were largely insignificant. In these models, the incarceration slope was constrained to zero. The parameter of major interest is the average within-individual causal effect of incarceration derived from the between-person model. That is, the average time-varying effect of incarceration in the Level 1 model $\beta_{1,i}$ was captured in the between-person model by the term $\gamma_{1,0}$ (Horney et al., 1995, p. 661; Laub & Sampson, 2003, p. 310). All results refer to population average effects with robust standard errors.

Causal estimates

Before looking at the causal estimates generated through the use of our IPTW weighting strategy, we first present results from a set of bivariate logistic regression models predicting incarceration. These results, displayed in Table 3.1, are presented to examine the degree of confounding present. The results in Table 3.1 show that the vast majority of our baseline, time-invariant covariates did not predict receipt of the treatment,

Table 3.1 Logistic Regression Coefficients and Standard Errors
Bivariate Predictions of Person-Period Incarceration
from Ages 17 to 32 and 17 to 70

	Incarceration, ages 17–32	Incarceration, ages 17–70
Individual differences, < 17 years		
Measured IQ	−0.003	0.011
	(0.005)	(0.011)
Competence	−0.150*	0.078
	(0.065)	(0.112)
Delinquent behavior	−0.044**	0.036
	(0.017)	(0.034)
Age at first arrest	−0.006	−0.036
	(0.033)	(0.066)
Days incarcerated	0.001***	0.001***
up to age 17	(0.0002)	(0.0003)
Extroversion	0.093	0.030
	(0.139)	(0.360)
Adventurousness	0.097	−0.140
	(0.138)	(0.298)
Egocentricity	0.271	−0.561*
	(0.197)	(0.239)
Aggressiveness	0.189	0.114
	(0.193)	(0.350)
Stubbornness	0.015	−0.059
	(0.138)	(0.278)
Family/parental background		
Family poverty	0.036	−0.096
	(0.040)	(0.076)
Parental education	0.084	−0.195
	(0.151)	(0.278)
Residential mobility	0.037*	−0.020
	(0.015)	(0.033)
Mother's supervision	−0.036	−0.0004
	(0.113)	(0.239)
Immigrant status	−0.355*	−0.181
	(0.139)	(0.275)
Family size	0.031	−0.019
	(0.033)	(0.057)

(Continued)

Table 3.1 Logistic Regression Coefficients and Standard Errors:
Bivariate Predictions of Person-Period Incarceration
from Ages 17 to 32 and 17 to 70 (Continued)

	Incarceration, ages 17–32	Incarceration, ages 17–70
Erratic/threatening	−0.001	0.015
discipline	(0.043)	(0.095)
Family disruption	0.161	0.240
	(0.140)	(0.278)
Criminality/alcoholism	0.089	0.040
of parent(s)	(0.056)	(0.116)
Mental disorder of	−0.011	0.061
parents	(0.095)	(0.199)
Adult time-varying covariates		
Age	−0.111***	−0.056***
	(0.010)	(0.008)
Age squared	−0.002***	−0.009***
	(0.0002)	(0.0002)
Married in last	−1.291***	−1.823***
person-period	(0.137)	(0.378)
Cumulative sum of	−0.197***	−0.102***
years married up to last	(0.030)	(0.032)
person-period		
Any arrest in last	1.412***	N/A
person-period	(0.081)	
Cumulative sum of	0.095***	−0.009
criminal events up to	(0.010)	(0.007)
last person-period		
Incarcerated in last	3.610***	4.799***
person-period	(0.106)	(0.153)
Cumulative sum of	0.293***	0.024
person-periods	(0.023)	(0.015)
Incarcerated up to last		
person-period		
In military in last	−0.781***	N/A
person–period	(0.157)	
Cumulative sum of in	−0.263***	N/A
military person-periods	(0.046)	
up to last person-period		

Table 3.1 Logistic Regression Coefficients and Standard Errors: Bivariate Predictions of Person-Period Incarceration from Ages 17 to 32 and 17 to 70 (Continued)

	Incarceration, ages 17–32	Incarceration, ages 17–70
Had a child in last person-period	−0.608*** (0.144)	N/A
Cumulative sum of number of children in household in past person-periods	−0.050*** (0.016)	N/A
Steady employment in last person-period	−2.229*** (0.151)	N/A
Cumulative sum of steady employment in past person-periods	−0.497*** (0.052)	N/A
Lagged pooled violent crime count	N/A	1.057*** (0.289)
Lagged pooled property crime count	N/A	1.452*** (0.160)
Lagged pooled drug crime count	N/A	−0.054 (0.144)
Cumulative sum of steady cohabitating relationship in past person-periods	N/A	−0.303 (0.210)

Note: N/A, not applicable since covariates included in the models generating the IPTW weights differed between the two samples due to data availability.

$+p < .10$ $*p < .05$ $**p < .01$ $***p < .001$

incarceration. In the full aged 17–32 sample, only 4 of 20 baseline covariates significantly predicted incarceration, and in the long-term follow-up sample, only 2 of 20 baseline covariates significantly predicted incarceration. Time-invariant covariates, however, were not a primary concern for the current analyses as the IPTW strategy is designed to eliminate biases stemming from time-varying confounders. Table 3.1 reveals that time-varying confounding is a major issue for the current analysis. In the full sample, all 14 time-varying measures significantly predicted incarceration,

Table 3.2 Hierarchical Variable-Exposure Poisson Models of Total Crime, Ages 17–32: Estimation of Incarceration Effects on Within-Individual Changes (N = 410 Men; 4,153 Observations)

Incarceration effect	Coefficient (*SE*)	*p* value	Event rate ratio	Confidence interval
Unweighted, freed slope, naïve estimate	0.550 (0.093)	0.000	1.73	(1.44–2.08)
IPTW noninteractive, freed slope	−0.031 (0.131)	0.821	0.97	(0.74–1.26)
IPTW fully interactive, freed slope	0.490 (0.092)	0.000	1.63	(1.36–1.96)

while in the long-term follow-up sample, 7 of 11 significantly predicted incarceration. This means that, in both our samples, there was a high degree of potential time-varying confounding, which indicates that IPTW is a promising strategy to reduce this potential bias.

Table 3.2 presents the hierarchical Poisson count models that account for exposure time (days not incarcerated) and persistent heterogeneity in unobserved causes of offending. We began with the larger sample of delinquent boys followed for a shorter period: ages 17 to 32 (N = 4,153 person-years). As in the logic of an experiment, we focused on the single estimate of the average causal effect of incarceration on crime, lagged 1 year. However, to assess robustness, we display the results from a "naïve" model followed by two models reflecting variations in IPTW specification for the weighting procedures.

The estimates of causal effects in Table 3.2 show that on implementing our IPTW weighting strategy, the estimated effects of incarceration were at least reduced, if not eliminated, when compared to an unweighted naïve model. Using this unweighted naïve model, the causal effect estimate is .550 ($p < .001$), with an exponentiated event rate of 1.73, indicating that incarceration is associated with large *increases* in subsequent criminal offending. This large estimated effect, however, was reduced when applying the IPTW weights. Using the fully interactive IPTW weights reduced the estimated effect of incarceration to an event ratio of 1.63, ($p < .001$). Using the more common form of noninteractive IPTW weights completely eliminated the estimated effect generated by the unweighted model. Taking the average of the two IPTW estimation strategies suggests a materially reduced "effect" of incarceration on later offending compared to the model in which we did not take into account nonrandom selection into incarceration.

Table 3.3 Hierarchical Variable-Exposure Poisson Models of Total Crime, Ages 17–70: Estimation of Incarceration Effects on Within-Individual Changes (N = 52 Men; 2,090 Observations)

Incarceration effect	Coefficient (*SE*)	*p* value	Event rate ratio	Confidence interval
Unweighted, freed slope, naïve estimate	1.488 (0.212)	0.000	4.43	(2.90–6.77)
IPTW noninteractive, freed slope	0.895 (0.216)	0.000	2.45	(1.59–3.78)
IPTW fully interactive, freed slope	−0.014 (0.468)	0.977	1.01	(0.40–2.59)

Note: SE, standard error.

Table 3.3 presents the results of analogous models for the long-term follow-up sample of 52 men, exploiting the life course data collected up to age 70 (*N* = 2,090 person-years). Here, the unweighted naïve estimate was again large, positive, and statistically significant (1.49, event ratio of 4.43, *p* < .001), which would again imply that incarceration led to increased propensities toward offending subsequent to release. Applying IPTW, however, revealed inconsistent and greatly reduced estimates. In this sample, the noninteractive IPTW weights reduced the coefficient by roughly 40%, although the estimated effect remained positive and significant (0.90, event ratio of 2.45, *p* < .001). The fully interactive weights, however, completely eliminated any estimated causal effect of incarceration. Taking the average of the two IPTW estimates, the naïve estimate was reduced by almost two-thirds. Note also that, in this sample, it was the fully interactive and not the noninteractive weights that eliminated the effect, suggesting that it is not likely that one specification is resulting in more "correct" estimates. Taken together, our IPTW estimates suggested that, when properly taking account of time-varying confounders, naïve estimates of causal effects of incarceration may be greatly reduced, although much uncertainty regarding the "true" causal effect still remains. We thus prefer to focus on the bounded "range" of causal estimates rather than any one point estimate, but either way the IPTW results suggested an attenuation of the estimated role of incarceration.

Conclusion

Perhaps the major issue at stake in the identification of turning points is whether the events identified as turning points in fact have true causal effects on subsequent behavior. This chapter addressed this problem directly by illustrating a flexible method for assessing the causal impact of time-varying turning points in the presence of time-varying confounders and time-varying outcomes. Our application employed a counterfactual life course approach that applied inverse probability of treatment weighting (IPTW) to the research question of whether incarceration increased or decreased later criminal offending. Using variation over the life course in incarceration, crime, and theoretically relevant covariates as a concrete example, we demonstrated how analysts can exploit IPTW to confront serious biases that arise from traditional methods that rely on controlling for lagged values of the treatment and covariates. Because even propensity score matching cannot properly incorporate time-varying covariates such as marriage and incarceration, the IPTW method is likely to have wide application in a variety of settings of interest to life course researchers who study turning points.

Our results showed that the causal effect of incarceration on later criminal offending was reduced considerably when nonrandom selection of incarceration was properly taken into account. These reductions suggest that many prior claims of causality put forth in the literature for the effect of incarceration on later crime, or for turning points in general, were likely overestimated due to complex processes of selection and bias generated by time-varying confounding in traditional naïve (i.e., unweighted) models. In the absence of viable opportunities to randomly assign subjects to turning points, we believe the IPTW method is thus of considerable importance to the further development of life course inquiry.

Acknowledgment

We thank the Russell Sage Foundation (Grant 85-01-23) for funding support.

References

Barber, J. S., Murphy, S. A., & Verbitsky, N. (2004). Adjusting for time-varying confounding in survival analysis. *Sociological Methodology, 34,* 163–192.

Blumstein, A., Cohen, J., Roth, J., & Visher, C. (Eds.). (1986). *Criminal careers and career criminals.* Washington, DC: National Academy Press.

Bushway, S., Piquero, A., Broidy, L., Cauffman, E., & Mazerolle, P. (2001). An empirical framework for studying desistance as a process. *Criminology, 39,* 491–515.

Glueck, S., & Glueck, E. (1950). *Unraveling juvenile delinquency.* New York: Commonwealth Fund.

Glueck, S., & Glueck, E. (1968). *Delinquents and nondelinquents in perspective.* Cambridge: Harvard University Press.

Harding, D. J. (2003). Counterfactual models of neighborhood effects: The effect of neighborhood poverty on dropping out and teenage pregnancy. *American Journal of Sociology, 109,* 676–719.

Hernán, M. Á., Brumback, B., & Robins, J. M. (2000). Marginal structural models to estimate the causal effect of zidovudine on the survival of HIV-positive men. *Epidemiology, 11*, 561–570.

Hernán, M. Á., Brumback, B., & Robins, J. M. (2002). Estimating the causal effect of zidovudine on CD4 count with a marginal structural model for repeated measures. *Statistics in Medicine, 21*, 1689–1709.

Horney, J. D., Osgood, W., & Marshall, I. H. (1995). Criminal careers in the short-term: Intra-individual variability in crime and its relation to local life circumstances. *American Sociological Review, 60*, 655–673.

Ko, H., Hogan, J. W., & Mayer, K. H.. (2003). Estimating causal treatment effects from longitudinal HIV natural history studies using marginal structural models. *Biometrics, 59*, 152–162.

Laub, J. H., & Sampson, R. J. (1998). The long-term reach of adolescent competence: Socioeconomic achievement in the lives of disadvantaged men. In A. Colby, J. James, & D. Hart (Eds.), *Competence and character through life* (pp. 88–112). Chicago: University of Chicago Press.

Laub, J. H., & Sampson, R. J. (2003). *Shared beginnings, divergent lives: Delinquent boys to age 70.* Cambridge: Harvard University Press.

MacKenzie, D. L. (2006). *What works in corrections.* New York: Cambridge University Press.

Matsueda, R. L., & Heimer, K. (1997). A symbolic interactionist theory of role-transitions, role-commitments, and delinquency. In T. P. Thornberry (Ed.), *Developmental theories of crime and delinquency* (pp. 223–276). New Brunswick, NJ: Transaction.

Moffitt, R. (2005). Remarks on the analysis of causal relationships in population research. *Demography, 42*, 91–108.

Morgan, S. L. (2001). Counterfactuals, causal effect heterogeneity, and the Catholic school effect on learning. *Sociology of Education, 74*, 341–374.

Nagin, D. S. (1998). Criminal deterrence research: A review of the evidence and a research agenda for the outset of the 21st century. *Crime and Justice: A Review of Research, 23*, 1–42.

Pettit, B., & Western, B. (2004). Mass imprisonment and the life course: Race and class inequality in U.S. incarceration. *American Sociological Review, 69*, 151–169.

Raudenbush, S. W., & Bryk, A. S. (2002). Hierarchical linear models: Applications and data analysis methods (2nd ed.). Thousand Oaks, CA: Sage.

Raudenbush, S. W., Bryk, A. S., Cheong, Y. F., & Congdon, R. (2000). *HLM 5: Hierarchical linear and nonlinear modeling.* Lincolnwood, IL: Scientific Software International.

Raudenbush, S. W., Hong, G., & Rowan, B. (in press). Studying the causal effects of instruction with application to primary-school mathematics. In J. M. Ross, G. W. Bohrnstedt, & F. C. Hemphill (Eds.), *Instructional and performance consequences of high poverty schooling.* Washington, DC: National Council for Educational Statistics.

Robins, J. (1986). A new approach to causal inference in mortality studies with a sustained exposure period: Application to the healthy worker survivor effect. *Mathematical Modeling, 7*, 1393–1512.

Robins, J. (1987). Addendum to "A new approach to causal inference in mortality studies with a sustained exposure period: Application to the healthy worker survivor effect." *Computers and Mathematics with Applications, 14,* 923–945.

Robins, J. (1999). Association, causation, and marginal structural models. *Synthese, 121,* 151–179.

Robins, J. M., Hernán, M. A., & Brumback, B. (2000). Marginal structural models and causal inference in epidemiology. *Epidemiology, 11,* 550–560.

Rosenbaum, P. R. (1984). The consequences of adjustment for a concomitant variable that has been affected by the treatment. *Journal of the Royal Statistical Society, Series A, 147,* 656–666.

Rosenbaum, P. R. (2002). *Observational studies* (2nd ed.). New York: Springer-Verlag.

Rosenbaum, P., & Rubin, D. (1983). The central role of the propensity score in observational studies for causal effects. *Biometrika, 70,* 41–55.

Sampson, R. J., & Laub, J. H. (1993). *Crime in the making: Pathways and turning points through life.* Cambridge: Harvard University Press.

Sampson, R. J., & Laub, J. H. (1994). Urban poverty and the family context of delinquency: A new look at structure and process in a classic study. *Child Development, 65,* 523–540.

Sampson, R. J., Laub, J. H, & Wimer, C. (2006). Does marriage reduce crime? A counterfactual approach to within-individual causal effects. *Criminology, 44,* 465–508.

StataCorp. 2003. Stata Statistical Software: Release 8.0. College Station, TX: Stata.

Winship, C., & Morgan, S. L. (1999). The estimation of causal effects from observational data. *Annual Review of Sociology, 25,* 659–707.

Endnotes

1. It is important to note that the weight-generating formula calls for the estimation of the cross-product of the function across all person-periods. That is, the time-dependent weights for each k are multiplied through time.

2. Because the focus of this chapter is on estimating the causal effects of incarceration on subsequent crime, we started with the group of high-rate offenders defined by the delinquent group sample in the Gluecks' original design, a group that generated almost 10,000 offenses over the life course (Laub & Sampson, 2003, p. 86). Although the question of incarceration and crime may be of interest in the nondelinquent group, we did not pursue counterfactual estimates in this group because incarceration and crime were so rare.

3. Military service was coded as 1 if the person was in the military for any portion of the yearly period and 0 otherwise. Employment at each age to 32 takes on the value 1 if the person had one job and was employed for at least 8 months during the year and 0 otherwise. Marriage at each age was coded as 1 if married and as 0 if not married. If a child was born during the age-year, children in the household was coded as 1 and as 0 otherwise.

4. Applying the stable unit treatment value assumption (SUTVA; see Rosenbaum, 2002), we made the reasonable assumption of no interaction across units—one man's response to incarceration was not conceived as

dependent on another subject's response. (The study started with 500 boys spread across the entire city of Boston and, in adulthood, extending well beyond.) Incarceration is also defined equivalently across all subjects even though the incarceration experience (e.g., number of days incarcerated, type of facility, etc.) varied. Within-subject correlation of errors was explicitly accounted for in our hierarchical change model described in the next section. We further assumed "sequential ignorability and randomization" or that incarceration propensity did not depend on unobservables after accounting for observed covariates, prior treatment history, and outcomes—the thought experiment was that incarceration is randomized within levels of prior variables for each person.

5. In all initial models, we allowed for overdispersion in the Poisson distribution, similar to the negative binomial model with unobserved heterogeneity often used in the criminology literature. The difference is that we did not impose any distributional assumptions (e.g., gamma distributed) on the extra-Poisson variance parameter. We used the HLM 6.0 software to estimate population-average model parameters with robust standard errors. Consistent with the logic and technical requirements of the Poisson model with variable exposure (Raudenbush et al., 2000, pp. 148–150), we examined observations in which men were free on the street at least 1 day (which is greater than 0) in the year of observation. The overwhelming majority of observations (96%) met this requirement and thus contributed to the analysis. We experimented with models in which these observations were included and exposure time was ignored. We also ran comparable negative binomial models using Stata. The results were very similar.

6. Considering the rarity of many specific crimes like violence along with much research showing versatility in offending, our analysis focused on total crime propensity (For fuller discussion, see Sampson et al., 2006).

chapter four

Turning points in family contact during emerging adulthood

David Rindskopf
City University of New York

Joel R. Sneed
Columbia University and the New York State Psychiatric Institute

Contents

Introduction 61
Data 64
Preliminary analyses.. 65
Data analysis sequence.. 68
    Who changed level of family contact?.. 68
    What differentiates nonchangers at each level?.............................. 70
    Characterizing overall change 70
    Within-person change and its determinants..................................... 71
Conclusion... 77
References 79

Introduction

The period referred to as *emerging adulthood*, the years between 18 and 29, are characterized by profound role changes across multiple life domains (Arnett, 2000). Prior to those years, most individuals live at home with parents and are enrolled in school, financially dependent, unmarried, and without children. However, after age 30, many are residentially and financially independent, no longer in school but working, in a committed romantic relationship, and parenting. Such normative changes conceal individual differences in change across the emerging adulthood period. Not all emerging adults consolidate their identities at the same time, and not all pursue higher education. Although most begin experimenting with romantic relationships in adolescence, during emerging adulthood some engage in committed long-term relationships; others continue dating and experimenting in transient romances. Emerging adults move out of the home at varying times and into different housing conditions. For example, some choose to move in with romantic partners, whereas others live with roommates or leave home for college living in dormitories. Now more than ever do such transitions, reflecting existential life course decisions, rest on the shoulders of emerging adults as prescribed roles and normative expectations have been abandoned in favor of continued exploration (Arnett, 2000).

One of the important changes that takes place during this period is the gradual development of autonomy. *Autonomy* has been identified as an intrinsic psychological need that, when realized, promotes mental health and well-being. The failure to develop autonomy, it has been hypothesized, may lead to decreased motivation and lowered self-esteem (Ryan & Deci, 2000). According to Boles (1999), the development of autonomy allows emerging adults to initiate assumption of increasingly adult levels of responsibility, including romantic relationship development and financial independence. Research has indicated that emerging adults tend to consider taking responsibility for the self, making independent decisions, and becoming financially independent as the most important criteria for developing a subjective sense as a fully functioning, autonomous adult (Arnett, 2000).

As might be expected, autonomy represents a cornerstone of most psychological theories of personality development. For example, Mahler, Pine, and Bergman (1975) maintained that the development of an autonomous and psychologically healthy person resulted from the processes of separation (i.e., emergence from a sense of oneness with the mother) and individuation (i.e., development of individuality). It has been hypothesized that the separation and individuation process is elaborated during a "second individuation" in adolescence and resolved during a "third individuation" that tends to take place during early-to-middle adulthood (Colarusso, 1990).

As people become more autonomous, they tend to have less contact with their family members. This general trend was shown nicely by Sneed et al. (2006). As can be seen in Figure 4.1, the average level of family contact for the 17-year-olds estimated from the average growth curve was approximately 95, reflecting the high rate of contact with family at this age. Family contact, however, decreased in a curvilinear manner throughout the emerging adulthood period, with men separating more quickly

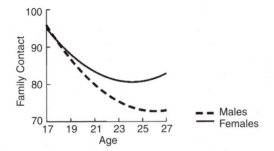

Figure 4.1 Change in family contact over emerging adulthood for men and women.

than women and maintaining less contact with their families overall at age 27.

This decline was expected on the basis of Mahler et al.'s (1975) separation-individuation theory, and the gender difference in this decline was expected on the basis of Gilligan's (1979, 1982) developmental theory. According to Gilligan, psychological theories of development emphasizing autonomy (i.e., instrumentality and separation) may more adequately describe the development of men rather than women. She suggested that attachment, connectedness, empathy, and intimacy may tend to play a more prominent role in women's personality development. Indeed, Cross and Madson (1997) noted that parents are more likely to discuss emotions with girls than boys, and parents are more likely to assign child care responsibilities to girls than to boys. Moreover, girls' relationships are characterized by intimate friendships and cooperation, whereas boys' groups are characterized more by competitiveness and rough play. Consequently, women tend to value family affiliation and closeness more than men do and to view their parents as a more important source of emotional support than men do (Kenny & Donaldson, 1991).

Such differences in socialization have important implications for the development of autonomy in emerging adulthood. To function independently, an increasing amount of time and energy must be devoted to activities and relationships outside the family (separation). This requires becoming emotionally and functionally independent from the family (Hoffman & Weiss, 1987). According to Gilligan (1979, 1982), women tend to struggle with the development of instrumentality (as traditionally conceived) and separation during adolescence and early adulthood because they tend to be more relationally oriented, whereas men tend to have more difficulty in developing and maintaining emotional relationships.

Of course, general trends may not apply to individuals; furthermore, both general age trends and group differences (such as that between males and females) may be functions of other, more basic, influences. To take a simple example, suppose that contact was dichotomized into two categories, high and low. Suppose further that everyone starts out at the high level, and that different people drop to the low level at different ages. If we examine, at each age, the proportion in the "high" category, we see that it starts at 1.00 and gradually drops to 0 as more and more people move to the "low" category. The general trend, then, is a relatively smooth decline, even though for each individual the pattern is extremely nonlinear, involving a sharp drop from high to low.

In addition to gender, one might envision a number of other variables that might predict change in contact with the family. As indicated, developmental milestones that are typically achieved during the emerging adulthood period include becoming residentially and financially independent, no longer enrolled in school but working, having a committed romantic relationship, and parenting. As a result, one might expect that life events such as going to college, coming home from college, obtaining a full-time job, marriage, and birth of children might significantly alter family contact and lead to (semi-) permanent changes in those relationships (i.e., turning points).

What we would like is a model for each individual: How (if at all) does that person's family contact change as a function of living outside the home, obtaining a job, getting married, or having children? Is such change gradual, as might be expected from the trend in Figure 4.1, or is it relatively sudden (indicating at least a change point and possibly a turning point in the person's life)? Once we have a model for each individual, we can also ask about similarities and differences among individual models. For example, does living at home have the same effect on level of family contact for everyone, or, for example, do males respond differently from females? Thus, we ask questions at two different levels: that of determinants of individual behavior and as determiners of differences across individuals in patterns of behavior. Our goal throughout this chapter is to highlight the utility of this modeling approach to the analysis of turning points while not getting lost in the complexities of the technical details. Therefore, we minimize the mathematical level of our presentation, realizing that statistically sophisticated readers can fill in the details for themselves, whereas statistically unsophisticated readers will be able to appreciate the usefulness of the approach.

Data

The data from this study came from a narrative interview of participants, 240 young adults ranging in age from 27 to 30, who are ongoing participants in a larger ($N = 800$) general population, longitudinal cohort study designed to examine risk factors for the development of mental and physical illness (Cohen & Cohen, 1996). The original sample was randomly selected on the basis of residence in one of two upstate New York counties that collectively were generally representative of the northeastern United States with regard to most demographic variables. However, they also reflected the sampled region, with a high proportion of Caucasians (91%) among those interviewed as characterized the region at the time of original sampling (Cohen & Cohen, 1996).

The dependent variable of interest (family contact) was assessed in the context of narrative interviews by trained interviewers (see Chapters 9 and 10 for details of the methods and variables in this study). Ratings of contact with the family of origin (i.e., parents or siblings) were obtained for each of the 120 months in the transitional period between age 17 and 27. Rating ranged from 0 to 100. Face-to-face meetings, telephone calls, letters, and electronic mail were all considered evidence of family contact. A rating of 0 indicated contact with a family member no more than twice per year. A rating of 25 indicated contact with one or more family members more than twice per year but no more than twice per month. A rating of 50 indicated contact with a family member more than twice per month but no more than twice per week. A rating of 75 indicated contact with a family member more than twice per week. A rating of 99 indicated daily contact with one or more family members.

As can be seen in Figure 4.2, the nature of the family contact variable strongly suggests that it be treated as ordinal, with cut points at certain natural places on the scale. For this sample, very few responses are at the low end of the scale; in fact, nearly half are at or near the very top of the scale. After some exploration and preliminary analyses, we decided to retain only three categories and used a compressed scale (with cut points at 75 and 90) to reflect that we wished to make distinctions at the high end of the contact scale. With such a categorical variable, we defined any change from one category to another as representing a meaningful amount of change.

Preliminary analyses

We began our examination of transitions by determining how many times people changed from one level of family contact to another. If most people had few changes, the modeling process (and explanatory model) might be simpler. We also looked at the overall number of changes for each possible transition from one month to the next.

Level of contact had three (ordered) categories. Table 4.1 shows, for all changes, how many were of each size (including zero). Each person contributed 120 values to the total. (Note that missing values are due to not

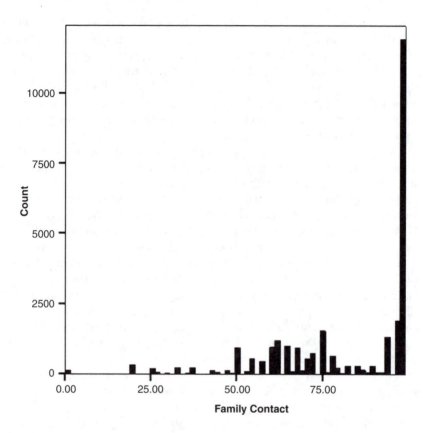

Figure 4.2 Histogram of family contact on its original scale.

Table 4.1 Number of Changes of Each Size and Direction
(Each Person Is Represented Up to 120 Times)

Number of changes	Frequency	Percentage	Cumulative percentage
− 2.00	192	0.7	0.7
− 1.00	38	0.1	0.8
0.00	27,121	97.8	98.7
1.00	63	0.2	98.9
2.00	307	1.1	100.0
Total	27,721	100.0	100.0

knowing when change occurred after the final report prior to the narrator's 27th birthday.) Almost all observations were zero; that is, there was no change from one month to the next. When change occurred, it was more likely a drastic change (two steps up or down) rather than a more minor change (only one step up or down).

Table 4.2 shows how many times each person changed (regardless of the direction of the change). Overall, 23% did not change at all over the 10-year period, whereas 77% did change at least once. Of the 77%, about 32% changed only once. Thus, by narrative report, the frequency of family contact was extremely stable between the 17th and 27th birthdays, changing little (if at all) over months and years.

The data in these tables not only illustrate that change was rare, they also validate the decision to categorize contact (instead of trying to treat it as continuous), and they validate the cut points used. If contact should have been treated as continuous, and individuals were near a cut point on the continuum, we would have seen a great deal of vacillation between the categories determined by that cut point. That is, one month a person might be just over the cut point, and the next month just below the cut point, thereby ending up in different categories. There were only a handful

Table 4.2 Number of Times People Changed Frequency
of Contact (Divided into Three Categories)

Number of changes in level of contact (categorized)	Frequency	Percentage	Cumulative percentage
0.00	54	22.6	22.6
1.00	60	25.1	47.7
2.00	34	14.2	61.9
3.00	35	14.6	76.6
4.00	8	3.3	79.9
5.00	18	7.5	87.4
6.00	8	3.3	90.8
7.00	9	3.8	94.6
8.00	3	1.3	95.8
9.00	4	1.7	97.5
10.00	1	0.4	97.9
11.00	1	0.4	98.3
12.00	2	0.8	99.2
14.00	1	0.4	99.6
15.00	1	0.4	100.0
Total	239	100.0	100.0

of cases with more than seven transitions, so the continuum model did not seem necessary.

Data analysis sequence

We now divided the issues into a sensible sequence: Who changed and who did not, and were there characteristics of individuals (e.g., gender, race, attending college or graduate school) that might have determined or predicted that change? Of those who remained stable, were there predictors that could account for the level of family contact? Finally, of those who changed, were there predictors that could account for changes within a person as well as different patterns of change between people?

To investigate the first of these issues, we created a file with one line for each person that indicated the following: sex; race; whether they ever attended (1) high school, (2) college, (3) graduate or professional school; age at which they first left home (if ever); highest age at which they were living at home (maximum 27 at end of the study); whether the level of contact ever changed during the study (yes/no); how many times the level of contact changed; and age at first change in level of contact. Notice that in these analyses the direction of changes in contact (if any) were ignored and are considered later.

Who changed level of family contact?

To answer the question of who changed level of family contact, we performed a logistic regression to predict who did and did not change; the results are displayed in Table 4.3. The predictor variables were race (black = 1 if black, 0 otherwise); sex (male = 1 if male, 0 if female); whether the person attended high school, college, or graduate/professional school (each coded 1 if yes, 0 if no); whether the person finished the highest level of education in which he or she enrolled (1 if yes, 0 if no); and age at which the person first left home (centered at 17 years, the beginning of the study). We tested whether the age of leaving home had a curvilinear effect by adding its square to a logistic regression; the square term was nowhere near significant and was not used in the more complete analysis.

A non-black female at the lowest educational level had a nearly 50% chance of changing. Race was not a significant predictor (although there were few blacks, so power was low). Males had a much higher probability of changing: The log odds for a male changing level of contact increased by 1.29 over females, so that a low-education non-black male had a .76 probability of changing.

Attending college (regardless of whether the person graduated) increased the log odds of change by .981; a male who attended college

Table 4.3 Logistic Regression to Predict Change versus No Change

Variables	B (SE)	Wald	df	p	Exp (B)	95% CI for Exp (B)
Male	2.37 (0.51)	21.40	1	<.01	10.70	3.92–29.20
Black	−0.42 (0.73)	0.33	1	.57	0.66	0.16–2.74
High school	−0.12 (.76)	0.03	1	.87	0.89	0.20–3.95
College	0.94 (0.43)	4.82	1	.03	2.55	1.11–5.88
Graduate school	19.61 (5,740.38)				^{a}	
Finish	0.79 (0.91)	0.75	1	.39	2.20	0.37–13.06
Age left home	−0.52 (0.09)	32.86	1	<.01	0.56	0.50–0.71
Constant	0.76 (0.93)	0.67	1	.41	2.14	

Note: Male = 1 if male, 0 if female; black = 1 if black, 0 otherwise; high school = 1 if attended high school, 0 otherwise; college = 1 if attended college, 0 otherwise; graduate school = 1 if attended graduate or professional school, 0 otherwise; finish = 1 if finished highest-level school attended, 0 otherwise; age left home = age at which the person first left home minus 17 (age = 27 if never left home). CI, confidence interval; Exp (B) = change in log (odds); *SE* = standard error.

^{a}The parameter and SE for this variable go to infinity and are not estimable; the z-ratio and test of significance are not computable by the usual asymptotic methods. See Rindskopf (2002) for details.

had a probability of .90 that contact would change. But, by far the largest effect was for attending graduate school; if an individual went to graduate school, the probability that level of family contact would change was predicted to be 1. This was confirmed by examining the sample; all 40 of those who attended graduate school did change.

Some technical notes follow for those interested; others may skip this paragraph without loss of continuity: (1) The significance level for attending graduate school makes it appear that this effect was not significant. This is incorrect; the parameter goes to infinity, as does the standard error, so the typical hypothesis testing procedure of dividing the parameter estimate by the standard error does not work here. A correct test is done by comparing either −2 log likelihood or the χ^2 accounted for by the model when the variable was included versus excluded from the model; here, the difference was about 16 with 1 df (degree of freedom), which is highly significant (see Rindskopf, 2002, for details). (2) For those who worry that the interaction term might be collinear with either race or sex, we ran the model with the interaction omitted. The fit of the model, of course, did not change, but neither did the coefficients, standard error, or p value for any other predictor change by very much.

What differentiates nonchangers at each level?

Now, we consider the issue of the status of those who did not change their level of contact over the 10-year period of the study. Of the 54 such people, 53 were at the highest level of contact throughout the 10-year period. Therefore, there is no meaningful variation to explain: Those who were stable were consistently at the highest levels of contact.

Characterizing overall change

Before performing more detailed analyses, we examine a very simple table that gives a great deal of information about changes in contact. We already know that a large proportion of respondents indicated no changes at all or just one change over the 10-year period of the study. Because of the great stability (small probability of change), we chose to cross-tabulate the level of contact at the first point of data (age 17) with the level of contact at the last point of data (age 27); this is displayed in Table 4.4.

The first important aspect of these results is that the marginal distribution of contact at age 17 is almost totally at the highest value: Of the respondents, 95% started at the highest level of contact, with only 2.5% at each of the other two values. Next, just over half of the respondents ended up (at age 27) at the lowest level of contact, another 12% in the middle

Table 4.4 Cross-tabulation of Level of Family Contact at
First Time of Measurement (17 Years of Age) by
Last Time of Measurement (27 Years of Age)

Age 17 level of family contact	Age 27 level of family contact			
	Low	Moderate	High	Total
Low	4	1	1	.025
Moderate	5	0	1	.025
High	113	28	86	.95
Total	.51	.12	.37	

category, and about 37% at the highest level. The net result is that a large proportion of people declined in contact between the first and last period of measurement, from nearly everyone having a high level of contact down to just over one-third having a high level of contact.

Within-person change and its determinants

Because we have data on each individual for (nearly) each month from age 17 through 27, we can track changes in family contact over that 10-year interval. It would seem sensible to write a model for the behavior of each individual in the sample who changed contact level at least once during this 10-year interval and then to compare models across individuals; for this purpose, a multilevel model would be the ideal tool. (To be clear, we must exclude from these analyses the 54 individuals who did not change, so there is no change in contact to model, that is, there is no variability to explain.)

Each person had a particular time course of contact; many respondents' patterns fell into one of a small number of patterns. One such pattern, as we have seen, was one of a constant level of contact; when it occurred, it was almost always at the highest level of contact. Another common pattern started at the highest level and suddenly switched to (and remained at) a lower level. This is not what would be expected from looking at population age trends, which show gradually decreasing levels of contact. This result is well known in some areas of psychology; in learning theory, for example, it is how proponents of all-or-none learning of individual items explained gradual learning of a list of words.

Although this general trend toward less contact with increasing age is apparent (see Figure 4.1), could we trace its cause? We distinguished two levels of potential explanatory variables: age invariant and age varying, which are also called between person and within person (or in multilevel modeling terminology, Level 2 and Level 1, respectively). Examples of age-invariant (between-person) predictors are gender and race; because they are constant within a person, they can only explain variation between people. For these data, examples of age-varying predictors were (in addition to actual age, of course) whether a person was living at home, held a job, was enrolled in school, and was taking responsibility for financial and romantic decision making.

The statistical model can be written in terms of a series of equations. For presentation, we only table and discuss the substantive implications of the final model. There are a variety of approaches to model fitting; for details, see the work of Raudenbush and Bryk (2002) or Singer and Willett (2003). The approach we chose was to start with a reasonable statistical model that included plausible variables based on substantive theory and to remove variables depending on the results until we reached a model that seemed to be plausible and had no obvious estimation problems.

In multilevel modeling, one equation (generally called the Level 1 equation in the multilevel modeling literature) describes the relationship between the dependent variable (contact, coded as a three-level ordinal variable) and various time-varying predictors. The other equations, called Level 2 equations, model the relationships between the regression coefficients in the Level 1 equation and the (time-invariant) predictors at the between-person level.

For the present study, the Level 1 equation for the fullest model is

$$Contact_{ij}^* = \pi_{0j} + \pi_{1j}AtHome_{ij} + \pi_{2j}Work_{ij} + \pi_{3j}Finance_{ij} + \pi_{4j}Romance_{ij}$$
$$+ \pi_{5j}(Age_{ij} - 27) + \pi_{6j}(Age_{ij} - 27)^2$$

The subscript i indicates the month of observation, and j indicates the individual. We put an asterisk on contact to indicate that this is an unobserved (continuous) variable that underlies a division into three observed categories. The variable *AtHome* is a dummy variable, coded 1 when the person was living at home during month i and 0 when the person was not living at home during month i. The variable *Work* is a dummy variable that refers to whether the respondent was working full time. The variable *Romance* is a dummy variable that refers to whether the respondent was in a relationship. The *Finance* variable is a dummy coded variable that refers to whether the primary source of financial support was the family. The variable *Age* is the actual age, and we subtracted 27 so that the intercept represents contact at that age for a particular individual (i.e., at the end of the study). We also included the square of *Age* as a predictor to check for nonlinearity (on the log-odds scale).

The Level 2 equations for the full model are as follows:

$$\pi_{0j} = \beta_{00} + \beta_{01}Male_j + \beta_{02}Black_j + u_{0j}$$

$$\pi_{1j} = \beta_{10} + \beta_{11}Male_j + \beta_{12}Black_j + u_{1j}$$

$$\pi_{2j} = \beta_{20} + \beta_{21}Male_j + \beta_{22}Black_j + u_{2j}$$

$$\pi_{3j} = \beta_{30} + \beta_{31}Male_j + \beta_{32}Black_j + u_{3j}$$

$$\pi_{4j} = \beta_{40} + \beta_{41}Male_j + \beta_{42}Black_j + u_{4j}$$

$$\pi_{5j} = \beta_{50} + \beta_{51}Male_j + \beta_{52}Black_j + u_{5j}$$

$$\pi_{6j} = \beta_{60} + \beta_{61}Male_j + \beta_{62}Black_j + u_{6j}$$

These equations show that the intercepts, the effects of living at home, work, finance, and romance, as well as the effect of age, could all vary from person to person; furthermore, some of this variation between people might be accounted for by knowing whether the person was male or female or whether he or she was black.

When we tried to fit the above model, it had severe problems due to at least two factors: (1) For many individuals, there was not enough variability in either the outcome or the predictors to get good estimates of the parameters. This created a problem for estimating Level 2 variances, many of which were so large they were unbelievable. (2) There may be collinearity among the predictors, causing estimation problems. For example, people may have left home and become financially independent at (about) the same time. For this reason, we took steps to simplify the model. First, because there were few blacks and the gender effects proved nonsignificant or small, we eliminated those predictors from the model. Even after these changes, the estimates of residual variances in the Level 2 equations (tau for users of the HLM software package) were still so large they were suspect, so we fixed all random effects but the intercept to zero.

The Level 1 equation for the final model was

$$contact^*_{ij} = \pi_{0j} + \pi_{1j}AtHome_{ij} + \pi_{2j}Finance_{ij} + \pi_{3j}(Age_{ij} - 27)$$

$$+ \pi_{4j}(Age_{ij} - 27)^2$$

      Applied data analytic techniques for turning points research

and the Level 2 equations for the final model were

$$\pi_{0j} = \beta_{00} + u_{0j}$$

$$\pi_{1j} = \beta_{10}$$

$$\pi_{2j} = \beta_{20}$$

$$\pi_{3j} = \beta_{30}$$

$$\pi_{4j} = \beta_{40}$$

The revised model gave much more believable estimates of parameters; the results for this final model are displayed in Table 4.5. The intercept −3.09 is the log odds of a high level of contact (rather than a low or medium level) for a 27-year-old not living at home and not dependent on parents as the primary source of financial support. In this case, the odds a high level of family contact would be $e^{-3.09} = 0.045$ (95% CI 0.032–0.063), and the probability is .04/1.04 = .038. If we added the threshold estimate to the intercept, we get a logistic regression equation with a different intercept, but the same effects of each predictor variable. This equation represents the log odds of having either the medium or high (rather than low) level of

Table 4.5 Parameter Estimates for The Final (Simplified) Model

	Fixed effects				
	Coefficient	SE	t ratio	df	p
Intercept	3.09	0.17	18.24	184	<.001
At home	5.16	0.081	63.95	21608	<.001
Finance	0.60	0.083	7.25	21608	<.001
Age	0.41	0.032	12.92	21608	<.001
Age 2	0.052	0.0032	16.424	21608	<.001
Threshold	1.22	0.026	47.036	21608	<.001

	Variance components				
	VC	SD	df	χ^2	p
Intercept	4.87	2.21	184	11,378.14	<.001

Note: Age is centered at 27 so that intercept corresponds to the end of the study. SD, standard deviation; SE, standard error; VC, variance component. The coefficient for threshold refers to the quantity to be added to the intercept to obtain the probability of being in the high family contact category versus the moderate-to-low family contact category.

family contact. The restriction that the regression coefficients remain the same (parallel slopes assumption) is what makes this model appropriate for an ordered outcome variable.

Although all the fixed effects are significant in this model, it is clear that one stands out as much larger than the others: whether the person was living at home. Living at home multiplied the odds of a high level of family contact by $e^{5.16} = 175.03$ (95% CI 149.40–205.05).

To illustrate the relative magnitude of the effects of each of the fixed effects, examine the plots in Figures 4.3 and 4.4. The largest effect is clearly whether a person was living at home at the time; if so, the probability of a high level of contact was extremely high, and if not, the probability of a high level of contact was relatively low. Financial independence changed these results very slightly, as did age. The most noticeable effect of age was that at ages 17 or 18, those not living at home had a slightly higher probability of more contact than at later ages.

A simple display shows the role that "at home" had in predicting contact with family. Table 4.6 contains the cross-tabulation of being at home with level of contact (0 = highest, 2 = lowest). This table aggregates across

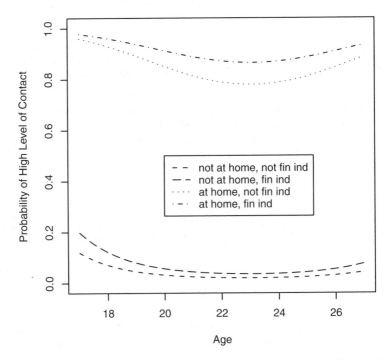

Figure 4.3 Probability of high level of contact as a function of age, whether living at home, and whether financially independent (fin ind).

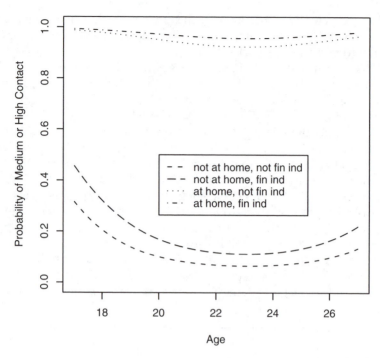

Figure 4.4 Probability of medium or high level of contact as a function of age, whether living at home, and whether financially independent (fin ind).

all respondents and all time periods but reflects accurately the general trend shown in the multilevel analyses. When respondents were not at home, the probability of the highest level of contact was about .25; when respondents were living at home, the probability of a high level of contact was over .9.

Table 4.6 Cross-tabulation of Being at Home with Level of Contact

		\multicolumn{4}{c}{Family contact}			
		High	Moderate	Low	Total
Not at home	Count	3,870	1695	9915	15480
	Percentage	25	11	64	100
At home	Count	11,391	310	779	12,480
	Percentage	91	3	6	100
Total	Count	15,261	2,005	10,694	27,960
	Percentage	55	7	38	100

Conclusion

Emerging adulthood is a time of great fluctuation and change as the individual moves from a state of relative dependency on the family of origin to a state of relative independence. One measure of this shift is reflected in one's level of family contact. In this chapter, we asked the following questions about family contact over the period of emerging adulthood: Who changed and who did not, and what characteristics of individuals (e.g., gender, race, attending college, graduate school) might determine change? Of those who remained stable, are there predictors accounted for the level of family contact? Finally, of those who changed, are there predictors that accounted for changes within a person as well as different patterns of change between people?

We found that men tended to change level of family contact more than women. Although we included race in the model, it is likely that there were too few blacks in the sample to make this a meaningful test. Education (attending college and graduate school) also had an impact on whether a person changed, with higher levels of education associated with greater likelihood of change.

We also found that 98% of nonchangers stayed at the highest level of family contact, leaving no variability among nonchangers (in their level of family contact) to predict. That is, people who remained stable consistently maintained the highest level of contact with their family of origin over the course of the study.

By far the most important predictor of change in the level of family contact within a person was whether the person was living at home. Although parental financial support and time (as well as its square) contributed significantly to the model, the impact of whether a person lived at home far outweighed the contribution of these other variables.

This last analysis revealed an important point that should be highlighted. For data such as these, multilevel models are usually written so that the dependent variable (family contact) is primarily a function of time or age. This is appropriate if there are no other good time-varying predictors or if such predictors are not sufficient to explain much variation in a person's level of family contact. If, however, we can identify predictors that can explain a large percentage of variation in a person's level of family contact, then age or time becomes relatively unimportant. This is the case in the present example; after accounting for whether a person lived at home, the effects of age and its square were no longer meaningfully large, although still statistically significant. By viewing time or age as means to an end rather than an end in itself, the researcher goes beyond simple description of *how* something like family contact changes with age to the issue of *why* it changes with age. This is particularly relevant to developmental psychology; it helps move from a purely descriptive (age-based) research agenda to one that involves searching for explanatory variables.

We found in this study that men tended to change level of family contact more than women. We also found in the analysis of changers that gender was not predictive of change in level of family contact. Figure 1 from Sneed et al. (2006) showed men decreasing more than women in family contact over the period of emerging adulthood. Reflecting on this figure in the context of the present findings suggests it is the product of two processes: whether you change, and if you do change, what does the change depend on. The difference between men and women in their trajectory of change in family contact (Figure 1) is not due to differences among changers (because changers change in the same way regardless of gender), it results from men changing more than women. These findings are still consistent with Gilligan's (1979; 1982) hypothesis that women struggle with separation more than men because they are relationally oriented, whereas men struggle with maintaining emotional relationships.

There are differences between analyzing change points and analyzing turning points that have implications for the statistical models that are chosen to fit the data. Turning points are generally thought of as nonreversible major life events, while change points may reflect life events but are reversible. In our study, family contact is obviously reversible, as are several of our predictors, with the exception of age (and for the most part race and gender). If family contact only changed once (nonreversible event), then we might have been interested in when it occurred rather than whether it occurred and what predicted its occurrence (the focus of this chapter). Event–history (survival) analysis of repeatable or nonrepeatable events provides a useful analogy. In event–history analysis, the focus is on the time until an event (for nonrepeatable events) or the time between occurrences of events (for repeatable events). Although it is beyond the scope of the present discussion, these differences have implications for the types of analyses used.

We should also point out that the analyses we have done are explanatory rather than predictive; prediction is important, but secondary. Had we merely wanted to attain maximal prediction, we most likely could have done so by using one of psychology's most famous principles: The best predictor of future behavior is past behavior. In our case, we would predict contact in any month to be the same as it was in the previous month. Remember that most people did not change at all (which would result in zero errors of prediction for that person) or a very small number of times (which would result in a very small number of errors of prediction). If our only interest were the practical issue of prediction, we would use that rule, but it would not help explain why the person's level of family contact was at a certain level. For explanation, we need a different variable (or variables) thought to have a causal influence on family contact.

We hope to have elucidated the use of multilevel modeling with an ordered categorical outcome to examine turning points in family contact during emerging adulthood. Although there are many ways of analyzing such data, the benefit of the approach demonstrated here is that it is relatively straightforward yet able to answer some of the most complicated questions in the analysis of change.

References

Arnett, J. J. (2000). Emerging adulthood: A theory of development from the late teens through the 20s. *American Psychologist, 55,* 469–480.

Boles, S. A. (1999). A model of parental representations, second individuation, and psychological adjustment in late adolescence. *Journal of Clinical Psychology, 55,* 497–512.

Cohen, P., & Cohen, J. (1996). *Life values and adolescent mental health.* Mahwah, NJ: Erlbaum.

Colarusso, C. A. (1990). The third individuation: The effect of biological parenthood on separation-individuation processes in adulthood. *Psychoanalytic Study of the Child, 45,* 179–194.

Cross, S. E., & Madson, L. (1997). Models of the self: Self-construals and gender. *Psychological Bulletin, 122,* 5–37.

Gilligan, C. (1979). Woman's place in man's life cycle. *Harvard Educational Review, 49,* 431–446.

Gilligan, C. (1982). *In a different voice: Psychological theory and women's development.* Cambridge, MA: Harvard University Press.

Hoffman, J., & Weiss, B. (1987). Family dynamics and presenting problems in college students. *Journal of Counseling Psychology, 34,* 157–163.

Kenny, M. E., & Donaldson, G. A. (1991). Contributions of parental attachment and family structure to the social and psychological functioning of first-year college students. *Journal of Counseling Psychology, 38,* 479–486.

Mahler, M., Pine, F., & Bergman, A. (1975). *The psychological birth of the human infant.* New York: Basic Books.

Raudenbush, S. W., & Bryk, A. S. (2002). *Hierarchical linear models: Applications and data analysis methods* (2nd ed.). Newbury Park, CA: Sage.

Rindskopf, D. (2002). Infinite parameter estimates in logistic regression. *Journal of Educational and Behavioral Statistics, 27,* 147–161.

Ryan, R. M., & Deci, E. L. (2000). Self-determination theory and the facilitation of intrinsic motivation, social development, and well-being. *American Psychologist, 55,* 68–78.

Singer, J. D., & Willett, J. B. (2003). *Applied longitudinal data analysis: Modeling change and event occurrence.* New York: Oxford University Press.

Sneed, J. R., Johnson, J. G., Cohen, P., Crawford, T. N., Chen, H., & Kasen, S. (2006). Gender differences in the age-changing relationship between family. Contact and instrumentality in emerging adulthood. *Developmental Psychology, 42,* 787–797.

chapter five

Testing turning points using latest growth curve models: Competing models of substance abuse and desistance in young adulthood

Andrea M. Hussong
University of North Carolina at Chapel Hill

Patrick J. Curran
University of North Carolina at Chapel Hill

Terrie E. Moffitt
University of London and University of Wisconsin–Madison

Avshalom Caspi
University of London and University of Wisconsin–Madison

Contents

Introduction 82
Testing snares 82
Chapter aims 88
Sample and measures 88
Analytic strategy 90
    Trajectories of antisocial behavior in young adulthood 92
    Test of the launch hypothesis 94
    Test of the snares hypothesis 95
    Test of the general deviance hypothesis 97
Conclusion 99
Acknowledgment 101
References 101

Introduction

Multiple terms denote the twists and turns that mark the life course of youth as they move from risk to resilience or maladjustment. From Rutter (1987), we have vulnerabilities and protective factors that denote mechanisms turning these adaptive trajectories away from or toward resilience, respectively. Among those youth who may not start from a clear point of risk, however, evidence of psychopathology clearly indicates the potential for turning points to lead away from an expected course of healthy adjustment. Within the study of antisocial behavior, theoretical writings and empirical studies recognized these mechanisms as influencing trajectories of problem behaviors. The concept of *snares*, offered by Moffitt (1993), fills a unique niche in this literature and refers to those mechanisms responsible for prolonging what might otherwise be a developmentally normative pattern of desisting antisocial behavior. Snares thus define a turning point away from an expected course of adaptation. Given the pattern of desistance that typifies the course of antisocial behavior in young adulthood, factors that serve to prolong antisocial behavior during this developmental period inform our search for ensnaring mechanisms. The current chapter examines the role of a potential snare, substance abuse, in interfering with the normative pattern of desistance from antisocial behavior during young adulthood.*

Testing snares

The test of ensnaring mechanisms presents several methodological and analytic challenges. One set of guidelines for conducting these tests came from Rutter (1996), based on the premise that snares constitute one form of turning points. In this framework, methodological considerations include the need (1) to measure intraindividual change over time, (2) to relate that change to specific circumstances, (3) to focus on a relevant segment of the population in which there has been an opportunity for the hypothesized variable to operate, and (4) to rule out heterotypic continuity. In this chapter, we provide one example of how this framework might be used to guide the test of snares that have an impact on trajectories of antisocial behavior in young adulthood.

The first consideration is the need to measure intraindividual change over time, such that turning points are references with respect to individual

---

* This chapter expands on previously reported analyses in the work of Hussong, Curran, Moffit, Caspi, and Carrig (2005).

rather than group patterns of change. Multilevel modeling (also known as hierarchical linear modeling and mixed modeling) and latent growth curve (LGC) modeling (within the structural equation modeling tradition) are both powerful methods for modeling interindividual differences in intraindividual change over time. Although these two methods have substantial overlap in their capabilities, they also have some notable areas of difference (e.g., Bauer, 2003; Curran, 2003; Willett & Sayer, 1994). Through the inclusion of either time-varying or time-invariant predictors within either of these models, we can address the second consideration of testing turning points, namely, the need to relate intraindividual change to specific circumstances. To retain focus in our demonstration, we adopt the latent curve-modeling approach to permit us greater flexibility in model testing and comparison.

The third consideration of testing turning points is the need to evaluate the hypothesis within a relevant population. To examine the ensnaring mechanism of substance abuse within antisocial behavior, we must study (1) those who are likely to show normative decrements in antisocial behavior over time in the absence of the snare and (2) those who are likely to evidence the snare and thus to have the opportunity to show deviations from the expected pattern of desistance. Two consistent findings help us define a population of interest meeting these requirements. First, robust support for the age–crime curve indicates that both incidence and prevalence of crime are highest during late adolescence and begin to drop off only in young adulthood (Blumstein, Cohen, & Farrington, 1988; Farrington, 1986). However, several theorists posit that this population curve comprises interindividual differences in intraindividual change over time (Laub & Sampson, 2001; Moffitt, 1993), and emerging evidence supports this contention (Bushway, Piquero, Broidy, Cauffman, & Mazerolle, 2001; Piquero, Blumstein, et al., 2001). Second, within this developmental period, gender differences in rates of substance abuse indicate that men are more likely than women to evidence alcohol and substance disorders (Hanna & Grant, 1997; Robins & Reiger, 1991). Together, this evidence suggests that men passing through the period of young adulthood form an ideal population within which to test the snares hypothesis.

The fourth consideration in testing turning points is the need to rule out heterotypic continuity. To broaden this consideration within the realm of classic methodological design (Shadish, Cook, & Campbell, 2001), evidence for the snares hypothesis is strongest if we are able to rule out other alternative relations between substance abuse and antisocial behavior. To meet this objective, we first must clearly define the concept of developmental snares as it may be tested within the LGC framework. In this regard, we propose two hypotheses in which substance abuse acts as a snare that serves to entrench young adult men in prolonged patterns of antisocial behavior during a period of normative desistance.

The first, captured by the "launch" hypothesis, posits that substance abuse early in young adulthood may both identify young men who are on a *long-term* course of elevated antisocial behavior and set men on such a course. According to this mechanism, substance abuse on entry into young adulthood defines different trajectories of antisocial behavior over time. Perhaps the most common method for examining individual development over time, the launch method, is "analogous to a catapult, in which the initial forces of the contextual antecedent are the major determinants of the shape of the curve of the outcome" (Kinderman & Skinner, 1992, p. 166). In such models, launching factors serve as distal predictors of change over time under the assumption that such time-lagged influences are more salient predictors of course than are time-varying or contextual factors. The role of such distal factors, though often described in causal terms, may also be one of early identification, which belies the effects of selection resulting from prior developmental processes. In either case, when applied to the study of crime desistance and substance abuse in young adulthood, this model posits that early signs of substance abuse predict maintenance of elevated antisocial behavior over young adulthood. This prediction is thus concerned with individual differences in the intercepts and slopes characterizing the trajectories of antisocial behavior over time (see Figure 5.1).

Previous studies showed support for the launch model as an explanation for antisocial behavior during adolescence, when such trajectories reflect a rise in antisocial behavior. For example, Munson, McMahon, and Spieker (2001) showed that greater maternal depression predicted steeper escalations in children's externalizing symptoms over time, especially among children with avoidant insecure attachments. However, to our knowledge, the role of substance abuse as a launching factor in young adulthood, when the expected pattern is desistance, has yet to be examined.

The second, for which we retain the term *snares hypothesis*, posits that substance abuse acts through a series of proximal influences on crime desistance such that *short-term* alterations in the course of antisocial behavior are impacted by substance abuse. Snares may then be defined in reference to protective factors as studied in the work of developmental criminologists and life course researchers (Laub & Sampson, 2001; Moffitt, 1993). "Protective" factors hasten the process of desistance among men at risk for continued antisocial behavior. Supporting the role of protective factors in crime desistance, several studies suggested that reduced involvement in antisocial behavior coincides with entry into good

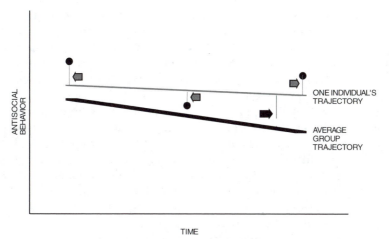

Figure 5.1 Contrast of snares versus launch hypotheses.

marriages and good jobs during young adulthood (Horney, Osgood, & Marshall, 1995; Laub, Nagin, & Sampson, 1998; Quinton, Pickles, Maughan, & Rut.ter, 1993). In contrast, "ensnaring" factors interfere with the normative deceleration of antisocial behavior that is observed in the population. As defined here, snares exert a contemporaneous or short-term effect on antisocial behavior, such that the local effects of snares alter the normative course of antisocial behavior when they or their sequelae are present. Unlike protective factors, the importance of snares in the maintenance of antisocial behavior has rarely been empirically evaluated (though see Piquero, Brame, Mazerolle, & Haapanen, 2001).

Ensnaring factors and protective factors are thought to play different roles in modifying antisocial behavior during young adulthood (Rutter, 1987). While the protective influences offered by a good marriage or a good job may serve to actively promote desistance during young adulthood, snares may serve to actively retard desistance during young adulthood. As such, a snare is posited to be more than merely the opposite of a protective factor. By distinguishing between these two influences, we are able to differentiate how the presence of various factors has a direct impact on young adults' lives. This distinction also has important potential implications for interventions. For example, desistance research that focuses on protective factors in marriage and at work necessarily suggests that interventions should focus on acquiring and promoting new adult roles and responsibilities. In contrast, research that focuses on snares suggests that, if snares can be identified, interventions should focus on removing those barriers to crime desistance that are likely to impede a healthy transition to adulthood.

Despite their potential importance for interventions targeting antisocial behavior, to our knowledge, little research has examined such protective factors, and no research has directly tested the snares hypothesis. The paucity of studies focusing on these factors is expected given the relatively recent introduction of the constructs to the literature and the lack of data sets that can meet demands for studies of desistance to include self-report data assessed repeatedly during young adulthood. Nonetheless, substance abuse has been hypothesized to be a potent snare (Moffitt, 1993). Several mechanisms may account for the ensnaring role of substance abuse within trajectories of antisocial behavior.

First, substance abuse has been associated with difficulties in conventional adult roles, the same protective factors that have been found to precede desistance in antisocial and criminal behavior (e.g., good marriages; Bachman, Wadsworth, O'Malley, Schulenberg, & Johnston, 1997; Leonard & Rothbard, 2000). Second, substance abuse has been associated with interrupted education and incarceration (Sher & Gotham, 1999; Vaillant, 1995), both of which have been proposed as additional snares forestalling normative desistance. Third, substance abuse may reflect a physiological dependence that motivates antisocial behavior necessary to purchase, obtain, and use substances. Fourth, the social nature of substance abuse during young adulthood may serve to maintain common activities and ties with a deviant peer context. And, fifth, the disinhibiting properties of alcohol and other drugs may increase the odds that poor judgment and impulsivity will lead to antisocial activities.

Each of these pathways may result in greater antisocial behavior for those who abuse substances during a developmental period in which most individuals are curbing their involvement in deviant behavior. Across these pathways, substance abuse may serve as either a marker variable for a process influencing substance abuse or as either a direct or indirect causal factor. Our goal here is not to distinguish these roles of substance abuse but rather to examine whether there is support for substance abuse to function in any one of these roles based on its prediction of crime desistance.

In contrast to the launch hypothesis, this basic prediction of the snares hypothesis is concerned with time-varying deviations in antisocial behavior away from the expected pattern of desistance over time. Whereas snares are expected to alter time-specific variation in antisocial behavior within the course of desistance, launching factors provide a more global prediction in which substance abuse alters the actual trajectory of antisocial behavior (see Figure 5.1). However, the launch and snares hypotheses are not necessarily incompatible; for example, substance abuse early in young adulthood may both decelerate an individual's overall pattern of crime desistance relative to others during this period (a launch prediction) and increase the likelihood of antisocial behavior within certain points in young adulthood relative to that individual's expected level of antisocial behavior (a snares prediction).

In light of these two definitions of snares, we now define an alternate hypothesis that addresses Rutter's fourth consideration for appropriately testing turning points, namely, ruling out the potential for heterotypic continuity. Both the launch and snares hypotheses posit that, during the transition from adolescence to adulthood, substance abuse serves to perpetuate continuity in antisocial behavior over time. An alternate, more parsimonious, explanation for the observed relation between substance abuse and antisocial behavior over time is offered by "general deviance" or "common propensity" hypotheses based on a sociogenic approach. These theories take as their starting point the empirical observation that problem behaviors in adolescence and adulthood are positively correlated (e.g., Elliott, Huizinga, & Menard, 1989; Osgood, Johnston, O'Malley, & Bachman, 1988). The fact that multiple problem behaviors tend to cluster among the same persons has led psychologists, sociologists, and criminologists to theorize that correlated problem behaviors (e.g., alcohol abuse, drug abuse, criminal participation) may have a common etiology. For example, problem behavior theory (Donovan & Jessor, 1985; Jessor & Jessor, 1977) posits that many different deviant behaviors form a "syndrome" that is caused by an underlying latent trait called *psychosocial proneness*. Similarly, Gottfredson and Hirschi (1990) hypothesized that participation in various correlated antisocial behaviors is caused by the same latent propensity factor at every age across the life span. Rather than substance abuse serving to influence continuity in antisocial behavior over time, general deviance or common propensity theories suggest that continuity in both substance abuse and antisocial behavior is a manifestation of an underlying propensity to engage in deviant activities.

General deviance models offer testable hypotheses about the structure of correlations among problem behaviors during adolescence and young adulthood. For example, these models predict that elevated substance abuse is an index of a heightened propensity toward deviancy that is similarly manifested in elevated antisocial behavior within time. Likewise, general deviance models predict that changes in substance abuse and antisocial behavior over time will mirror one another in synchrony because they are both thought to be developmental manifestations of the same underlying propensity toward problem behaviors. This prediction thus defines substance abuse and antisocial behavior as multiple indicators of a single trajectory. We test this model using a multiple-indicator, second-order LGC model. Because a general theory is the most parsimonious model, it is a compelling alternate explanation to the snares hypothesis (Osgood & Rowe, 1994).

Chapter aims

The aims of this chapter are thus to demonstrate the use of LGC techniques for testing turning points, defined as the ensnaring role of substance abuse within the expected pattern of desisting antisocial behavior in young adulthood. Reflecting Rutter's (1996) guidelines for conducting such tests, we adopted statistical techniques that model intraindividual change over time as applied to a longitudinal data set able to reflect these patterns of change; we defined our sample as men passing through young adulthood, a developmental period when desistance is normative and thus the role of substance abuse as a snare is more obvious; we considered several alternate hypotheses, including that mirroring the assumption of heterotypic continuity. Specifically, our analyses tested (1) the launch hypothesis, in which substance abuse is tested as a time-invariant predictor of intraindividual differences in the intercepts and slopes defining trajectories of antisocial behavior over time; (2) the snares hypothesis, in which substance abuse is tested as a time-varying predictor of elevated antisocial behavior against an expected pattern of desistance over time; and (3) a general deviance hypothesis, in which substance abuse and antisocial behavior are multiple indicators of a single construct characterized by an underlying trajectory of problem behavior spanning young adulthood.

Sample and measures

Participants are members of the Dunedin Multidisciplinary Health and Development Study, a longitudinal investigation of health and behavior in a complete birth cohort (Silva & Stanton, 1996). The study members were born in Dunedin, New Zealand, between April 1972 and March 1973. Of these, 1,037 children (91% of eligible births; 52% males) participated in the first follow-up assessment at age 3, and they constitute the base sample for the remainder of the study. Cohort families represent the full range of socioeconomic status in the general population of New Zealand's South Island and are primarily white; fewer than 7% self-identified at age 18 as Maori or Pacific Islanders. Assessments have been conducted at ages 3 ($n = 1,037$), 5 ($n = 991$), 7 ($n = 954$), 9 ($n = 955$), 11 ($n = 925$), 13 ($n = 850$), 15 ($n = 976$), 18 ($n = 993$), 21 ($n = 961$), and at age 26 ($n = 980$, 499 males; 96%

of living cohort members). The current study focused on self-report data gathered from men at ages 18, 21, and 26. Rates of diagnosed conduct disorder, substance dependence, and self-reported delinquent offending in New Zealand were similar to those obtained for surveys of same-age epidemiological samples in the United States; for documentation supporting generalization from the Dunedin cohort to other settings, see the work of Moffitt, Caspi, Rutter, and Silva (2001).

For the current study, men with incomplete data at age 18 ($n = 64$) or who were missing data at both ages 21 and 26 ($n = 10$) were omitted from analyses (final $n = 461$ of 535 male respondents at age 18, including 438 with completed data and 23 with partially missing data). The t tests showed no significant differences between retained and omitted cases, where available, on antisocial behavior, alcohol symptoms, or marijuana symptoms at ages 18, 21, or 26. Detailed analyses comparing groups of study members who did not take part in assessments versus those who did on a variety of family and individual characteristics have revealed no group differences (as reported in Moffitt et al., 2001).

Alcohol abuse and marijuana abuse were assessed by symptoms from the Diagnostic Interview Schedule (DIS; Robins, Helzer, Cottler, & Goldring, 1989). The DIS was administered to participants at ages 18 (DIS-IIIR), 21 (DIS-IIIR), and 26 (DIS-IV). Antisocial behaviors were assessed via the self-report offending interview, which ascertains illegal behaviors and conduct problems (Moffitt, Silva, Lynam, & Henry, 1994). Antisocial behaviors and substance abuse symptoms were ascertained on the same day but in separate, counterbalanced sessions conducted by interviewers who were blind to the other assessment. Because we were interested in examining changes in both the mean and variance of behavior over time, continuity in item content for each scale was very important. For this reason, parallel items were selected from each assessment age to measure antisocial behavior, alcohol abuse, and marijuana abuse.

We used eight parallel items assessing conduct disorder (*Diagnostic and Statistical Manual of Mental Disorders* [*DSM-IV-TR*], American Psychiatric Association, 1994) to create a variety score for antisocial behavior within each period. Variety scores index the total number of different forms of antisocial behavior in which a participant has engaged as opposed to, for example, the total frequency of antisocial acts. Previous studies suggested that variety scores may better reflect the extent or severity of antisocial involvement, and these scores are consistent with a diagnostic approach to assessing conduct problems (Gottfredson & Hirschi, 1995; Robins, 1978). Our variety scores were the total number of forms of antisocial behavior in which each participant had engaged over the past 12 months. Eight forms of antisocial behavior were assessed: breaking and entering; destroying property (illegal acts of vandalism); fighting (simple assault, aggravated assault, or gang fighting); setting fires (arson); lying (criminal fraud); stealing with confrontation (robbery); stealing without confrontation (criminal theft); and carrying or using a weapon. Psychometric properties of the resulting variables are reported in Table 5.1.

Nineteen items from the DIS assessed symptoms of alcohol abuse and dependence, and 10 items assessed symptoms of marijuana abuse and dependence across the three assessments. These symptoms largely reflect those for substance abuse and dependence as stated in the *DSM-IV-TR* (e.g., unable to stop using, tolerance, continued use despite health or social problems; American Psychiatric Association, 2000). Each symptom was coded as present or absent within the previous year. The total number of symptoms endorsed for each scale served as the alcohol abuse and marijuana abuse scores, respectively, for the current study. Table 5.1 contains psychometric properties for these variables.

Analytic strategy

To test our hypotheses, we examined a series of LGC models. LGC, also referred to as growth curve analyses or random effects modeling, extends latent variable analyses within the structural equation modeling framework to provide a flexible tool for testing hypotheses of change over time and of predictors of such change (McArdle, 1988; Meredith & Tisak, 1984, 1990). First, we estimated an unconditional linear growth model to examine whether the characteristics of individual trajectories of antisocial behavior varied across men. Second, we tested the launch hypothesis through a conditional latent trajectory model in which substance abuse at age 18 served as an exogenous predictor of change over time in antisocial behavior. Third, we tested the snares hypothesis through a time-varying covariate LGC that considered the repeated measures of substance abuse as time-varying covariates to test their time-specific influences on antisocial behavior above and beyond the influence of each individual's underlying trajectory of antisocial behavior. The time-varying covariate LGC allowed for a direct test of our hypothesis about developmental snares given the simultaneous estimation of (1) variability across men in individual trajectories of antisocial behavior and (2) the association of substance abuse with time-specific deviations away from this predicted trajectory for each man's antisocial behavior within time (see, e.g., Bryk & Raudenbush, 1992, p. 151; Curran & Hussong, 2002; Curran, Muthén, & Harford, 1998). Fourth, we tested the general deviance hypothesis using a second-order LGC as described by Bollen and Curran (2005) and McArdle (1988).

To avoid bias due to the limited attrition in the sample, we estimated all models using the direct maximum likelihood procedure available in Mplus (Muthén & Muthén, 1998) and thus included all cases who had

Table 5.1. Correlation Matrix

Variable	1	2	3	4	5	6	7	8	9
1 Antisocial behavior at 18	—								
2 Antisocial behavior at 21	.56	—							
3 Antisocial behavior at 26	.51	.53	—						
4 Marijuana symptoms at 18	.55	.37	.36	—					
5 Marijuana symptoms at 21	.50	.54	.46	.55	—				
6 Marijuana symptoms at 26	.42	.40	.49	.42	.57	—			
7 Alcohol symptoms at 18	.53	.37	.35	.46	.42	.31	—		
8 Alcohol symptoms at 21	.44	.48	.34	.34	.53	.36	.52	—	
9 Alcohol symptoms at 26	.34	.32	.40	.20	.30	.48	.34	.46	—
M	1.95	1.57	1.50	0.63	1.07	1.08	2.32	3.54	2.78
SD	1.59	1.71	1.46	1.61	2.02	1.98	2.85	3.68	3.23
Reliability	.67	.74	.67	.86	.86	.85	.82	.86	.84
n	461	451	455	461	446	456	461	451	456

Note: Due to missing data, n = 440–461 across correlations reported above; all correlations are significant at p < .0001. M, mean; SD, standard deviation.

complete data at age 18 and at least one subsequent time point (final $n = 461$). The adequacy of model fit was evaluated using the likelihood ratio test (i.e., model χ^2) and associated p value. Given that our large sample size might lead to excessive power of the χ^2 test to detect even small misspecifications (MacCallum, 1990), we also used two incremental fit indices that are less dependent on sample size (Comparative Fit Index [CFI]; Bentler, 1990; Incremental Fit Index [IFI]; Bollen, 1989).

Trajectories of antisocial behavior in young adulthood

To examine the fixed and random components of growth in antisocial behavior, we estimated an unconditional LGC for the repeated measures of antisocial behavior reported at ages 18, 21, and 26. Two latent factors were estimated: one to define the intercept of the developmental trajectory of antisocial behavior (with all factor loadings fixed to 1.0) and one to define the linear slope of the trajectory (with factor loadings set to 0, 3, and 8 to define an annual metric of time). A mean was estimated for the intercept and slope factors, and these values represented the mean model-implied developmental trajectory pooled over all individuals. A variance was also estimated for the intercept and slope factors, representing the degree of individual variability in trajectories around the group mean values. The covariance between the two factors represented the covariation between initial level and rate of change. Larger variance estimates imply greater individual variability in the starting point and the rate of change over time. Finally, residual variances were estimated for each repeated measure, and these values represented variability in the time-specific measures not accounted for by the underlying random trajectories.

The unconditional LGC was estimated and found to fit the observed data well, with $\chi^2(1) = 9.31$, $p = .002$, IFI = .98, and CFI = .98. The means of the latent factors showed that the model-implied trajectory for the group was characterized by a significant intercept of 1.90 different types of antisocial behavior at the first time period ($t = 26.33$, $p < .001$) and a significantly decreasing slope of 0.05 units per year ($t = -5.84$, $p < .001$; see Figure 5.2). Thus, the model-implied mean rate of antisocial behavior significantly decreased from 1.90 to 1.50 types of behavior over the period of study. Further, significant variance estimates for both the intercept ($\hat{\psi} = 1.77$, $t = 8.96$, $p < .001$) and slope ($\hat{\psi} = 0.02$, $t = 2.69$, $p < .01$) factors indicated substantial interindividual variability in intraindividual developmental trajectories of antisocial behavior. Finally, the negative correlation between the intercept and slope factors ($r = -0.44$, $t = -3.20$, $p < .01$) indicated that higher initial values were associated with steeper decreases over time.

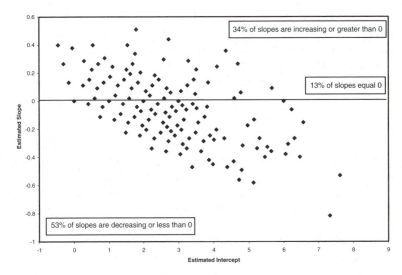

Figure 5.2 Pattern of trajectory parameters based of regression analyses within individual.

To examine whether men who were incarcerated during the 12-month periods before assessments at ages 21 and 26 accounted for this pattern of desistance (Piquero, Blumstein, et al., 2001), we reestimated these models by dropping the 14 men who had been incarcerated for more than 1 month prior to either assessment point. No meaningful changes in the findings occurred. We also reestimated these models to explore whether cases that showed a notable drop in antisocial behavior at age 21 relative to ages 18 and 26 served as influential outliers. Again, no meaningful changes in the findings occurred.

Overall, these results indicate that the mean developmental trajectory of antisocial behavior for the sample was significantly decreasing over time, consistent with previous findings on the age–crime curve. However, we also found that there were substantial individual differences in both the initial level and rate of change over time. Figure 5.2 depicts such variation by plotting the intercept and slope values for each participant's estimated trajectory against one another. (Note that these individual case-by-case estimates are for descriptive visualization purposes only.) These trajectories were estimated by conducting separate regression models within each case with complete data (see Carrig, Wirth, & Curran, 2004, for further details). As indicated, 53% of participants showed decreasing trajectories over time (i.e., slopes greater than 0), 13% showed no change, and 34% showed increasing slopes. These results further underscore the notable variation in individual trajectories. Although the growth trajectories

explained 70%, 49%, and 78% of the variance in the time-specific indicators of antisocial behavior at ages 18, 21, and 26, respectively, significant
residual variances remained at each age. Thus, the underlying trajectory
process is accounting for only a portion of the observed variability in antisocial behavior within each time period.

Test of the launch hypothesis

We next estimated a conditional LGC that tested the hypothesis that substance abuse at age 18 predicts a slowed or dampened pattern of desistance in the overall developmental trajectory of antisocial behavior over
young adulthood. In other words, this model tested whether the magnitude of intercepts and slopes underlying antisocial behavior varied as a
function of age 18 substance abuse. Both marijuana and alcohol abuse at
age 18 were included as exogenous predictors of the intercept and slope
factors defining the trajectories of antisocial behavior over ages 18, 21, and
26 (see Figure 5.3). The resulting model provided a good fit to the data,
with $\chi^2(3) = 11.33$, $p = .01$, CFI = .99, and IFI = .99. Greater alcohol and marijuana abuse at age 18 both significantly predicted higher intercepts of the
trajectories of antisocial behavior ($\hat{\beta} = .44$, $t = 9.63$, $p < .001$ and $\hat{\beta} = .40$,
$t = 8.81$, $p < .001$, respectively). Both marijuana ($\hat{\beta} = -.21$, $t = -3.24$, $p <
.001$) and alcohol ($\hat{\beta} = -.19$, $t = -2.86$, $p < .001$) abuse were also negatively
related to the slope of the antisocial behavior trajectories, meaning that
higher age 18 substance abuse predicted lower or increasingly negative
slope values. Because such negative predictions may reflect a variety of
relations, we further probed this effect by plotting model-implied trajectories of antisocial behavior one standard deviation above and below the
mean of the predictor (i.e., substance abuse). This procedure is similar in
many respects to probing interactions in multiple regression and formally
recognizes the interaction inherent in these models between time and
substance abuse, reflected in the growth factor prediction (Curran, Bauer,
& Willoughby, 2004).

Results indicated that men with the highest substance symptoms at age
18 also showed steeper negative slopes in their trajectories of antisocial
behavior ($M = -.03$, $-.02$, and $-.01$ for those high, medium, and low, respectively, in substance abuse at age 18), although this finding reflects a change
of less than one type of antisocial acts difference between each of the
three groups over the 8-year period. Importantly, probing of this relation
by recoding the trajectory factors such that the intercept factor represents
average antisocial behavior at age 26 also revealed that men who reported
greater substance abuse at age 18 showed greater antisocial behavior at
even the final time points ($\beta = .17$, $.09$; $z = 5.13$, 4.80, $p < .001$ for marijuana
and alcohol abuse, respectively). Taken together, these results indicate that

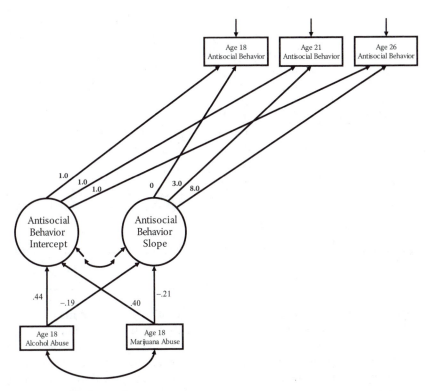

Figure 5.3 Conditional latent growth curve (LGC) testing launch hypothesis.

men elevated in substance abuse at age 18 reported higher initial levels of and steeper decreases in antisocial behavior over time but were signifi- cantly elevated in antisocial behavior across all periods of observation.

Test of the snares hypothesis

The extent to which substance abuse symptoms accounted for time- specific elevations in antisocial behavior over young adulthood was examined through a time-varying covariate model in which indicators of substance abuse (e.g., alcohol and marijuana abuse) at ages 18, 21, and 26 served as predictors of within-time individual variability in antisocial behavior that was not accounted for by the underlying individual trajec- tories of such behavior (see Figure 5.4 and Curran et al., 1998, for more detail). This strategy evaluated whether higher levels of substance abuse uniquely predicted a time-specific elevation or "shock" in antisocial behavior above and beyond what was expected based on the individual- specific underlying trajectory of antisocial behavior (Curran & Bollen,

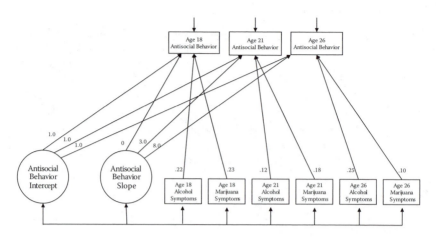

Figure 5.4 Time-varying covariate latent growth curve (LGC) testing snares hypothesis.

2001). In other words, significant prediction of time-specific measures of antisocial behavior, above and beyond the decreasing individual trajectories, from the measures of substance abuse indicate that substance abuse maintained a higher level of antisocial behavior than would be expected for that individual given his overall pattern of antisocial behavior during young adulthood. In this manner, the time-varying covariate model examined whether substance abuse was either a marker variable for a causal process or a causal variable itself in relation to antisocial behavior.

The hypothesized model with the time-varying effects of alcohol and marijuana abuse fit the observed data well, with $\chi^2(1) = 10.59$, $p = .001$, CFI = .99, and IFI = 1.0. At the age 18 and 21 assessment periods, men with more symptoms of alcohol or marijuana abuse reported significantly higher levels of antisocial behavior than would be expected based on their individual trajectories alone (at age 18 $\hat{\beta} = .22$, $t = 2.93$, $p < .001$ and at age 21 $\hat{\beta} = .12$, $t = 2.58$, $p < .001$ for alcohol; at age 18 $\hat{\beta} = .23$, $t = 2.92$, $p < .001$ and at age 21 $\hat{\beta} = .18$, $t = 3.25$, $p < .001$ for marijuana). At the age 26 assessment, this effect of alcohol abuse was marginally significant ($\hat{\beta} = .25$, $t = 1.83$, $p = .07$), and this effect for marijuana abuse was nonsignificant ($\hat{\beta} = .10$, $t = 0.68$, $p > .10$). These results suggest that, during the periods when these young men experienced more symptoms of substance abuse, they did not decline in their antisocial behavior to the extent that we would expect based on their antisocial behavior throughout young adulthood. Rather, substance abuse appeared to ensnare these young men within elevated patterns of antisocial behavior. This effect became weaker as men aged through this period of crime desistance.

To examine whether the snaring effects of substance abuse persisted over the subsequent measurement interval, we modified our LGC model to include (1) covariances (rather than structural pathways) between substance abuse indices and antisocial behavior within each measurement period that were constrained to be equal within time (e.g., the age 18 covariance between marijuana abuse and antisocial behavior was equated with the age 18 covariance between alcohol abuse and antisocial behavior) and (2) structural pathways from substance abuse at ages 18 and 21 predicting subsequent time-specific variations in antisocial behavior at ages 21 and 26, respectively. To identify this model, these paths were constrained to be equal within time (e.g., the path between age 18 marijuana abuse and age 21 antisocial behavior was equated with the path between age 18 alcohol abuse and age 21 antisocial behavior). The resulting model fit the data well, with $\chi^2(2) = 9.50$, $p = .01$, CFI = .99, and IFI = .99. All lagged predictions of time-specific deviations in antisocial behavior above and beyond the influences of the underlying trajectory process, and the covariances among substance abuse and antisocial behavior were nonsignificant ($\hat{\beta} = -.07$, $t = -1.86$ from ages 18 to 21; $\hat{\beta} = -.06$, $t = -0.95$). These results suggest that, as predicted by the snares hypothesis, substance abuse exerted a contemporaneous, rather than a lagged, effect on time-specific deviations away from individual trajectories of antisocial behavior.

Test of the general deviance hypothesis

A competing hypothesis is that substance abuse is not uniquely related to antisocial behavior, but instead antisocial behavior and substance abuse are interrelated over time due to a single underlying shared factor. Although we cannot directly observe such an underlying influence, we can estimate a model that would be consistent with this general deviance hypothesis. We estimated a second-order LGC in which alcohol abuse, marijuana abuse, and antisocial behavior each served as indicators on latent factors representing deviance proneness traits at ages 18, 21, and 26. Consistent with the work of Bushway et al. (2001) and Duncan, Duncan, Strycker, Li, and Alpert (1999), we then modeled growth in these three latent factors as a function of a higher-order intercept (with loadings set to 1.0) and slope (with loadings set to 0, 3, and 8) factor, reflecting individually varying trajectories of deviance proneness over time (see Figure 5.5).

We estimated this model in two steps. First, we tested just the longitudinal measurement model in which the three indicators of antisocial behavior, alcohol abuse, and marijuana abuse each loaded on a single underlying latent factor within each of the three time periods (Sayer & Cumsille, 2001). To identify this model, we set the factor loadings for the antisocial behavior indicator equal to 1.0 for each deviance proneness

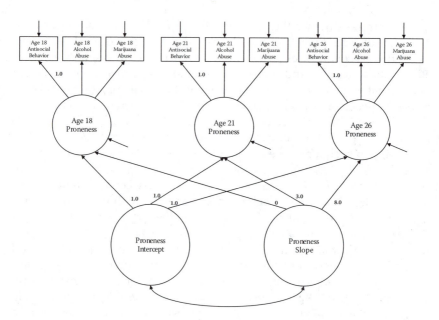

Figure 5.5 Second-order latent growth curve (LGC) testing general deviance hypothesis.

factor and fixed the intercept of this item to zero (Bollen & Curran, 2005). We also estimated means for each latent factor within time and freely correlated errors of measured variables across like indicators over time (e.g., errors for alcohol abuse at ages 18, 21, and 26 were correlated). The resulting model provided an adequate fit to the data, with $\chi^2(15) = 28.14$, $p = .02$, CFI = .99, and IFI = .99.

We extended this measurement model within the LGC framework to test whether individuals varied from one another in their trajectories of deviance proneness over time. As described by Bollen and Curran (2005), such second-order LGCs require that factor loadings within the measurement model be constrained to be equal over time for like constructs (e.g., factor loadings for marijuana abuse at ages 18, 21, and 26 were constrained to be equal). This constraint is necessary so that changes over time captured through the latent growth model are not confounded with changes over time in the contributions of individual indicators to the construct for which growth is modeled over time (see Sayer & Cumsille, 2001). After imposing these constraints, latent trajectory factors were initially estimated to reflect the intercept and slope of the trajectory underlying the three deviance proneness factors estimated within each assessment period. As before, errors of measured variables were correlated across like indicators over time. The mean and variance of each trajectory factor were initially estimated. However, serious estimation problems indicated that the variance of the slope factor was near zero, suggesting no individual variability in the slope of general deviance over time. Following recommendations based on the work of Bryk and Raudenbush (1992), we reestimated the second-order LGC, fixing the variance of the slope factor to zero. However, the resulting model provided a poor fit to the data, with $\chi^2(22) = 98.06$, $p < .001$, CFI = .95, and IFI = .95.

We next explored whether poor fit in this final model was due either to the inability of the latent trajectory model to adequately capture change in the deviance proneness factors over time or to constraints posed on the measurement structure (which were necessary to estimate the second-order LGC but also consistent with the general deviance model's hypothesis that the relations between the indicators of deviant behavior and the underlying deviance proneness factor were constant over time). To do so, we returned to the longitudinal measurement model to test whether these constraints contributed to significant decrements in model fit. We estimated the same longitudinal measurement model as described above, but we also constrained the factor loadings of like constructs to be equal over time (as we did for the second-order LGC). The resulting model provided a similarly poor fit to the data, with $\chi^2(19) = 62.07$, $p < .001$, CFI = .97, and IFI = .97. A nested χ^2 test indicated that the addition of these constraints to the longitudinal measurement model produced significant decrements in model fit, with $\chi^2(3) = 33.93$ and $p < .001$. These results indicate that, although a general deviance factor is a tenable model within any given assessment period, the manifestations of this construct were variable over young adulthood. Given such changes in the nature of the construct over time, a model of growth in this construct over time is untenable. For this reason, we concluded that the general deviance hypothesis is not consistent with these data.

Conclusion

The current findings confirm a long-standing but largely untested assumption in developmental research on antisocial behavior; namely, that there are significant individual differences in intraindividual patterns of crime desistance during the transition from adolescence to adulthood. Although a gradual, linear decline in antisocial behavior typified the process of desistance for men in the Dunedin sample, these men differed significantly from one another both in the extent of antisocial behavior that they showed in late adolescence and in the rate at which their antisocial behavior declined as they entered adulthood. Moreover, alcohol and marijuana abuse each accounted for significant interindividual variability in antisocial behavior over time through two mechanisms. Our analyses of the launch model showed that men with greater substance abuse at the end of adolescence showed greater antisocial behavior across young adulthood, although their trajectories showed greater decline than those of their peers. In essence, these men started young adulthood with a very high level of antisocial involvement; thus, they had further to fall as they desisted. Supporting the snares hypothesis, we also found that men who abused substances during young adulthood showed greater antisocial behavior than would be expected based on their estimated individual trajectories of antisocial behavior over time. In other words, periods in which men reported greater symptoms of substance abuse corresponded to elevated antisocial behavior with respect to that individual's pattern of antisocial behavior over time. Further, this conclusion was most strongly supported in our younger adult assessments. As such, substance abuse appears to exert both proximal and distal effects on desistance in antisocial behavior over young adulthood.

We offer this conclusion in the context of limitations in the current study. First, longitudinal studies of desistance suffer from the lack of information beyond the study window, leaving open to question whether those showing decelerated antisocial behavior will continue on a path toward cessation or later return to further antisocial behavior (Laub & Sampson, 2001). Second, we sampled eight behaviors from among those that index antisocial behavior during young adulthood. The extent to which substance abuse varies as an ensnaring factor across other types of antisocial behaviors is a question left for future study. Third, we focused on the ensnaring role of substance abuse among men. However, differences in the timing and, potentially, the predictors of crime desistance suggest that gender-specific hypotheses may need to be tested to more fully understand the normative process of desistance in women as well as men (Moffitt et al., 2001). Fourth, we studied only one cohort in one part of the world, and the findings require replication, although we have good reason to be optimistic because previous findings from the Dunedin study have been replicated in and generalized to other samples and developmental settings (e.g., Moffitt, Caspi, Silva, & Stouthamer-Loeber, 1995). Fifth, although the present study identified the snaring effects of both alcohol abuse and marijuana abuse, further research is needed to explore the mechanisms that mediate these effects.

As evidenced by the present findings, LGC modeling offers a powerful alternative to traditional methods that study change over time and that examine hypotheses about intraindividual development. Using these techniques, the current study offers significant insights into the developmental associations that may emerge over time between substance abuse and antisocial behavior. These hypotheses suggest a direction of causality in which substance abuse serves to maintain engagement in antisocial behavior. Alternatively, the direction of effect may be reversed, reflecting self-selection in which the maintenance of antisocial behavior over time increases the likelihood of substance abuse. This possibility cannot be ruled out for our test of the launch hypothesis. However, although self-selection and the snares hypothesis may coexist (Moffitt, 1993), results from our time-varying covariate analyses offer evidence that self-selection does not account for the impact of snares as an impediment to crime desistance during young adulthood. Because predictions of antisocial behavior within time held above and beyond predictions based on the underlying trajectory of individual behavior, effects of substance abuse on antisocial behavior were residualized from the effect of continuity and developmentally normative change in antisocial behavior over time. Thus, previous antisocial behavior cannot account for these associations.

More broadly, LGC models offer a useful approach to the study of turning points. Their flexibility to incorporate different forms of influence on individually varying trajectories of behavior permits comparisons, as demonstrated here, across differing definitions of turning points. However, such flexibility also imposes a burden for theory development, which must rise to the challenge of specifying which of these points of inflection and forms of influence within the LGC best capture that proposed to underlie our turning points. Through continuing to push this exchange between developmental researchers and quantitative methodologists, we better approach a productive confluence of theory and methods.

Acknowledgment

We thank the Dunedin study members, Dunedin Unit Director Richie Poulton, unit research staff, and study founder Phil Silva. Research assistance was provided by HonaLee Harrington. The Dunedin Multidisciplinary Health and Development Research Unit is supported by the New Zealand Health Research Council. This research received support from Grants US-NIDA DA15398, US-NIDA DA13148; US-NIMH Grants MH45070 and MH49414; the William T. Grant Foundation; and Air New Zealand.

References

American Psychiatric Association. (1994). *Diagnostic and statistical manual of mental disorders* (4th ed.). Washington, DC: Author.

American Psychiatric Association. (2000). *Diagnostic and statistical manual of mental disorders* (text revision). Washington, DC: Author.

Bachman, J. G., Wadsworth, K. N., O'Malley, P. M., Schulenberg, J., & Johnston, L. D. (1997). Marriage, divorce and parenthood during the transition to young adulthood: Impacts on drug use and abuse. In J. Schulenberg, J. L.

Maggs, & K. Hurrelmann (Eds.), *Health risks and developmental transitions during adolescence* (pp. 246–282). New York: Cambridge University Press.

Bauer, D. J. (2003). Estimating multilevel linear models as structural equation models. *Journal of Educational and Behavioral Statistics, 28*, 134–167.

Bentler, P. M. (1990). Comparative fit indexes in structural models. *Psychological Bulletin, 107*, 238–246.

Blumstein, A., Cohen, J., & Farrington, D. P. (1988). Criminal career research: Its value for criminology. *Criminology, 26*, 1–35.

Bollen, K. A. (1989). A new incremental fit index for general structural equation models. *Sociological Methods and Research, 17*, 303–316.

Bollen, K. A., & Curran, P. J. (2005). *Latent trajectory models: A structural equation approach.* New York: Wiley.

Bryk, A. S., & Raudenbush, S. W. (1992). *Hierarchical linear models: Applications and data analysis methods.* Newbury Park, CA: Sage.

Bushway, S., Piquero, A., Broidy, L., Cauffman, E., & Mazerolle, P. (2001). An empirical framework for studying desistance as a process. *Criminology, 39*, 491–515.

Carrig, M. M., Wirth, R. J., & Curran, P. J. (2004). A SAS macro for estimating and visualizing individual growth curves. *Structural Equation Modeling, 11*, 132–149.

Curran, P. J. (2003). Have multilevel models been structural equation models all along? *Multivariate Behavioral Research, 38*, 529–569.

Curran, P. J., Bauer, D. J., & Willoughby, M. T. (2004). Testing main effects and interactions in latent curve analysis. *Psychological Methods, 9*, 220–237.

Curran, P. J., & Bollen, K. A. (2001). The best of both worlds: Combining autoregressive and latent curve models. In L. M. Collins, & A. G. Sayer (Eds.), *New methods for the analysis of change* (pp. 105–136). Washington, DC: American Psychological Association.

Curran, P. J., & Hussong, A. M. (2002). Structural equation modeling of repeated measures data. In D. Moskowitz & S. Hershberger (Eds.), *Modeling intraindividual variability with repeated measures data: Methods and applications* (pp. 59–86). Mahwah, NJ: Erlbaum.

Curran, P. J., Muthén, B. O., & Harford, T. C. (1998). The influence of changes in marital status on developmental trajectories of alcohol use in young adults. *Journal of Studies on Alcohol, 59*, 647–658.

Donovan, J. E., & Jessor, R. (1985). Structure of problem behavior in adolescence and young adulthood. *Journal of Consulting and Clinical Psychology, 53*, 890–904.

Duncan, T. E., Duncan, S. C., Strycker, L. A., Li, F., & Alpert, A. (1999). *An introduction to latent variable growth curve modeling: Concepts, issues, and applications.* Mahwah, NJ: Erlbaum.

Elliott, D. S., Huizinga, D., & Menard, S. (1989). *Multiple problem youth: Delinquency, substance use, and mental health problems.* New York: Springer-Verlag.

Farrington, D. P. (1986). Age and crime. In M. Tonry and N. Morris (Eds.), *Crime and justice: An annual review of research* (Vol. 7, pp. 189–250). Chicago: University of Chicago Press.

Gottfredson, M., & Hirschi, T. (1990). *A general theory of crime.* Stanford: Stanford University Press.

Gottfredson, M., & Hirschi, T. (1995). Control theory and the life-course perspective. *Studies on Crime and Crime Prevention, 4,* 131–142.

Hanna, E. Z., & Grant, B. F. (1997). Gender differences in *DSM-IV* alcohol use disorders and major depression as distributed in the general population: Clinical implications. *Comprehensive Psychiatry, 38,* 202–212.

Horney, J., Osgood, D. W., & Marshall, I. H. (1995). Criminal careers in the short-term: Intra-individual variability in crime and its relation to local life circumstances. *American Sociological Review, 60,* 655–673.

Hussong, A. M., Curran, P. J., Moffit, T. E., Caspi, A., & Carrig, M. (2005). Substance abuse hinders desistance in young adults' antisocial behavior. *Development and Psychopathology, 16,* 1029–1046.

Kinderman, T. A., & Skinner, E. A. (1992). Modeling environmental development: Individual and contextual trajectories. In J. B. Asendorpf & J. Valsiner (Eds.), *Stability and change in development: A study of methodological reasoning* (pp. 155–190). Newbury Park, CA: Sage.

Jessor, R., & Jessor, S. L. (1977). *Problem behavior and psychosocial development: A longitudinal study of youth.* New York: Academic Press.

Laub, J. H., Nagin, D. S., & Sampson, R .J. (1998). Trajectories of change in criminal offending: Good marriages and the desistance process. *American Sociological Review, 63,* 225–238.

Laub, J. H., & Sampson, R. J. (2001). Understanding desistance from crime. In M. Tonry (Ed.), *Crime and justice: An annual review,* 28 (pp. 1–69), Chicago: University of Chicago Press.

Leonard, K. E., & Rothbard, J. C. (2000). Alcohol and the marriage effect. *Journal of Studies on Alcohol, Supplemental, 13,* 139–146.

MacCallum, R. C. (1990). The need for alternative measures of fit in covariance structure modeling. *Multivariate Behavioral Research, 25,* 157–162.

McArdle, J. J. (1988). Dynamic but structural equation modeling of repeated measures data. In J. R. Nesselroade & R. B. Cattell (Eds.), *Handbook of multivariate experimental psychology* (2nd ed.), (pp. 561–614), Plenum Press: New York.

Meredith, W., & Tisak, J. (1984). *"Tuckerizing" curves.* Paper presented at the annual meeting (June) of the Psychometric Society, Santa Barbara, CA.

Meredith, W., & Tisak, J. (1990). Latent curve analysis. *Psychometrika, 55,* 107–122.

Moffitt, T. E. (1993). Adolescence-limited and life-course persistent antisocial behavior: A developmental taxonomy. *Psychological Review, 100,* 674–701.

Moffitt, T. E., Caspi, A., Rutter, M., & Silva, P. A. (2001). *Sex differences in antisocial behaviour: Conduct disorder, delinquency, and violence in the Dunedin longitudinal study.* Cambridge, UK: Cambridge University Press.

Moffitt, T. E., Caspi, A., Silva, P. A., & Stouthamer-Loeber, M. (1995). Individual differences in personality and intelligence are linked to crime: Cross-context evidence from nations, neighborhoods, genders, races, and age-cohorts. In J. Hagan (Ed.), *Current perspectives on aging and the life cycle* (Vol. 4, pp. 1–34). Greenwich, CT: JAI Press.

Moffitt, T. E., Silva, P. A., Lynam, D. R., & Henry, B. (1994). Self-reported delinquency at age 18: New Zealand's Dunedin Multidisciplinary Health and Development Study. In J. Junger-Tas & G. J. Terlouw (Eds.), *The International Self-report Delinquency Project* (pp. 354–369). Amsterdam: Kugler.

Munson, J. A., McMahon, R. J., & Spieker, S. J. (2001). Structure and variability in the developmental trajectory of children's externalizing problems: Impact of infant attachment, maternal depressive symptomatology, and child sex. *Development and Psychopathology, 13,* 277–296.

Muthén, L. K., & Muthén, B. O. (1998). Mplus: The comprehensive modeling program for applied researchers. User's Guide. Los Angeles: Muthén & Muthén.

Osgood, D. W., Johnston, L. D., O'Malley, P. M., & Bachman, J. G. (1988). The generality of deviance in late adolescence and early adulthood. *American Sociological Review, 53,* 81–93.

Osgood, D. W., & Rowe, D. C. (1994). Bridging criminal careers theory and policy through latent variable models of individual offending. *Criminology, 32,* 517–554.

Piquero, A., Blumstein, A., Brame, R., Haapanen, R., Mulvey, E. P., & Nagin, D. S. (2001). Assessing the impact of exposure time and incapacitation on longitudinal trajectories of criminal offending. *Journal of Adolescent Research, 16,* 54–74.

Piquero, A., Brame, R., Mazerolle, P., & Haapanen, R. (2001). *Crime in emerging adulthood.* Unpublished manuscript.

Quinton, D., Pickles, A., Maughan, B., & Rutter, M. (1993). Partners, peers, and pathways: Assortative pairing and continuities in conduct disorder. *Development and Psychopathology, 5,* 763–783.

Robins, L. N. (1978). Sturdy predictors of adult antisocial behaviour: Replications from longitudinal studies. *Psychological Medicine, 8,* 611–622.

Robins, L. N., Helzer, J. E., Cottler, L., & Goldring, E. (1989). *Diagnostic Interview Schedule, Version III-R.* St. Louis, MO: Washington University.

Robins, L. N., & Reiger, D. A. (Eds.) (1991). *Psychiatric disorders in America: The epidemiologic catchment area study.* New York: The Free Press.

Rutter, M. (1987). Psychosocial resilience and protective mechanisms. *American Journal of Orthopsychiatry, 57,* 316–331.

Rutter, M. (1996). Transitions and turning points in developmental psychopathology: As applied to the age span between childhood and mid-adulthood. *International Journal of Behavioral Development, 19,* 603–626.

Sayer, A. G., & Cumsille, P. (2001). Second-order latent growth models. In L. Collins & A. Sayer (Eds.), *New methods for the analysis of change* (pp. 179–200). Washington, DC: APA Books.

Shadish, W. R., Cook, T. D., & Campbell, D. T. (2001). *Experimental and quasi-experimental designs for generalized causal inference.* Boston: Houghton Mifflin.

Sher, K. J., & Gotham, H. J. (1999). Pathological alcohol involvement: A developmental disorder of young adulthood. *Development and Psychopathology, 11,* 933–956.

Silva, P. A., & Stanton, W. R. (1996). *From child to adult: The Dunedin Multidisciplinary Health and Development Study.* Auckland, New Zealand: Oxford University Press.

Vaillant, G. E. (1995). *The natural history of alcoholism revisited.* Cambridge: Harvard University Press.

Willett, J. B., & Sayer, A. G. (1994). Using covariance structure analysis to detect correlates and predictors of individual change over time. *Psychological Bulletin, 116,* 363–381.

chapter six

Modeling age-based turning points in longitudinal life-span growth curves of cognition

John J. McArdle
University of Southern California

Lijuan Wang
University of Virginia

Contents

Introduction 105
Methods... 110
    Participants.. 110
    Measurements... 110
    Models.. 113
    Fitting the linear and nonlinear models 116
Results.. 117
    Univariate models 117
    Bivariate model results 121
Conclusion... 123
Acknowledgment.. 125
References 125

Introduction

The purpose of this study was to explore and compare several different methods for estimating unknown turning points in longitudinal data, employing the Bradway-McArdle longitudinal life-span data for crystallized (Gc) and fluid (Gf) intelligence scores (Cattell, 1998). Life-span studies are often designed to investigate age changes in characteristics (e.g., Nesselroade & Baltes, 1979). The focal data for life-span studies can be described as nested, repeatedly measured, multilevel, or longitudinal. Initial analyses may characterize the relationship among the occasions by the average change trajectory. At a second stage of analysis, the differences between the average group curve and the individual curves can be characterized in many different ways. A typical way to analyze both intraindividual change and variability and interindividual differences is to use mixed-effects models (Davidian & Giltinan, 1995; Diggle, Liang, & Zeger, 1994; McArdle, Ferrer-Caja, Hamagami, & Woodcock, 2002; Verbeke & Molenberghs, 2000). However, it is not always reasonable to use a single and simple dynamic function to capture the entire process. For example, in the processes of cognitive aging over the life span, some researchers suggest that cognitive development has several different stages (i.e., an infant development stage, a child development stage, an adolescent development stage, an adult development stage, an older adult decline stage, and a final decline toward death phase). If we take these substantive issues seriously, we need to investigate the age-based change points at which one trajectory stops and the next begins.

Two theoretical examples are presented in Figure 6.1 to set the stage for the current longitudinal analyses. In both cases, we draw the trajectories of the latent scores $Y[t]$ of $n = 4$ individuals as a function of age $A[t]$ at that time. In the first example (Figure 6.1a), we have drawn growth curves in which all four individuals have very similar true scores $Y[t]$ up until about age $\alpha[t] = 18$ but then seem to go in different directions after this age. Because the individuals were largely indistinguishable before age 18 but easily distinguishable after age 18, $\tau = 18$ might be considered the *age-based turning point* for this function. Of course, there is a question about whether these differences could be detected even before age 18, and the issue of *earliest prediction age* needs to be considered. Figure 6.1b gives an alternative possibility in which the $n = 4$ individuals all have similar functional form, but the approach to this asymptote starts at different ages for each individual. In this case, there is no common turning point for the group, and the variation in the age-based turning point is a key feature of interest. Further combinations of these two basic models allow for many additional classes of turning points with growth curves of these combinations as in Figure 6.1c. Although we focus on cognition scores here, these theoretical statements could apply to any variables measured in the same units over all ages.

One of the challenges for contemporary statistical research has been to create growth curve models that allow for the estimation of these complex but reasonable possibilities. Variations of multiphase regression analysis

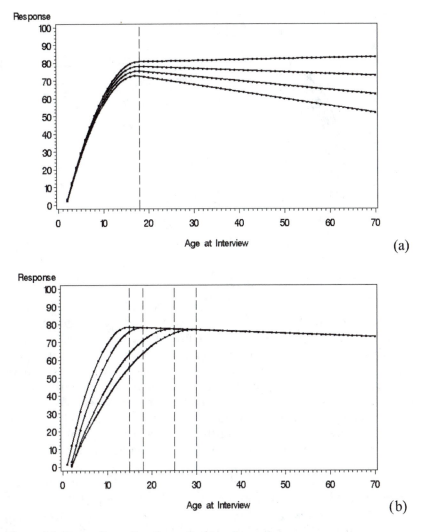

Figure 6.1 Some alternative theoretical turning point processes.

have been proposed to locate change points (Gallant & Fuller, 1973; Smith & Cook, 1980). But, since this model could not deal with nested data or repeated measures, a multiphase mixed-effects model beginning with known change points was designed and employed (Bryk & Raudenbush, 1992; Diggle et al., 1994). Multiphase mixed-effects models with unknown change points are a more recent extension of this work (Cudeck & Du Toit, 2003; Cudeck & Klebe, 2002; Hall, Lipton, Sliwinski, & Stewart, 2000;

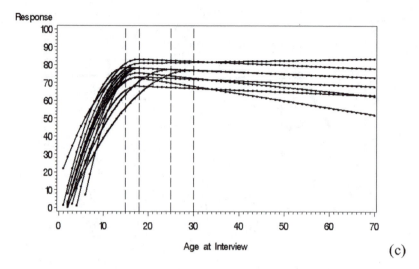

(c)

Figure 6.1 (Continued)

Hall et al., 2001). In this model, there are two or more different "phases." Cudeck and Klebe (2002) specifically defined the term *change point* as the time when development "switches from one phase to another" and listed several examples of such change points, such as a skill learning curve. They further suggested: "This kind of behavior addressed in this article develops in phases in a way that cannot be summarized satisfactorily by a standard nonlinear regression model of low complexity (p. 41)." Because the model includes the product of the random change point parameter and the random slope, it is also a special case of general nonlinear mixed-effects models.

One of the simplest statistical solutions proposed for estimating the unknown change points is based on trying a range of possibilities for a turning point. For example, it is possible to fit a two-piece linear spline model in which the turning point is either $\tau = 10$, $\tau = 11$, $\tau = 12$, ... , $\tau = 30$, and so on. This method successfully avoids the problem of interpreting covariance associated with the product (interaction) of a random change point parameter and a random slope parameter. Thus, the model becomes a linear mixed-effects model instead of a nonlinear mixed model. After fitting alternative models, we can use a comparison of their fits to the data to determine the best location of an age-based turning point τ. This piece-meal approach was formally expressed as the profile likelihood method. While it is necessarily limited by the interval size, it has been shown to be practically useful by Hall et al. (2001), who used this method to assess the age-based turning point associated with Alzheimer's disease.

When the model estimates turning points as fixed parameters, no inter-individual differences in the turning points are allowed. But, for many phenomena it seems reasonable to suggest that key changes may be triggered by other events or experiences at different ages for different persons. If so, we must extend the standard mixed model to include random effects for individual differences in the turning points, Indeed, these may be the most important set of parameters in the longitudinal analysis.

Turning points can also be estimated by methods that estimate non-linear mixed-effects models. Davidian and Giltinan (2003) systematically reviewed such methods. Of two major categories, one comes from the frequentist school of statistics based on classical methods. Here, analyses approximate a likelihood function, including first-order Taylor series expansions by expanding the random coefficients around zero (Beal & Sheiner, 1982), first-order Taylor Series expansion around the current estimates of the random effects (Lindstrom & Bates, 1990), and second-order Laplace approximation (Vonesh, 1996; Wolfinger, 1993). Pinheiro and Bates (1995) proposed exact likelihood functions to estimate the parameters by an adaptive Gaussian quadrature (AGQ) using the first-order method of Beal and Sheiner (1982).

In previous studies based on this approach, Morrell, Pearson, Carter, and Brant (1995) used a first-order linearization method (Lindstrom & Bates, 1990) to estimate the unknown change points in men with prostate cancer. Hall et al. (2000) used profile likelihood estimation to fit the linear mixed models under different known change points, and Hall et al. (2001) used a MCMC (Markov Chain Monte Carlo, [metropolis algorithm]) to estimate the unknown change points of two cognitive aging variables and compared the results to the profile likelihood methods. Cudeck and Klebe (2002) and Cudeck and Du Toit (2003) used AGQ to estimate the unknown change points of nonverbal performance over life span, including analyses based on Bradway-McArdle longitudinal data used here.

Another category of multivariate model fitting has been developed from techniques in Bayesian estimation. In the Bayesian framework, both the likelihood of the model and the prior distributions of the parameters need to be specified. These analyses can be carried out with a free computer package, winBUGS (Congdon, 2001, 2003; Spiegelhalter, Thomas, Best, & Lunn, 2003). Davidiin and Giltinan (1995, 2003) and Gilks, Richardson, and Spiegelhalter (1996) provided detailed information on these estimation methods. Usually, the prior distributions are specified using noninformative distributions because there is no clear prior information, that is, considering age-based turning points in a uniform distribution (e.g., $U[0,100]$). If there is prior information, constraints can be employed in specifying the prior distributions and be expected to improve the accuracy and efficiency of the estimation. For example, if we believe the change points of age must lie in the range 10 to 40, we could specify an informative prior (e.g., $U[10,40]$. In the current study, we assumed no relevant prior information regarding the fixed parameters.

These analyses compared these contemporary statistical methods in the analysis of real longitudinal cognitive data. Several linear and nonlinear mixed-effects models are proposed on different measures of cognition from the Bradway-McArdle longitudinal life-span data (described next). These models were fitted and compared using three estimation methods for turning points: (1) profile likelihood methods, (2) the first-order method of Beal et al. (1982), and (3) Bayesian methods. In a companion paper (Wang and McArdle, 2008), we present technical overviews of the methods used here and examine statistical simulations from known populations. In this chapter, we focus on the application to the Bradway-McArdle data using standard goodness-of-fit indices to compare the multiphase mixed models with alternative models in our search for significant change points in the life-span cognitive measures. These comparisons also provide information regarding individual differences in cognitive change points.

Methods

Participants

These data came from the Bradway-McArdle longitudinal data (McArdle & Hamagami, 1996; McArdle, Hamagami, Meredith, & Bradway, 2001). The participants were drawn from an original sample ($N = 231$) of children living in the Bay area of northern California in connection with the standardization of the two forms of the Revised Stanford-Binet (S-B) Intelligence Scale. In 1931, there were 231 children, aged 2 to 7 years, tested on both L and M forms of the Revised S-B Scale. In 1941, 136 of the same children were tested using the S-B L form. In 1956, 111 participants were retested on the revised S-B Scale as well as on the Wechsler Adult Intelligence Scale (WAIS). In 1969, 48 of these participants were measured on the S-B and WAIS; in 1984 and 1992, 51 of these participants were measured on the WAIS and Woodcock-Johnson Revised (WJ-R) test.

Measurements

Item response theory (IRT) models were used in previous work to create semicomparable measurements over time (Hamagami, 1998; McArdle et al., 2007). The data used here were the Rasch-scaled fluid intelligence (Gf) and crystallized intelligence (Gc) scores of participants ($n = 111$) on the six occasions. The individual scores for Gf and Gc longitudinal data are plotted against age at testing in Figure 6.2.

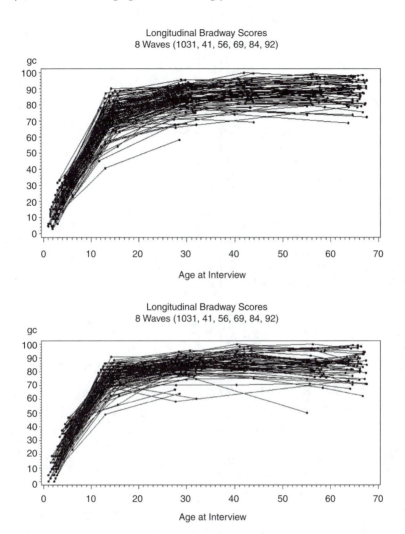

Figure 6.2 Raw data on growth curves with change points of Gc and Gf from the Bradway-McArdle longitudinal life-span data.

Table 6.1a is a list of the summary statistics (mean, standard deviation, range, and number of participants) of Rasch-scaled *Gc* and *Gf* of this sample on the six occasions. Table 6.1b displays the correlation matrix of *Gc* and *Gf* over the six occasions. From Figure 6.2 and Table 6.1a, we can see that the participants gained rapidly in *Gc* and *Gf* over the first two or three occasions. In adulthood, the *Gc* and *Gf* means were relatively stable. From

Table 6.1 Statistical Summary of Rasch-Scaled Gc and Gf

a. Means and standard deviations (SDs) at six ages

Test year	N	Age, mean (SD)	Gc, mean (SD)	Gf, mean (SD)
1931	110	3.90 (1.44)	22.13 (9.85)	24.59 (12.96)
1941	111	13.91 (1.44)	72.21 (9.34)	75.84 (7.74)
1956	110	29.51 (1.48)	84.35 (6.99)	83.79 (6.21)
1969	49	41.86 (1.43)	87.87 (6.69)	88.77 (6.37)
1984	51	57.12 (1.44)	88.89 (5.85)	84.43 (8.40)
1992	51	65.36 (1.44)	88.11 (7.14)	84.94 (8.68)

b. Correlations of Rasch-scaled Gc and Gf by rounded mean age

	Gc_4	Gc_14	Gc_30	Gc_42	Gc_57	Gc_65	Gf_4	Gf_14	Gf_30	Gf_42	Gf_57
Gc_4	1.00										
Gc_14	.55	1.00									
Gc_30	.23	.68	1.00								
Gc_42	.19	.38	.81	1.00							
Gc_57	.30	.49	.80	.80	1.00						
Gc_65	.08	.47	.76	.66	.91	1.00					
Gf_4	.91	.45	.10	.05	.19	.00	1.00				
Gf_14	.43	.82	.67	.51	.44	.36	.35	1.00			
Gf_30	.20	.46	.77	.67	.54	.45	.11	.58	1.00		
Gf_42	-.08	.13	.45	.45	.42	.38	-.05	.26	.77	1.00	
Gf_57	.09	.20	.38	.47	.55	.42	.05	.38	.74	.85	1.00
Gf_65	.03	.20	.49	.43	.40	.50	-.02	.25	.67	.83	.84

Table 1.2, the measurements of *Gc* or *Gf* are correlated relatively higher among the last four occasions than the first two occasions (see Table 6.1a). And, the relationships of *Gc* and *Gf* on the same occasion are also positive correlated, which is relatively higher in the earlier occasions than the later occasions. The largest set of incomplete data in this study came from longitudinal attrition and mortality, which were the main reasons why some participants ($n = 36$) were not measured on the last three occasions.

Models

Several linear mixed models and nonlinear mixed models can be used to describe the changes of *Gc* and *Gf* in the Bradway-McArdle longitudinal data over age. In the notation used here, the dependent variables in these models are either *Gc* or *Gf*, and indexed by $Y[t]_n$ (the Rasch-scaled *Gc* or *Gf* of nth individual at tth occasion) in the following equations. The independent variable in these models is chronological age, which is indexed by $A[t]_n$ (the test age of nth individual at tth occasion). The common structure of all the mixed-effects models to follow can be written as

$$Y[t]_n = f(Age[t]_n, b_n) + e[t]_n \text{ with } e[t]_n \sim N(0, \sigma_e^2) \text{ and } b_n \sim N(\beta, \Phi)$$

The change function as expressed above can be linear or nonlinear. The random parameter vector is indexed by b, and β indexes the fixed-parameter vector; Φ is the variance-covariance matrix representing interindividual differences in these parameters; and σ_e^2 is the variance of the residual $e[t]$. $Age[t]$ may be rescaled in advance of the data analysis (i.e., to center the age variable).

Several different models can be used to characterize the change process, and we examine the following: (1) linear mixed-effects model, (2) quadratic mixed-effects model, (3) cubic mixed-effects model, (4) exponential mixed-effects model, (5) dual-exponential mixed-effects model, (6) linear-linear mixed-effects model, (7) quadratic-linear mixed-effects model, and (8) a bivariate version of model 7.

Model 1: Linear mixed-effects model

In Model 1, the change over age is assumed to be linear. The model can be expressed as

$$Y[t]_n = b_{0n} + b_{1n} Age[t]_n + e[t]_n$$

This model predicting the observed variable *Y* at time *n* or $Y[t]_n$ has two fixed parameters: the average performance level at zero β_0 and the average linear slope for a one-unit change in *Age* β_1. The interindividual differences in the (random-level) mean parameter b_{0n} and slope parameter b_{1n} are represented by a 2 × 2 variance-covariance matrix Φ.

Model 2: Quadratic mixed-effects model

The change over age was fitted by a quadratic curve written as

$$Y[t]_n = b_{0n} + b_{1n} Age[t]_n + \tfrac{1}{2} b_{2n} Age[t]_n^2 + e[t]_n$$

This model has three fixed parameters: an average performance level β_0, the average linear slope β_1, and the average quadratic slope β_2. The inter-individual differences in the random parameters of b_{0n}, b_{1n}, and b_{2n} is estimated by a 3 × 3 variance-covariance matrix Φ.

Model 3: Cubic mixed-effect model

Model 3 adds the fixed and random cubic slopes into the model, now expressed as

$$Y[t]_n = b_{0n} + b_{1n} Age[t]_n + \tfrac{1}{2} b_{2n} Age[t]_n^2 + 1/3\, b_{3n} Age[t]_n^3 + e[t]_n$$

This yields four fixed parameters, and the interindividual differences are estimated by a 4 × 4 variance-covariance matrix.

Model 4: Exponential mixed-effect model

In Model 4, a nonlinear exponential function is used to fit the change process, written as

$$Y[t]_n = b_{0n} - b_{1n} \exp\{- b_{2n}{}^*Age[t]_n\} + e[t]_n$$

Fixed parameter β_0 estimates the average peak level of the population; β_1 estimates the average difference between the peak level and initial level at age zero; β_2 estimates the average rate of improvement or decline. The interindividual differences and intraindividual variability are also estimated in the model (after McArdle & Hamagami, 1996).

Model 5: Dual-exponential mixed-effect model

Model 4 used a single parameter to characterize the change rate as a function of a power of age that would necessarily describe a curve that either increases or decreases. To allow some flexibility here, we add a second power of age that permits a more complex curve in Model 5.

$$Y[t]_n = b_{0n} + b_{1n}(\exp\{- b_{2n}{}^*Age[t]_n\} - \exp\{- b_{3n}{}^*Age[t]_n\}) + e[t]_n$$

Here, b_{3n} may estimate the rate of age decline in fluid or crystallized intelligence to be combined with b_{2n}, used to estimate the increase rate. In previous work, this model was found to be a useful way to characterize the change of cognitive performances over the life span (McArdle et al., 2002).

Model 6: Linear-linear mixed-effect model

In place of a single function, the next model uses two different linear functions to characterize the change. This model is expressed as

$$Y[t]_n = b_{0n} + b_{1n} Age[t]_n + b_{2n}(Age[t]_n - \tau_n) + e[t]_n$$

$$(Age[t]_n - \tau_n) = 0 \text{ iff } Age[t]_n < \tau_n$$

$$(Age[t]_n - \tau_n) = Age[t]_n - \tau_n \text{ iff } Age[t]_n > \tau_n$$

Here, the b_{0n} estimates the initial ability of each individual at age 0. The b_{1n} estimates the linear slope before the change point τ_n for each individual. The sum, $b_{1n} + b_{2n}$ is an estimate of the *linear slope after the change point*. Therefore, before the change point τ_n, there is a linear function to characterize the change, and after the change point τ_n, there is another linear function to characterize the change. The functions used in the two phases are both linear, but their values are allowed to be different.

Model 7: Quadratic-linear mixed-effects model

The next model uses a quadratic-linear function, which was presented by Cudeck and Klebe (2002). This model is expressed in our notation as

$$Y[t]_n = b_{0n} + b_{1n} Age[t]_n + b_{2n}(\tau_n - Age[t]_n)^2 + e[t]_n$$

$$(\tau_n - Age[t]_n)^2 = 0 \text{ iff } Age[t]_n > \tau_n$$

$$(\tau_n - Age[t]_n)^2 \neq 0 \text{ iff } Age[t]_n < \tau_n$$

A quadratic function is used for the first phase and a linear function for the second phase. Thus, before the change point τ_n, the function may be curved, but after the change point, the function becomes linear. In this way, b_{2n} estimates the individual quadratic slope in the first phase; b_{1n} estimates the individual linear slope in the second phase; and $b_{0n} + b_{1n}\tau_n$ is an estimate of the individual performances at the change point.

Model 8: Bivariate quadratic-linear mixed-effects model

From the correlation matrix displayed in Table 6.1, the *Gc* and *Gf* measured on the same occasions are highly correlated with each other. So, the performance level at the change point for these two constructs, and the change points themselves, could be also correlated. Besides estimating the change points for these two variables separately, we are interested in estimating the change points for both simultaneously by including the correlated information in the model. Thus, the model includes the correlation between τ_{gf} and τ_{gc}, as well as the correlations of these parameters with other variables (for more detail, see Wang & McArdle, 2008). The difference between Model 8 and Model 7 is simultaneous estimation of multiple change points along with tests of hypotheses across variables (i.e., is $\tau_{gf} = \tau_{gc}$).

Fitting the linear and nonlinear models

Models 1 to Model 6 were estimated in PROC MIXED (Model 1 to Model 3), or NLMIXED (Model 4 to Model 6, first-order method) using traditional maximum likelihood estimation (MLE) methods and in winBUGS using a Bayesian method.

Univariate quadratic-linear models (Model 7) were estimated using three estimation methods noted above. For the profile likelihood method, age-based turning points were fixed from 10 to 30. This method was implemented by using a PROC MIXED macro. For the first-order method (implemented in PROC NLMIXED with METHOD=FIRO) two starting value sets were used. One set of estimates was generated from the profile likelihood method, and the other used the profile likelihood estimates plus 1.96 times the parameter standard error.

To compare the fit of the models such as Model 7 with any fixed turning points, the likelihoods can be used. These models have the same number of parameters, so the model with the minimum fitting function value (–2 LL [Log Likelihood]) can be selected. To compare the goodness of fit of the change point model (Model 6 and Model 7) to another linear or nonlinear mixed model (Model 1 to Model 5), we used the MLE for linear mixed models and first-order method for nonlinear mixed models. The equation $AIC = -2 \log L + 2r$ can be used to compare these nonnested models (models with smaller AICs (Akaike Information Criterion) are considered better fit).

The winBUGS syntax for estimating the quadratic-linear mixed-effects model using three methods are provided in the appendix. In implementing the Bayesian method, we also used two sets of different starting values. The bivariate quadratic-linear model is easier to estimate using Bayesian methods than the other two. Before obtaining the Bayes estimates, the Gelman-Rubin statistic and autocorrelation plots (Plummer, Best, Cowles, & Vines, 2005) were used in testing the convergence problem and assurance of satisfaction of the convergence criteria. (In this analysis, 100,000 iterations after 10,000 burn-in iterations were updated, and 1 sample in every 20 samples was used in calculating the estimates.) The goodness-of-fit index in Bayesian framework is termed the *deviance information criterion* (*DIC*; the sum of the posterior mean deviance $D(\theta)$ and twice the model complexity index pD; see Spiegelhalter, Best, Carlin, & Linde, 2002).

In this context, the *DIC* is similar to the *AIC* (and BIC [Bayesian Information Criterion]) used in the classical framework (Congdon, 2003), and a
smaller *DIC* indicates that the model has a better fit to the data.

Results

Univariate models

The results of univariate longitudinal analyses of *Gc* and *Gf* are displayed
in Table 6.2. The second column shows the fit from PROC MIXED/PROC

Table 6.2 Goodness of Fit of Linear and Nonlinear Univariate
Mixed-Effects Models on *Gc/Gf*

	MLE/FIRO	Bayesian indices of model fit and complexity		
	AIC	Dbar	pD	DIC
Goodness-of-fit for *Gc*				
Linear mixed model	4,172.6	4,131.8	4.34	4,136.2
Quadratic mixed model	3,676.9	3,655.7	13.2	3,668.9
Cubic mixed model	3,308.6	3,124.1	114.3	3,238.4
Exponential mixed model	3,087.3	2,842.8	175.6	3,018.3
Dual-exponential mixed model	3,069.8	2,618.1	192.2	2,810.3
Linear-linear mixed model	3,020.0	2,596.4	200.5	2,796.9
Quadratic-linear mixed model	3,010.1	2,493.5	247.7	2,741.2
Goodness-of-fit for *Gf*				
Linear mixed model	4,220.0	4,221.2	5.17	4,226.3
Quadratic mixed model	3,772.0	3,771.9	14.0	3,785.9
Cubic mixed model	3,409.3	3,328.3	84.5	3,412.8
Exponential mixed model	3,180.3	2,937.0	165.7	3,102.7
Dual-exponential mixed model	3,160.6	2,851.0	174.9	3,026.0
Linear-linear mixed model	3,208.8	2,866.8	106.1	2,993.0
Quadratic-linear mixed model	3,127.3	2,704.8	230.3	2,935.1

Note: MLE is maximum likelihood estimation, which was used to estimate the linear mixed models
from Model 1 to Model 3; FIRO is first-order method of Beal and Sheiner (1982), which was used
to estimate the nonlinear mixed models from Model 4 to Model 7. Dbar is the post mean of −2 log
likelihood values pD is a measure of model complexity. DIC, deviance information criterion.

NLMIXED in the classical framework. The last three columns gave the fit information from winBUGS in the Bayesian framework.

Generally, these results suggest the model estimation became more complex if a nonlinear component was included in the model. For example, there were three random parameters in both the quadratic mixed model and exponential model, but the model complexity (pD) of these two models showed that the exponential model is more complex than the quadratic model (175.6 vs. 13.2 for Gc, 165.7 vs. 14.0 for Gf). According to the fit indices of AIC and DIC in Table 6.2, the Cudeck and Klebe (2002) quadratic-linear mixed-effects model fit relatively better than other models for both the Gc and Gf scores.

When fitting the quadratic-linear change point model, three estimation methods were used. The parameter estimates and standard errors from these three methods are displayed in Tables 6.3 and 6.4 separately for Gc and Gf, respectively. For the simple profile likelihood estimation, after comparing the likelihood values from the quadratic-linear models with fixed change points from 10 to 30, the models with the fixed turning point at age 21 for Gc and 19 for Gf yielded the best fits (Figure 6.3). Since the turning points were fixed points in each run of the profile likelihood estimation, there were no variances and covariances associated with the turning points here.

Overall, the estimates for the fixed effects from these three methods were similar. The change points of the average person for Gc was about 21 years old, and for Gf was about 19 years old. The average linear slope in the second phase after the change point for Gc is around 0.10 (with standard error = 0.02) and for Gf is around 0.03 (with standard error = 0.03). However, at the individual level, different participants exhibited different linear slopes in the second phase; some people showed flat change, some showed decreasing change, and others showed increasing change.

The interindividual differences in the change points can be characterized by allowing a variance of the individual change points. However, for the first-order estimation from PROC NLMIXED, the estimates and standard errors were found to be extremely sensitive to different starting values, and this was especially true for the variance components. For instance, the estimated variances of the random change point parameter from two sets of starting values for Gc were $\sigma_\tau^2 = 4$ and $\sigma_\tau^2 = 2$. But, from the Bayesian estimation, the estimates of the variance of the random change point were much less sensitive, with $\sigma_\tau^2 = 1.17$ and $\sigma_\tau^2 = 1.19$ from two different sets of starting values (and with standard errors ~ 0.7). The same pattern holds for the Gf parameters as well (i.e., $\sigma_\tau^2 = 0.98$ and $\sigma_\tau^2 = 1.01$ with standard error = 0.8).

Table 6.3 Parameter Estimations From the Univariate Quadratic-Linear Mixed-Effects Models on Gc

	Profile likelihood estimation (MLE)		First-order estimation from PROC NLMIXED				Bayesian model estimation WinBUGS			
			Starting value 1		Starting value 2		Starting value 1		Starting value 2	
	Estimates	SE	Estimates	SE	Estimates	SE	Estimates	SE	Estimates	SE
Fixed effects										
β_0	81.27	0.96	82.16	1.15	82.98	1.24	80.74	0.97	80.68	1.00
β_1	0.11	0.02	0.09	0.03	0.08	0.02	0.12	0.02	0.12	0.02
β_2	-0.2	0	-0.19	0.02	-0.19	0.01	-0.21	0.01	-0.21	0.01
τ	21	—	21.48	1.13	21.71	0.37	20.70	0.33	20.67	0.35
Variance components										
σ_e^2	12.3	1.268	10.44	2.14	14.46	2.67	10.99	1.19	11.00	1.20
ϕ_{00}	73.86	14.06	73.72	28.65	100.97	0.25	43.86	12.61	43.67	12.84
ϕ_{11}	0.012	0.004	0.01	0.006	0.014	0.005	0.012	0.003	0.012	0.003
ϕ_{22}	0.001	0	0.003	0	0.002	0	0.003	0.001	0.003	0.001
$\phi_{\tau\tau}$	—	—	4.021	1.586	2.019	0.381	1.167	0.653	1.191	0.680
ϕ_{01}	-0.647	0.226	-0.546	0.392	-0.931	0.186	-0.245	0.186	-0.244	0.191
ϕ_{02}	-0.168	0.041	-0.198	0.201	-0.163	0.049	-0.257	0.058	-0.258	0.058
$\phi_{0\tau}$	—	—	-2.834	7.984	0.941	2.18	-6.503	1.806	-6.521	1.851
ϕ_{12}	0.002	0.001	0.023	0.303	0.001	0.002	0.002	0.001	0.002	0.001
$\phi_{1\tau}$	—	—	0.104	0.016	-0.013	0.07	0.032	0.023	0.032	0.024
$\phi_{2\tau}$	—	—	0.023	0.303	0.051	—	0.043	0.019	0.043	0.020

Note: Starting value 1 is based on the estimates from the profile likelihood estimation. Starting value 2 is based on the estimates from the profile estimates + 1.96*standard error (SE). MLE, maximum likelihood estimation.

Table 6.4 Parameter Estimations From the Univariate Quadratic-Linear Mixed-Effects Models on Gf

	Profile likelihood estimation (MLE)		First-order estimation from PROC NLMIXED				Bayesian estimation WinBUGS			
			Starting value 1		Starting value 2		Starting value 1		Starting value 2	
	Estimates	SE	Estimates	SE	Estimates	SE	Estimates	SE	Estimates	SE
Fixed effects										
β_0	83.25	0.86	84.18	1.23	84.54	1.26	82.53	0.97	82.57	1.03
β_1	0.02	0.02	0	0.03	-0.01	0.03	0.03	0.03	0.03	0.03
β_2	-0.25	0	-0.24	0.01	-0.24	0.01	-0.27	0.01	-0.27	0.01
τ	19	—	19.6	0.49	19.61	0.4	18.60	0.40	18.63	0.44
Variance components										
σ_e^2	16.27	1.76	16.01	2.52	16.38	2.09	16.24	1.87	16.18	1.86
ϕ_{00}	48.29	12.13	48.31	27.48	72.07	41.94	20.90	12.38	21.21	11.99
ϕ_{11}	0.021	0.006	0.028	0.012	0.035	0.017	0.019	0.005	0.019	0.005
ϕ_{22}	0.001	0	0.004	0	0.002	0	0.004	0.001	0.004	0.001
$\phi_{\tau\tau}$	—	—	3.396	—	1.072	—	1.015	0.772	0.989	0.725
ϕ_{01}	-0.544	0.263	-0.702	0.553	-1.138	0.831	-0.118	0.209	-0.124	0.207
ϕ_{02}	-0.163	0.051	-0.145	0.06	-0.231	0.017	-0.191	0.068	-0.194	0.066
$\phi_{0\tau}$	—	—	-0.001	0.003	0.002	0.002	-3.482	1.558	-3.567	1.468
ϕ_{12}	0.002	0.001	0.37	4.301	-0.041	5.148	0.001	0.002	0.001	0.002
$\phi_{1\tau}$	—	—	-0.106	0.12	-0.069	0.102	0.003	0.040	0.006	0.038
$\phi_{2\tau}$	—	—	0.101	—	0.034	—	0.046	0.029	0.045	0.028

Note: Starting value 1 is based on the estimates from the profile likelihood estimation. Starting value 2 is based on the profile estimates + 1.96*standard error (SE).

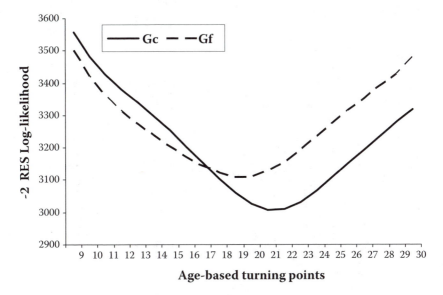

Figure 6.3 Profile likelihood values for age-based turning points.

Bivariate model results

Table 6.5 displays the parameter estimates from the bivariate quadratic-linear mixed model using Bayesian estimation. The estimates of fixed parameters from the bivariate model are close to the estimates from the univariate model for both the *Gc* and *Gf* scores. The average change points were estimated here to be τ_{gc} = 20.87 and τ_{gf} =18.77 years old. From the estimated covariance matrix, we found that the individual change points of *Gc* and *Gf* both have smaller variability ($\sigma_\tau^2 \sim$ 0.7) and are positively correlated (0.87). Also as expected, the individual performance levels of *Gc* and *Gf* at the change points were also highly positively correlated (>0.99), indicating a boundary condition was reached.

Simultaneously estimating the change points for *Gc* and *Gf* in one model provided some additional options, including the opportunity to *test the equality of change points across variables.* According to the loss of fit found when equating these change points (z = 17.68), the estimates from the bivariate quadratic-linear model suggest the average change point for *Gf* occurs at a significantly earlier age than for *Gc*: *The change in* Gf *occurs about 2 years earlier than the change for* Gc, and this is consistent with part of Cattell's (1971) original theory.

Table 6.5 Parameter Estimations from The Simultaneous Bivariate Quadratic-Linear Mixed-Effects Models on Both Gc and Gf

	Estimates	SE		Φ							
				b_{no1}	b_{n11}	b_{n21}	τ_{n1}	b_{no2}	b_{n12}	b_{n22}	τ_{n2}
$\hat{\beta}_{01}$	81.340	.817	b_{no1}	53.500							
$\hat{\beta}_{11}$	.102	.016	b_{n11}	-.363	.013						
$\hat{\beta}_{21}$	-.209	.006	b_{n21}	-.252	.002	.003					
$\hat{\tau}_{1}$	20.870	.160	τ_{n1}	-5.587	.038	.028	.676				
$\hat{\beta}_{02}$	83.120	.619	b_{no2}	39.430	-.265	-.184	-4.076	29.730			
$\hat{\beta}_{12}$	.016	.017	b_{n12}	-.271	.009	.002	.028	-.212	.018		
$\hat{\beta}_{22}$	-.266	.010	b_{n22}	-.313	.002	.002	.034	-.226	.002	.004	
$\hat{\tau}_{2}$	18.770	.228	τ_{n2}	-5.350	.037	.026	.599	-3.716	.024	.035	.690

$\sigma^2_{e1} = 10.71, \sigma^2_{e2} = 14.70.$

Conclusion

The goal of this chapter was to explore the application of three typical methods for estimating the change points for *Gc* and *Gf*. These methods were profile likelihood methods, first-order estimation, and Bayesian methods. According to any of the goodness-of-fit indices used here (*AIC* and *DIC*), the combined quadratic-linear model fit both *Gc* and *Gf* better than other proposed models, and this means that there may be some significant age-based turning points in life-span cognition. The average age-based turning points for *Gc* and *Gf* were found at age 21 and age 19, respectively, and this gap of 2 years represents a significant difference. On average, there was rapid growth in both *Gc* and *Gf* before the turning points, but after the turning points there was a slight increase for *Gc* and no development for *Gf* through the mid-60s.

We conclude that each of these three methods has some advantages and disadvantages in estimating unknown change points. For profile likelihood estimation, the main advantages of the technique include (1) The model is relatively easier to estimate since it turns to a linear mixed model, and the estimates and likelihood values are standard; (2) it does not depend on good starting values, so it is useful as the first-step procedure for other methods; (3) it can be easily implemented and runs fast in standard programs such as SAS MIXED and Splus LME. The main disadvantages of this method are that (4) there are no estimated individual differences in the change points, and (5) the fixed change points are discrete (i.e., not continuous) values.

For the first-order method in the MLE framework, the main advantages of this model include (1) an easy way to allow interindividual differences around the change points in the model; (2) it can be easily implemented in standard programs such as SAS NLMIXED, and if the starting values are reasonable, the computational speed is relatively fast. The disadvantages of the MLE method seems to be (3) the need for extremely good starting values because the estimates are sensitive to different starting values.

For the Bayesian estimation of the models used here, the main advantages include (1) it permits the estimation of the interindividual differences in turning points in the model (σ_τ^2 and associated covariances); (2) it can be implemented in standard programs (e.g., winBUGS), which seems to have low sensitivity to different starting values; (3) it makes some use of the previous information about the change points and other information to set informative priors; (4) it is relatively easier to extend the univariate model into the bivariate model in this framework. Of course, the disadvantages include (5) that an improper prior distribution could make the estimates inaccurate, especially if the model is complex, and (6) we need more burn-in iterations and the iteration speed is extremely slow (i.e., possibly from hours to days).

According to Cudeck and Klebe (2002) and Cudeck and Du Toit (2003), a subset of the Bradway-McArdle longitudinal data was used; the participants' data were not used if there were three missing data in the last three occasions, so only $n = 76$ were also used to estimate the change points. The goodness-of-fit index in this study showed that a quadratic-linear mixed-effects model fits the Gc and Gf data relatively better than other fitted models in this study, which is consistent with the findings from Cudeck and Klebe (2002). But, the parameter estimations from the quadratic-linear model (see Table 6.4) for Gf were substantially different from the report of Cudeck and Klebe, especially in the second-phase linear fixed-effects slope, the first-phase quadratic fixed-effects slope, and the intraindividual variability. For instance, the second-phase linear fixed-effects slope was 0.03 from Bayesian estimation and was also 0.3 from the first-order method in this study, but the estimation from the first-order method was -0.129 (Cudeck & Klebe, 2002) and the estimation from the AGQ was -0.141 (Cudeck & Du Toit, 2003). This is a nontrivial issue because differences of this magnitude could be of substantial consequence for change point analyses by a substantive researcher. Based on the preliminary results of separate simulation studies of different intraindividual variability and different second linear slope (Wang et al., 2008), *the estimation results from Bayesian methods are more reliable* in estimating the quadratic-linear mixed-effects models than the classical estimation methods.

On the whole, the substantive results presented here are largely consistent with predictions of Gf/Gc theory (e.g., Cattell, 1971; Horn, 1989). The most unexpected finding of the change point model was that there was no clear negative trend in fluid intelligence over the later ages. Among many possible reasons are the following: (1) These participants were from the high ability and geographically narrow population; (2) practice effects are possible since the participants were measured on the same tests more than once (Ferrer, Salthouse, Stewart, & Schwartz, 2004); (3) the potential of a third underlying phase or segment, requiring two turning points for each score, was not investigated in this study; (4) the oldest age tested was only 65. As seen in Table 6.1a, the average performance of Gf decreased from 87.8 at the age 42 to 84.4 at the age of 57. After that, the average performance of Gf showed no notable decline from age 57 to age 65. It follows that there could be a decline phase after another change point around 45, and it could be useful to investigate this third phase in future studies.

In sum, these analyses demonstrate three reasonable approaches to identify potential age-based turning points in life-span cognitive development. The profile likelihood estimation method was a good start to estimate the unknown change points. At the very least, this method can provide reasonable starting values for other nonlinear estimation methods, such as the first-order MLE method and Bayesian methods. Future studies interested in evaluating the performances of different estimation methods might consider the important issues surrounding multivariate turning points. This research suggested the multivariate models can bring more data into these problems, and the hope is that clearer and more stable results will work. Indeed, the most critical challenges of turning points research may not be solved until we recognize these are multivariate questions.

Acknowledgment

This work was supported by grants from the National Institute on Aging (AG02695, AG04704, and AG07137) and would not have been possible without the cooperation of the participants of the Bradway-Longitudinal Study. We thank Fumiaki Hamagami, John R. Nesselroade, and Zhiyong Zhang for their assistance and comments on manuscript drafts. This work is presented in more detail in the master's thesis of the second author and a 2005 presentation at the Society of Multivariate Experimental Psychology.

References

Beal, S. L., & Sheiner, L. B. (1982). Estimating population kinetics. *CRC Critical Reviews in Biomedical Engineering, 8,* 195–222.

Bryk, A. S., & Raudenbush, S. W. (1992). *Hierarchical linear models.* Newbury Park, CA: Sage.

Cattell, R. B. (1971). *Abilities: Their structure, growth and action.* Boston: Houghton-Mifflin.

Cattell, R.B. (1998). Where is intelligence? Some answers form the triadic theory. In J. J. McArdle & R. W. Woodcock (Eds.), *Human cognitive abilities in theory and practice* (pp. 29–38). Mahwah, NJ: Erlbaum.

Congdon, P. (2001). *Bayesian statistical modeling.* New York: Wiley.

Congdon, P. (2003). *Applied Bayesian modelling.* New York: Wiley.

Cudeck, R., & Du Toit, S. H. C. (2003). Nonlinear multilevel models for repeated measures data. In S. P. Reise & N. Duan (Eds.), *Multilevel modeling: Methodological advances, issues, and applications* (pp. 1–24). Mahwah, NJ: Erlbaum.

Cudeck, R., & Klebe, K. J. (2002). Multiphase mixed-effects model for repeated measure data. *Psychological Methods, 7,* 41–63.

Davidian, M., & Giltinan, D. M. (1995). *Nonlinear models for repeated measurement data.* London: Chapman and Hall.

Davidian, M., & Giltinan, D.M. (2003) Nonlinear models for repeated measurements: An overview and update. *Journal of Agricultural, Biological, and Environmental Statistics, 8,* 387–419.

Diggle, P. J., Liang, K.-Y., & Zeger, S. L. (1994). *Analysis of longitudinal data.* Oxford, UK: Oxford University Press.

Ferrer, E., Salthouse, T. A., Stewart, W. F., & Schwartz, B. S. (2004). Modeling age and retest processes in longitudinal studies of cognitive abilities. *Psychology and Aging, 19*, 243–259.

Gallant, A. R., & Fuller, W. A. (1973). Fitting segmented polynomial regression models whose join points have to be estimated. *Journal of the American Statistical Association, 68*, 144–147.

Gilks, W. R., Richardson, S., & Spiegelhalter, D. J. (1996). Introducing Markov chain Monte Carlo. In W. R. Gilks, S. Richardson, and D. J. Spiegelhalter (Eds.), *Markov chain Monte Carlo in practice* (pp. 339–357). London: Chapman and Hall.

Hall, C. B., Lipton, R., Sliwinski, M., & Stewart, W. F. (2000). A change point model for estimating the onset of cognitive decline in preclinical Alzheimer's disease. *Statistics in Medicine, 19*, 1555–1566.

Hall, C. B., Ying, J., Kuo, L., Sliwinski, M., Buschke, H., Katz, M., et al. (2001). Estimation of bivariate measurements having different change points, with application to cognitive ageing. *Statistics in Medicine, 20*, 3695–3714.

Hamagami, F. (1998). Developmental-based item factor analyses. In J. J. McArdle & J. R. Woodcock (Eds.), *Human abilities in theory and practice* (pp. 231–246). Mahwah, NJ: Erlbaum.

Horn, J. L. (1989) Models for intelligence. In R. Linn (Ed.), *Intelligence: Measurement, theory and public policy* (pp. 29–73). Urbana, IL: University of Illinois Press.

Lindstrom, M. J., & Bates, D. M. (1990). Nonlinear mixed effects models for repeated measures. *Biometrics, 46*, 673–687.

McArdle, J. J., Ferrer-Caja, E., Hamagami, F. & Woodcock, R.W. (2002). Comparative longitudinal structural analyses of the growth and decline of multiple intellectual abilities over the life span. *Developmental Psychology, 38*, 115–142.

McArdle, J. J., & Hamagami, F. (1996). Multilevel models for a multiple group structural equation perspective. In G. A. Marcoulides & R. E. Schumacher (Eds.), *Advanced structural equation modeling: Issues and techniques* (pp. 57–88). Mahwah, NJ: Erlbaum.

McArdle, J. J., Hamagami, F., Meredith, W., & Bradway, K. P. (2001). Modeling the dynamic hypotheses of *Gf-Gc* theory using longitudinal life-span data. *Learning and Individual Differences, 12*, 53–79.

McArdle, J. J., Grimm, K., Hagigami, F., Bowles, R., & Meredith, W. (2007). A longitudinal item response model of vocabulary abilities over the life-span. *Psychological Methods*, under review.

Morrell, C. H., Pearson, J. D., Carter, H. B., & Brant, L. J. (1995). Estimating unknown transition times using piecewise nonlinear mixed-effects model in men with prostate cancer. *Journal of the American Statistical Association, 90*, 45–53.

Nesselroade, J. R., & Baltes, P. B. (Eds.). (1979). *Longitudinal behavior and development.* New York: Academic Press.

Pinheiro, J. C., and Bates, D. M. (1995). Approximations to the log-likelihood function in the nonlinear mixed-effects model. *Journal of Computational and Graphical Statistics, 4*, 12–35.

Plummer, M., Best, N., Cowles, K., & Vines, K. (2005). Output analysis and diagnostics for MCMC. Retrieved from http://www-fis.iarc.fr/coda/. Retrieved June 1, 2005.

Smith, A. F. M., & Cook, D. G. (1980). Straight lines with a change-point: A Bayesian analysis of some renal transplant data. *Applied Statistics, 29*, 180–189.

Spiegelhalter, D. J., Best, N. G., Carlin, B. P., & Linde, A. (2002). Bayesian measures of model complexity and fit. *Journal of Statistical Society, 64*, 583–639.

Spiegelhalter, D., Thomas, A., Best, N., & Lunn, D. (2003). WinBUGS Manual (version 1.4.1). MRC Biostatistics Unit, Cambridge University, UK. Retrieved from: http://www.mrcbsu.cam.ac.uk/bugs/welcome.shtml. Retrieved December 1, 2004.

Verbeke, G., & Molenberghs, G. (2000). *Linear mixed models for longitudinal data.* New York: Springer.

Vonesh, E. F. (1996). A note on the use of Laplace's approximation for nonlinear mixed-effects models. *Biometrika, 83*, 447–452.

Wang, L., & McArdle, J. J. (2008). A simulation study comparision of Bayesian estimation with conventional methods for estimating unknown change points. *Structural Equation Modeling, 15*, 52–74.

Wolfinger, R.D. (1993). Laplace's approximation for nonlinear mixed models. *Biometrika, 80*, 791–795.

chapter seven

Bereavement as a potential turning point: Modeling between-person variability in adjustment to conjugal loss

Christopher T. Burke
New York University

Patrick E. Shrout
New York University

Niall Bolger
Columbia University

Contents

Introduction 130
Bereavement as a potential turning point 130
Modeling cross-sectional trends in adjustment 132
Modeling longitudinal trajectories of adjustment 135
Explaining individual differences in trajectories
of adjustment 137
Modeling changes versus levels: Reparameterizing
the longitudinal adjustment model 138
Future extensions of the adjustment model 144
Conclusion 146
References 147

Introduction

One of the most striking features of human development is the propensity to develop and maintain close relationships. The process of forming attachment bonds can be seen in the very first interaction between a neonate and his or her mother. As the caregiver relationship develops, so do other close relationships. Over time, relationships with caregivers are superseded by relationships with potential partners and later by relationships with one's own offspring. The human species is an especially social one, one whose development as a whole has been shaped by these types of relationships.

However, like other species, humans also experience mortality. Just as these attachment relationships blossom and grow, so must they all come to an end. The loss of a close other is an experience that nearly every person will experience at least once in his or her life. Some people experience this kind of loss multiple times, and people's experiences are far from uniform. In their review of the psychological literature on bereavement, Stroebe and Stroebe (1987) discussed the tremendous variability in the experiences of bereaved individuals: "We find anger and apathy, weight loss and weight gain, preoccupation with or suppression of memories of the deceased, and removal versus treasuring their possessions" (p. 8). Some individuals may experience phases of grief; others may not. Some individuals may recover quickly; some may recover slowly. Some individuals may experience grief reactions; others may experience *relief* reactions. For some individuals, bereavement may represent a true "turning point"; for others, it may not. For bereavement researchers interested in interindividual variability in how the process of grieving unfolds over time, one of the major challenges is to develop a statistical model that can account for this wide range of reactions to loss. In this chapter, we describe a model of adjustment to bereavement that flexibly accounts for much of the variability inherent in grief trajectories.

Bereavement as a potential turning point

A *turning point* may be defined as a qualitative change in a developmental trajectory brought on by some event (cf. Elder, 1986). Although seemingly simple, this definition has several important features. First, there is some exogenous event that triggers the turning point. The event may be the birth of a child, the loss of one's job, winning the lottery, or even a religious conversion. These may be obvious examples of potential turning points, but any event has the potential to lead to qualitative changes in developmental outcomes — even events that are purely subjective. Second, the event affects certain developmental trajectories but not others. Although winning the lottery may represent a turning point with respect to financial matters, it is unlikely to affect the route one takes to get to the market. Likewise, the construction of a new highway may affect the route to the market but not one's financial matters. By this definition, a researcher of turning points must therefore identify an event and specify the dimensions on which the event has an impact. Third, because the event leads to a qualitative change in the developmental trajectory, the researcher needs to have data about the process on both sides of the event. By having data on both sides of the event, the researcher can estimate the "pre-" and "post-" trajectories and examine what occurs at the time of the event. Fourth, to identify turning points, a researcher must have a model that can distinguish transient effects of the event from more lasting effects. Many events can have passing effects on developmental variables. Although these events may be of interest to psychology researchers, they do not represent turning points according to the definition provided here. In addition to these implications of the definition, we add that the model should allow for the event to have different effects on different individuals. That is, for some individuals, the event may represent a turning point, while for others it may cause only temporary changes, and for yet others it may have no effect at all. It is unlikely that a specific event represents a universal turning point for all who experience it. Rather, the event represents a potential turning point with an impact on a given individual that depends on psychological and contextual factors.

From our perspective, the loss of a close loved one is one of the best examples of a potential turning point with respect to a person's well-being. Bereavement can have a profound impact on well-being and health (see Stroebe, Hansson, Stroebe, & Schut, 2001, for a review), and the effects can last for months, if not years. In some cases, the bereaved individual never returns to preloss levels of well-being. Within psychology, research on bereavement has tended to focus on general outcomes, such as level of depressive symptoms, grief symptoms, and life satisfaction and has pointed to a wide range of reactions that bereaved individuals experience following the loss with respect to these outcomes. In the past, many bereavement researchers have assumed that bereaved individuals return to normal functioning rather quickly following the loss (Wortman & Silver, 1989; 2001). Failure to return to normal functioning within the allotted period of time was considered to be maladaptive. However, few attempts have been made to explicitly model the normative return to positive functioning, and to our knowledge these attempts have not distinguished individuals who never return to normal functioning from those who do return to normal functioning, but after a longer period of time.

Our group (Carnelley, Wortman, Bolger, & Burke, 2006; Burke, Bolger, & Shrout, 2007) has developed a flexible model of adjustment to loss that can account for the features of a turning point as outlined here and can also distinguish true turning points from the types of extended temporary disruptions just described. The model is a nonlinear mixed model (see Cudeck & Harring, 2007, for an excellent overview) that connects a preloss trajectory of well-being to a postloss trajectory of well-being. Because the loss represents a potentially traumatic event, we allow for a discontinuity at the time of the loss. We have modeled postloss patterns of adjustment with a negative exponential function, which specifies that adjustment should happen most rapidly just after the loss and slow over time, approaching an asymptote. We chose the negative exponential function because of its relationship to control systems approaches to self-regulation (Carver & Scheier, 1982). We proposed that bereavement results in a potential state of psychological disequilibrium for bereaved individuals, and that adjustment efforts (including both *intra*personal coping and *inter*personal social support processes) would be engaged in proportion to the current amount of disruption. Importantly, the patterns of preloss well-being and postloss well-being are uninfluenced by each other; that is, the eventual level of well-being that is attained is not required to have any particular relationship to well-being prior to the loss. Finally, our model can be implemented in a multilevel framework, so each individual is allowed to deviate from the average pattern of well-being estimated by the model. This framework allows the estimation of the magnitudes of the variances and covariances of these deviations. In the following sections, we describe the first two applications of our model before describing how our model can be reformulated to assess whether the loss corresponds to a turning point for some individuals.

Modeling cross-sectional trends in adjustment

Carnelley et al. (2006) first developed the bereavement model to describe normative trajectories of grief-related variables in a large, cross-sectional sample. As mentioned, many grief theorists in the past have assumed that the process of grieving runs its course within a couple of years of the loss, and that grief symptoms lasting longer are cause for clinical concern. While bereavement researchers have found some empirical evidence for this assumption (e.g., Bonanno et al., 2002), these studies have tended to focus on the psychological *outcomes* of the loss (e.g., depressive symptoms, life satisfaction), leaving variables related to the *process* of grieving (e.g., frequency of thoughts about the partner, intensity of anniversary reactions) relatively unstudied. The goal in this first article (Carnelley et al., 2006), then, was to examine the normative time course of adjustment in these process-related variables.

For a cross-sectional sample, the negative exponential model can be represented by the following equation:

$$Y_j = F + (L - F) \cdot e^{-S \cdot t_j} + \varepsilon_j \qquad (7.1)$$

In this equation, Y_j represents the grief-related outcome modeled for observation j. L represents the average level of the outcome at the time of the loss (i.e., the *at-loss* level), which is analogous to the intercept in a linear regression model. F represents the average final level of the outcome long after the loss (i.e., the asymptote of Y). The t_j variable is the time since loss for observation j, and S represents the decay constant — the rate at which the adjustment occurs — which must be greater than or equal to zero. Levels of S closer to zero indicate slower adjustment, while higher levels of S indicate more rapid adjustment. Finally, ε_j is a residual for each observation j. These residuals are assumed to be drawn from a normal distribution and to be independent and identically distributed. An example of the type of adjustment trajectory implied by this model is illustrated to the right of the vertical dotted line in Figure 7.1.

With this model, we (Carnelley et al., 2006) found evidence that a number of variables related to the process of grieving follow such a nonlinear trend. Our sample was from the Americans' Changing Lives survey (see House et al., 1990), a national probability sample of nearly 800 bereaved individuals who

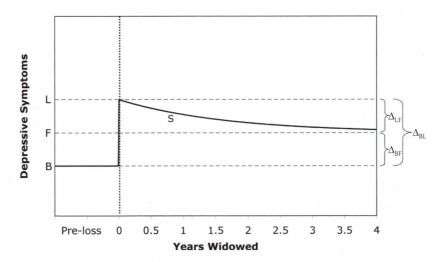

Figure 7.1 Example trajectory of depressive symptoms as a function of time according to our nonlinear model of adjustment. The vertical dotted line represents the time of the loss, with points to the left reflecting preloss depression and points to the right reflecting postloss depression.

had lost a spouse anywhere from a few months to 64 years prior to the interview. It was a large and diverse sample that allowed us to examine the process of adjustment. We compared the fit of the negative exponential model described above to a linear model of adjustment and a model that predicted no adjustment over time. Not only did the negative exponential model tend to provide the best fit to the data, but also we found evidence that many indicators of adjustment showed a much more gradual change over time than expected, with some taking decades to approach their normative set point. In addition, for many of these variables the average set point did not represent what would be considered complete recovery.

As an example, the extent to which thoughts of the deceased spouse led the respondent to feel sad or upset showed a negative exponential decline over time. Recently bereaved respondents reported experiencing negative affect when thinking of the spouse between "sometimes" and "often" (61.4 on a 0 to 100 scale), while those bereaved for many years reported experiencing negative affect between "rarely" and "sometimes" (37.4 on a 0 to 100 scale). It took respondents an average of 12.6 years to span 90% of the distance between the at-loss level and the final level, which is substantially longer than would be expected based on prior work. Figure 7.2 illustrates this result graphically. Many of the other variables that we examined showed this kind of pattern, although they varied greatly in the extent and rate of adjustment.

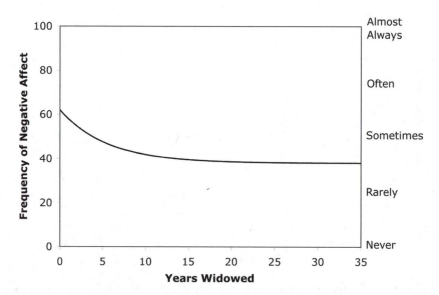

Figure 7.2 Normative trajectory of the frequency of sad or upsetting thoughts about the deceased partner as a function of time relative to the loss. The right vertical axis shows the verbal labels to which participants responded.

The analyses using the adjustment model in Equation 7.1 provided new insights into the process of grieving at a normative level. However, the cross-sectional sample limited our ability to make inferences about trajectories of grief per se. Instead, we could only describe the normative pattern of adjustment as a function of time since loss. We had to adjust for a number of variables correlated with time since loss (e.g., age of spouse at death, expectedness of death) to rule them out as potential confounds. These additions to the model helped to strengthen our argument that the negative exponential adjustment trajectories fit the data, but we still could not make strong statements about the patterns of adjustment expected within individuals or estimate variability in individual trajectories.

Modeling longitudinal trajectories of adjustment

To address these limitations, we (Burke et al., 2007) extended the model in Equation 7.1 to account for individual differences in adjustment trajectories. To do so, we developed a multilevel version of Equation 7.1. The Level 1 (i.e., within person; see Raudenbush & Bryk, 2002) equation is as follows:

Level 1: $$Y_{ij} = F_i + (L_i - F_i) \cdot e^{-S \cdot t_{ij}} + \varepsilon_{ij} \qquad (7.2)$$

Notice that Equation 7.2 only differs from Equation 7.1 in the addition of the i subscripts to the variables and parameters in the model. The i subscript indexes persons in the data set, so L_i and F_i represent model parameters that potentially vary across persons. The Level 2 (i.e., between person; Raudenbush & Bryk, 2002) equations are as follows:

Level 2:
$$L_i = \gamma_L + \zeta_{L,i}$$
$$F_i = \gamma_F + \zeta_{F,i} \qquad (7.3)$$

Here, γ_L and γ_F are the mean levels of at-loss and final adjustment (e.g., depression), respectively, within the population of bereaved individuals. They are often described as the fixed effects. The $\zeta_{L,i}$ and $\zeta_{F,i}$ terms represent person-level random variables (i.e., random effects) with means of zero, variances of σ_L^2 and σ_F^2, respectively, and covariance σ_{LF}. These were assumed to have a multivariate normal distribution:

$$\begin{bmatrix} \zeta_{L,i} \\ \zeta_{F,i} \end{bmatrix} \sim N\left(\begin{bmatrix} 0 \\ 0 \end{bmatrix}, \begin{bmatrix} \sigma_L^2 & \\ \sigma_{LF} & \sigma_F^2 \end{bmatrix} \right) \qquad (7.4)$$

The longitudinal data that we used to test our model came from the Changing Lives of Older Couples (CLOC) survey (see Carr et al., 2000). The CLOC was a *prospective* study of bereavement, containing one pre-loss and three postloss waves of data collection. The timing of the pre-loss assessment varied from person to person, occurring an average of 3 years before the loss. The postloss assessments occurred at 6, 18, and 48 months postloss. Given the presence of the preloss assessment, we were able to incorporate these data into the longitudinal model described by Equations 7.2 and 7.3:

Level 1:
$$Y_{ij} = d_{ij} \cdot B_i + (1 - d_{ij}) \cdot [F_i + (L_i - F_i)e^{-S \cdot t_{ij}}] + \varepsilon_{ij} \tag{7.5}$$

Level 2:
$$\begin{aligned} B_i &= \gamma_B + \zeta_{B,i} \\ L_i &= \gamma_L + \zeta_{L,i} \\ F_i &= \gamma_F + \zeta_{F,i} \end{aligned} \tag{7.6}$$

Here, the B_i in the Level 1 equation represents the predicted preloss level of the outcome for person i. The Level 2 model in Equation 7.6 shows that this breaks down into an average level (i.e., fixed effect) of γ_B and a random effect $\zeta_{B,i}$ for each person i. Finally, d_{ij} is a variable that indicates whether each observation is a preloss assessment or one of the postloss assessments. It is coded 1 for preloss assessments and 0 for postloss assessments. This technique is useful for specifying different functional forms on either side of a change point (see Cudeck & Klebe, 2002, and Singer & Willett, 2003, for more details). Because we had only one preloss time point, we specified the level of Y to be constant for each person before the loss. However, with more preloss time points it would be possible to specify more dynamic preloss trajectories. Similar to above, the distributions of the three random effects is as follows:

$$\begin{bmatrix} \zeta_{B,i} \\ \zeta_{L,i} \\ \zeta_{F,i} \end{bmatrix} \sim N \left(\begin{bmatrix} 0 \\ 0 \\ 0 \end{bmatrix}, \begin{bmatrix} \sigma_B^2 & & \\ \sigma_{BL} & \sigma_L^2 & \\ \sigma_{BF} & \sigma_{LF} & \sigma_F^2 \end{bmatrix} \right) \tag{7.7}$$

Here again, the effects are assumed to be multivariate normal, with variances σ_B^2, σ_L^2, and σ_F^2 and covariances σ_{BL}, σ_{BF}, and σ_{LF}.

We (Burke et al., 2007) used the nonlinear mixed model described by Equations 7.5 and 7.6 to estimate individual differences in trajectories of depressive symptoms surrounding conjugal loss. Depressive symptoms were measured by the Center for Epidemiological Studies Depression scale (CES-D; Radloff, 1977). We found a pattern of fixed effects indicating a relatively undramatic pattern of depression on average: moderately low levels of preloss depression (11.1 on the 0 to 60 scale of the CES-D), a small jump at the time of the loss to a level (15.2 on the 0 to 60 scale) that did not exceed the common clinical cut point for the CES-D, and a gradual decline over time to a level comparable to the preloss level (7.8 on the 0 to 60 scale). However, this pattern of fixed effects was qualified by significant (and strong) random effects of each of the three levels. That is, there was substantial interindividual variability in preloss, at-loss, and final levels of depressive symptoms. The analysis also revealed significant correlations among the random effects. While all three of the correlations were positive, the correlation between the preloss and final levels of depression (.56) was larger than the correlation between preloss and at-loss levels of depression (.35) or between at-loss and final levels of depression (.37). Taken together, these findings suggest that level of depressive symptoms is fairly stable over time; that bereavement disrupts normal functioning; and that individuals generally return to a level of depressive symptoms comparable to preloss levels over time.

Explaining individual differences in trajectories of adjustment

With such an expansive data set as the CLOC, we had at hand a number of variables that could potentially explain the individual differences described above. We therefore wanted to expand the multilevel adjustment model described by Equations 7.5 and 7.6 to incorporate this type of information. We (Burke et al., 2007) focused on variables assessed at the preloss interview (i.e., before respondents knew they would lose their spouses) and treated them as time-invariant covariates. As such, Level 1 Equation 7.5 remained unchanged, while Level 2 Equation 7.6 were modified to incorporate this new information.

We proposed two methods for incorporating these covariates into the model and recommended using the Akaike Information Criterion (AIC; Akaike, 1974) for choosing the most appropriate method in a given situation. In the first method, we assumed that the covariate M had the same relationship to depressive symptoms throughout the adjustment process:

Level 2:
$$B_i = \gamma_B + b_M \cdot M_i + \zeta_{B,i}$$
$$L_i = \gamma_L + b_M \cdot M_i + \zeta_{L,i} \tag{7.8}$$
$$F_i = \gamma_F + b_M \cdot M_i + \zeta_{F,i}$$

This set of Level 2 equations only differs from Equation 7.6 in the addition of the $b_M \cdot M_i$ term to each equation. M_i represents the level of covariate M for person i, and b_M represents the linear relationship between M and the outcome irrespective of time relative to the loss. This method has a familiar feel to it as it is how covariates are typically conceived. We found that the respondent's preloss level of perceived coping ability — how capable the person felt he or she was of dealing with a major stressor on his or her own — showed this relationship to depressive symptoms. The higher a person's perceived coping ability, the lower the person's level of depressive symptoms across time. Because perceived coping ability showed a strong negative skew, this effect is likely to be driven by the individuals with particularly low perceived coping ability.

The second method allows for the covariate M to have a time-varying relationship to Y. While this method is less parsimonious than the method described above, the added complexity may often be justified by the improvement in fit. The Level 2 equations for this model are

$$B_i = \gamma_B + b_B \cdot M_i + \zeta_{B,i}$$

Level 2: $$L_i = \gamma_L + b_L \cdot M_i + \zeta_{L,i} \qquad (7.9)$$

$$F_i = \gamma_F + b_F \cdot M_i + \zeta_{F,i}$$

Although this set of equations closely resembles Equation 7.8, the difference is that the relationship between M and Y is allowed to vary as a function of time relative to the loss. That is, M and Y have one relationship at preloss (i.e., b_B), a different relationship at the time of the loss (i.e., b_L), and yet another relationship ultimately (i.e., b_F). It is important to keep in mind that M itself does not vary over time, but its relationship to Y is allowed to vary over time with this method. In our analysis, preloss relationship quality showed this type of relationship to depressive symptoms. Respondents with better relationships had fewer depressive symptoms before the loss and ultimately, but relationship quality did not predict level of depressive symptoms at the time of the loss. Here again, a strong negative skew of relationship quality suggests that this effect was driven by the individuals with poor relationships having higher levels of depression before the loss and higher levels in the long run.

Modeling changes versus levels: Reparameterizing the longitudinal adjustment model

As we have discussed, in our analysis of the CLOC data (Burke et al., 2007), we used the negative exponential function as the basis of our postloss Level 1 growth model. With the addition of the preloss time point, the three parameters in the model that were allowed to vary between persons all represented *levels* of depressive symptoms at various times in the adjustment trajectory: the preloss level, the at-loss level, and the final level. For many developmental processes, however, researchers may be less interested in *levels* of some outcome than they are in *changes* in that outcome over time. For instance, between-person differences in level of preloss depression may be less interesting than variability in the size of people's reactions to the loss or in how much depressive symptoms change over time following the loss.

One of the benefits of nonlinear modeling is the potential for respecifying the model in equivalent forms to tap into different parts of the unfolding process. With respect to the adjustment model given by Equation 7.5, we can define a new parameter Δ_{BL} that represents the change in depressive symptoms from pre loss to at-loss (i.e., $L - B$). That is, Δ_{BL} represents the size of an individual's reaction to the loss. Through algebraic substitution, we can restate Level 1 Equation 7.5 in terms of B and Δ_{BL}, or Δ_{BL} and L, rather than B and L. Likewise, we can define Δ_{LF} as the change in depressive symptoms a person experiences over time after the loss (i.e., $F - L$). Again, the model can be restated in terms of L and Δ_{LF}, or Δ_{LF} and F, rather than L and F. Finally, we might consider a third new parameter Δ_{BF} that represents the difference between a person's preloss level of depressive symptoms and his or her predicted level of depression many years after the loss (i.e., $F - B$). The Δ_{BF} parameter may be of particular interest in the context of this volume as it indicates whether a person will restabilize at a level of depression comparable to the level prior to his or her spouse's death. The right margin of Figure 7.1 shows graphically how these parameters are defined.

With the definition of these three new parameters, which are simply linear combinations of old parameters, we now have 15 equivalent forms of the Level 1 model stated in Equation 7.5. For convenience, these equations are compiled in Appendix 2. As stated, Equations A1 to A15 represent mathematically equivalent forms of the negative exponential growth curve. Any pair will produce identical estimates of the parameters they have in common, and they will fit the data equally well. Ultimately, the choice of which form to use is up to the researcher. Below, we use the CLOC depression data to illustrate several benefits of fitting multiple forms of the same model, such as obtaining additional information about the interrelationships between the random effects and testing different associations between covariates and patterns of adjustment.

When estimating the multilevel model represented by Equations 7.5 and 7.6, we (Burke et al., 2007) obtained a 3×3 covariance matrix of random effects, corresponding to the variances of B, L, and F and the covariances between them. By estimating a few of the other parameterizations of the model, we can obtain what is effectively a 6×6 covariance matrix of

Table 7.1 Covariances and Correlations of Random
Effects from Reparameterizations of Adjustment Model
for Depressive Symptoms

Covariances

Parameter	B	Δ_{BL}	L	Δ_{LF}	F	Δ_{BF}
B	60.1*					
Δ_{BL}	−31.1*	119.4*				
L	29.0*	88.3*	117.3*			
Δ_{LF}	7.6	−89.9*	−82.3*	118.2*		
F	36.6*	−1.6	35.0	35.9	70.9*	
Δ_{BF}	−23.5*	29.5	6.0	28.4	34.3	57.9*

Correlations

Parameter	B	Δ_{BL}	L	Δ_{LF}	F	Δ_{BF}
B	1.00					
Δ_{BL}	−.37*	1.00				
L	.35*	.75*	1.00			
Δ_{LF}	.09	−.76*	−.70*	1.00		
F	.56*	−.02	.38	.39	1.00	
Δ_{BF}	−.40*	.36	.07	.34	.54	1.00

*$p < .05$.

random effects, corresponding to estimates of the population variances of
B, Δ_{BL}, L, Δ_{LF}, F, and Δ_{BF} and all of the covariances between them.

The top portion of Table 7.1 displays this covariance matrix based on the
CLOC data, and the bottom portion displays the correlation matrix. The
entries in this table were completed by fitting various alternative models
described above and estimating chunks of the covariance matrix using
models that contained alternative representations of the trajectory pattern
shown in Figure 7.1. Several values are worth noting in these matrices.
First, all three of the new change parameters (Δ_{BL}, Δ_{LF}, and Δ_{BF}) vary significantly and substantially across persons in the population. In fact, the
estimates of the variances of Δ_{BL} and Δ_{LF} are larger than the others that we
previously reported (Burke et al., 2007). In other words, people seem to
vary more in how much they change in depressive symptoms over time
(both at the time of the loss and afterward) than they vary in their static
levels of depression before the loss, at the time of the loss, or eventually.

The correlations in Table 7.1 also shed light on the adjustment process.
Three of the added correlations are very large, with absolute values of .70 or

greater. The first is a positive correlation of .75 between the change due to the loss and the level at the time of the loss. That is, individuals who experience a greater-than-average jump in depression at the time of the loss tend to have a greater-than-average level of depression at the time of the loss. This relationship may seem intuitive but note that the correlation between preloss level of depression and change due to the loss is much smaller, at −.37. The second large correlation is a negative correlation of −.76 between change due to the loss and change over time following the loss. This correlation can be interpreted as evidence for adjustment as a regulatory process as it suggests that individuals who experience a greater jump in depression due to the loss will experience the greatest drop in depression over time. The third large correlation is a negative correlation of −.70 between at-loss depression and change in depression over time following the loss. This correlation suggests that individuals with the highest levels of depression at the time of the loss drop the most over time following the loss, which is again consistent with our regulatory interpretation of the adjustment process.

The consideration of alternate parameterizations also allows researchers to explore different relationships between the growth trajectories and covariates of interest. In our adjustment model, this means that not only can we test the relationship between a covariate and the three levels of depression (preloss, at-loss, and final), but also we can test its relationship to the amount of change in depression a person experiences at the time of the loss, over time following the loss, and from preloss to the postloss set point.

We can consider incorporating a variable like this into the model by modifying the Level 2 Equations 7.8 or 7.9. In other words, the variable can have a consistent effect on depressive symptoms throughout the adjustment trajectory, or its effect can vary for different aspects of the trajectory. Extending Equation 7.9 for different parameterizations of the model is relatively straightforward: Whichever three parameters one includes in the model, the explanatory variable M is allowed to have different relationships to the between-person variability in those three parameters. As an example, say one were interested in estimating the model with Level 1 Equation A1 from Appendix 2, which includes parameters for preloss depression (B_i), change in depression at the time of the loss (Δ_{BL}), and change in depression over time following the loss (Δ_{LF}). The Level 2 equations according to Equation 7.9 would be

$$B_i = \gamma_B + b_B \cdot M_i + \zeta_{B,i}$$

Level 2:
$$\Delta_{BL,i} = \gamma_{\Delta_{BL}} + b_{\Delta_{BL}} \cdot M_i + \zeta_{\Delta_{BL},i} \tag{7.10}$$

$$\Delta_{LF,i} = \gamma_{\Delta_{LF}} + b_{\Delta_{LF}} \cdot M_i + \zeta_{\Delta_{LF},i}$$

As can be seen, the change parameters, like the level parameters, each get their own fixed effect (i.e., γ), random effect (i.e., ζ), and effect of variable M (i.e., b).

Modifying the Level 2 Equation 7.8 for the reparameterized model is a bit more nuanced. If the explanatory variable M has a constant relationship to depressive symptoms, as in Equation 7.8, it should actually be unrelated to the change parameters. That is, the equivalent form of the Level 2 model Equation 7.8 for parameters representing change rather than level has no M_i term. This result can be shown by algebraic substitution. For instance, we defined the $\Delta_{BL,i}$ parameter as

$$\Delta_{BL,i} = L_i - B_i$$

By substituting in the Level 2 equations for B_i and L_i based on Equation 7.8, we obtain the following result:

$$
\begin{aligned}
\Delta_{BL,i} &= (\gamma_L + b_M \cdot M_i + \zeta_{L,i}) - (\gamma_B + b_M \cdot M_i + \zeta_{B,i}) \\
&= (\gamma_L - \gamma_B) + (b_M \cdot M_i - b_M \cdot M_i) + (\zeta_{L,i} - \zeta_{B,i}) \\
&= (\gamma_{\Delta_{BL}}) + (0 \cdot M_i) + (\zeta_{\Delta_{BL},i})
\end{aligned}
$$

An analogous result obtains for the $\Delta_{LF,i}$ and $\Delta_{BF,i}$ parameters. Using the same example as above, with Level 1 Equation A1, the set of Level 2 equations corresponding to Equation 7.8 would therefore be

$$B_i = \gamma_B + b_M \cdot M_i + \zeta_{B,i}$$

Level 2: $$\Delta_{BL,i} = \gamma_{\Delta_{BL}} + \zeta_{\Delta_{BL},i} \tag{7.11}$$

$$\Delta_{LF,i} = \gamma_{\Delta_{LF}} + \zeta_{\Delta_{LF},i}$$

To demonstrate how these techniques can be used to better understand bereavement as a potential turning point, we now examine whether a new variable — respondents' self-reported dependence on their spouses — can help to explain some of the between-person differences in trajectories of depressive symptoms discussed above. One might expect that a respondent who is more dependent on his or her spouse will be more likely to experience the loss as a turning point; that is, that respondents who reported being more dependent on their spouses will experience a greater (more positive or less-negative) change in depressive symptoms from preloss to long after the loss. We can use the methods outlined above to test this hypothesis.

Dependence was assessed at the preloss time point via four items that tapped dependence on the spouse for (1) preparing meals, general housework, and laundry; (2) home maintenance and minor repairs; (3) keeping up with financial accounts and paying bills; and (4) making major financial and legal decisions ($\alpha = .64$). We averaged these four items for each respondent to create an index of preloss dependence on the spouse, which was centered at its grand mean before entering it in the following analyses.

For these analyses, we estimated a model with the Level 1 equation given by Equation A11 in the appendix. This Level 1 model allows for individual differences in reaction to the loss (i.e., $\Delta_{BL,i}$), level of depression at the time of the loss (i.e., L_i), and overall change in depression from preloss to long after the loss (i.e., $\Delta_{BF,i}$) (see Figure 7.1). Recall that this final parameter indicates one way that respondents can be said to experience bereavement as a turning point versus a transient disruption. Based on the above discussion, the model that assumes a constant relationship between preloss dependence and depressive symptoms has the following Level 2 equations:

$$\Delta_{BL,i} = \gamma_{\Delta_{BL}} + \zeta_{\Delta_{BL},i}$$

Level 2: $\qquad\qquad L_i = \gamma_L + b_M \cdot M_i + \zeta_{L,i}$ (7.12)

$$\Delta_{BF,i} = \gamma_{\Delta_{BF}} + \zeta_{\Delta_{BF},i}$$

where M_i represents centered preloss dependence on one's spouse. The model that allows the relationship between preloss dependence and depressive symptoms to vary for different parts of the adjustment trajectory has the following Level 2 equations:

$$\Delta_{BL,i} = \gamma_{\Delta_{BL}} + b_{\Delta_{BL}} \cdot M_i + \zeta_{\Delta_{BL},i}$$

Level 2: $\qquad\qquad L_i = \gamma_L + b_L \cdot M_i + \zeta_{L,i}$ (7.13)

$$\Delta_{BF,i} = \gamma_{\Delta_{BF}} + b_{\Delta_{BF}} \cdot M_i + \zeta_{\Delta_{BF},i}$$

As described above, we can run both models and choose between them based on which has the lower AIC fit statistic.

In the CLOC data, both models that include dependence on the spouse improve the fit over the original model that does not include dependence on the spouse. The AIC for the model with Level 2 Equation 7.12 is 5,842.1, and the AIC for the model with Level 2 Equation 7.13 is 5,830.8, compared to 5,846.7 for the original model. Comparing the AICs of the two models that include dependence, it seems that the more flexible model that allows the relationship between dependence and depression to vary over time fits the data better. This analysis reveals that there is a significant linear relationship between dependence on one's spouse and the total change in depressive symptoms resulting from the loss, $b_{\Delta_{BF}} = 3.99$, $t(247) = 3.40$, $p < .001$. That is, for each unit increase in dependence, the overall change in depressive symptoms from preloss to long after the loss is expected to be about 4 points greater. As a result of incorporating information about dependence, the amount of unexplained between-person variability in overall change in depressive symptoms $\sigma^2_{\Delta_{BF}}$ dropped from 57.9 to 49.2, a decrease of 15%. The relationship between dependence and the size of the reaction to the loss also approached significance [$b_{\Delta_{BL}} = 2.26$, $t(247) = 1.89$, $p = .06$], and the relationship between dependence and level of depressive symptoms at the time of the loss was nonsignificant [$b_L = -.86$, $t(247) = .78$, $p = .44$].

Researchers interested in factors that contribute to bereavement acting as a turning point should be pleased with the above results: Being more dependent on one's partner seems to predict qualitative shifts in one's set point of depressive symptoms. However, the last point we will make regarding the benefits of exploring reparameterizations is that they should be interpreted cautiously. The above result could have arisen because more dependent individuals end up with higher levels of depressive symptoms than others do, but it may also have arisen because more dependent individuals are less depressed before the loss (or a combination of these two possibilities). To unpack this result, we examined the role of dependence in other parameterizations of the model. It turns out that dependence is statistically unrelated to level of depressive symptoms long after the loss, $b_F = .87$, $t(247) = .76$, $p = .44$. Dependence on one's spouse is, however, related to *lower* levels of depressive symptoms prior to the loss, $b_B = -3.12$, $t(247) = 4.29$, $p < .001$. That is, for each unit increase in dependence on one's spouse, preloss levels of depression are expected to be a little over 3 points lower on the 0 to 60 scale of the CES-D. After taking dependence on one's spouse into account, the unexplained between-person variability in preloss depression decreases from 60.1 to 54.3, a drop of about 10%. Thus, the final added benefit of the ability to parameterize the nonlinear model in multiple ways is the ability to use different parameterizations to clarify ambiguous findings.

Future extensions of the adjustment model

In this chapter, we reviewed a procedure that we have developed for modeling adjustment to bereavement (Carnelley et al., 2006; Burke et al., 2007).

The basis of this model is a nonlinear function — the negative exponential function — that models the pattern of adjustment following the loss. We have described several variants of this basic model, such as incorporating preloss information, accounting for individual differences, and reparameterizing to examine *change* in adjustment rather than *level* of adjustment. Combining all of these elements, we were able to examine whether some individuals experienced the loss of their spouse as a turning point with respect to depression, and we were able to explore a possible mechanism determining whether bereavement acts as a turning point compared to a transient stressor. The flexibility of this model allows the potential for it to grow in complexity with increasingly rich data sets. In this section, we briefly mention some of these possibilities. ·

The reader may have noticed that one parameter in the model (e.g., Equation 7.5) was never allowed to vary across persons — the S parameter, which represents the rate at which people adjust to the loss. The reason for this constraint is not necessarily that we believe it is invariant in the population, but rather that we did not have enough within-person observations to estimate its variance. We had a maximum of four data points per person, so attempting to estimate four random effects would have led to a saturated model that fit the data perfectly. In principle, we could have estimated the variability in the rate of adjustment if we had constrained one of the other variances (e.g., σ_B^2, σ_L^2, or σ_F^2) to be zero, but these variances were so large that this constraint would have made the estimation difficult and could have biased the estimate of σ_S^2. The inclusion of additional postloss interviews would have made σ_S^2 estimable, although four random effects are often regarded as the computational limit for maximum likelihood estimation of nonlinear mixed models in programs like SAS NLMIXED (SAS Institute, 2004). In these cases, Bayesian estimation methods, such as those implemented in WinBUGS (Spiegelhalter, Thomas, Best, & Lunn, 2003), might still allow for estimation of these models.

Above, we alluded to another interesting extension of the adjustment model: modeling more complex preloss patterns. Because we only had a single preloss assessment, we were limited to assume that preloss levels of depressive symptoms were constant. With additional preloss time points, we could have estimated, for instance, a linear trend of depressive symptoms leading up to the loss. The slope of a person's preloss depression trajectory may be related in interesting ways to the parameters of the person's postloss trajectory of depression. These relationships can only be revealed with more preloss assessments.

On a similar note, the bereavement literature often makes reference to the process of "anticipatory grief" (e.g., Rando, 2000). Anticipatory grief occurs when a to-be-bereaved individual becomes aware of his or her partner's impending death before it actually occurs. When this happens, the process of grieving the loss can begin prior to the loss, which can soften the blow of the loss when it does occur. Our bereavement model assumes that the "event" is the loss, and that it therefore occurs at the time of the loss. For individuals who have the opportunity to begin grieving before the loss occurs, the event may instead be the initial realization that the partner is dying, which may occur some time before the actual loss. Cudeck and Klebe (2002) outlined a procedure for estimating the timing of an event as a person-level random effect. In the context of the above discussion, the timing of grief onset for an individual may have important implications for other aspects of the grief trajectory. In particular, allowing for anticipatory grief may help explain why some studies of grief trajectories (e.g., Bonanno et al., 2002) find that a sizable portion of the population fails to show evidence of grief reactions.

Conclusion

We examined a class of models that can be useful for studying a potential psychological turning point in people's life: the loss of a loved one. The model can reflect the initial change in well-being following a loss, and it can represent a variety of adjustment patterns following the loss. Embedded in a multilevel context, it explicitly recognizes that different people can have different experiences. The recovery process is modeled by the negative exponential function, which predicts initial rapid adjustment that slows over time, approaching an asymptote. We presented several forms of this basic model for modeling cross-sectional (Carnelley et al., 2006) as well as longitudinal (Burke et al., 2007) patterns of adjustment. In each of these situations, the model has fit data as well as or better than a comparable linear model that assumes a constant rate of adjustment.

In our previous work (Burke et al., 2007), we extended the basic model to include preloss information and suggested two methods for incorporating covariates into the model to explain individual differences in adjustment. Here, we added a discussion of how different parameterizations of the model (e.g., in terms of patterns of change rather than patterns of levels) can change the vantage point of the researcher with respect to the adjustment process and provide new information about how the process unfolds for different individuals. We also suggested three additional modifications of the original model to look at more complex patterns of individual differences in adjustment to loss.

The class of models that we considered here is by no means exhaustive. As researchers collect more intensive data on the bereavement processes, these models can be further refined to reflect possibly different phases of the bereavement process. Splines and other nonlinear functions can be considered if the additional data reveal systematic deviation of the more extensive data from the negative exponential function examined here. In the meanwhile, we recommend that the models we examined here can provide a flexible method for studying nonlinear adjustment and for helping to understand which people experience bereavement as a turning point experience as opposed to a difficult transient stress period.

References

Akaike, H. (1974). A new look at the statistical model identification. *IEEE Transactions on Automatic Control, 19,* 716–723.

Bonanno, G. A., Wortman, C. B., Lehman, D. R., Tweed, R. G., Haring, M. H., Sonnega, J., et al. (2002). Resilience to loss and chronic grief: A prospective study from pre-loss to 18-months post-loss. *Journal of Personality and Social Psychology, 83,* 1150–1164.

Burke, C. T., Bolger, N., & Shrout, P. E. (2007). Individual differences in adjustment to spousal loss: A nonlinear mixed model analysis. *International Journal of Behavioral Development, 31,* 405–415.

Carnelley, K. B., Wortman, C. B., Bolger, N., & Burke, C. T. (2006). The time course of grief reactions to spousal loss: Evidence from a national probability sample. *Journal of Personality and Social Psychology, 91,* 476–492.

Carr, D., House, J. S., Kessler, R. C., Nesse, R. M., Sonnega, J., & Wortman, C. (2000). Marital quality and psychological adjustment to widowhood among older adults: A longitudinal analysis. *Journal of Gerontology: Social Sciences, 55B,* S197–S207.

Carver, C. S., & Scheier, M. F. (1982). Control theory: A useful conceptual framework for personality-social, clinical, and health psychology. *Psychological Bulletin, 92,* 111–135.

Cudeck, R., & Harring, J. R. (2007). Analysis of nonlinear patterns of change with random coefficient models. *Annual Review of Psychology, 58,* 615–637.

Cudeck, R., & Klebe, K. J. (2002). Multiphase mixed-effects models for repeated measures data. *Psychological Methods, 7,* 41–63.

Elder, G. H. (1986). Military times and turning points in men's lives. *Developmental Psychology, 22,* 233–245.

House, J. S., Kessler, R. C., Herzog, A. R., Mero, R. P., Kinney, A. M., & Breslow, M. J. (1990). Age, socioeconomic status, and health. *Milbank Quarterly, 68,* 383–411.

Radloff, L. S. (1977). The CES-D scale: A self report depression scale for research in the general population. *Applied Psychological Measurement, 1,* 385–401.

Rando, T. A. (2000). *Clinical dimensions of anticipatory mourning: Theory and practice in working with the dying, their loved ones, and their caregivers.* Champaign, IL: Research Press.

Raudenbush, S. W., & Bryk, A. S. (2002). *Hierarchical linear models: Applications and data analysis methods* (2nd ed.). Thousand Oaks, CA: Sage.

SAS Institute. (2004). SAS/STAT® 9.1 user's guide. Cary, NC: SAS Institute.

Singer, J. D., & Willett, J. B. (2003). *Applied longitudinal data analysis: Modeling change and event occurrence.* New York: Oxford University Press.

Spiegelhalter, D., Thomas, A., Best, N., & Lunn, D. (2003). WinBUGS user manual: Version 1.4. Cambridge, UK: MRC Biostatistics Unit, Institute of Public Health.

Stroebe, M. S., Hansson, R. O., Stroebe, W., & Schut, H. (2001). *Handbook of bereavement research: Consequences, coping and care*. Washington, DC: American Psychological Association.

Stroebe, W., & Stroebe, M. S. (1987). *Bereavement and health: The psychological and physical consequences of partner loss*. New York: Cambridge University Press.

Wortman, C. B., & Silver, R. C. (1989). The myths of coping with loss. *Journal of Consulting and Clinical Psychology, 57*, 349–357.

Wortman, C. B., & Silver, R. C. (2001). The myths of coping with loss revisited. In M. S. Stroebe, R. O. Hansson, W. Stroebe, & H. Schut (Eds.), *Handbook of bereavement research: Consequences, coping, and care* (pp. 405–429). Washington, DC: American Psychological Association.

chapter eight

Application of change point theory to modeling state-related activity in fMRI

Martin A. Lindquist
Columbia University

Tor D. Wager
Columbia University

Contents

Introduction 150
Methods... 153
    Exponentially weighted moving averages.. 153
        EWMA statistic variance 157
        Correction for search across time................................. 157
        Estimating change points 158
        Dealing with multiple change points 159
    HEWMA: A hierarchical extension of EWMA 160
Simulations 163
    Simulation 1.. 163
    Simulation 2.. 164
    Simulation 3.. 165
Experimental fMRI data collection and analysis 165
    Participants... 165
    Task design 165
    Image acquisition.. 166
    Image analysis... 166
Results... 168
    Simulation results... 168
        Simulation 1 168

Simulation 2 168
Simulation 3 169
fMRI results.. 170
Discussion 175
Conclusion.. 177
Acknowledgment.. 178
References 178

Introduction

Neuroimaging, particularly functional magnetic resonance imaging (fMRI), is a useful and increasingly popular tool for studying the brain activity dynamics underlying human psychology. fMRI data consist of brain images — approximately 100,000 brain *voxels* (cubic volumes that span the three-dimensional space of the brain) — measured repeatedly every 2 sec or so, with images nested within task conditions and conditions nested within participants. Analysis of these complex data sets is the focus of intensive research and development in the scientific community.

Most previous approaches toward analysis assumed that the nature, timing, and duration of the psychological processes are known (Wager, Hernandez, Jonides, & Lindquist, 2007; Worsley & Friston, 1995). The analysis thus tests whether activity in a brain region (i.e., a voxel or set of voxels) is systematically related to the known input function. In these model-based approaches, the general linear model (GLM) is used to test for differences in activity among psychological conditions or groups of participants. For example, a task might require participants to inhibit an automatic tendency to make a motor response in favor of a less automatic one. The investigators might look for transient increases in brain activity when inhibition-demanding stimuli are presented and test whether activity is greater on trials that require inhibition compared with those that do not.

However, in many areas of psychological inquiry, the precise timing and duration of psychological events is hard to specify a priori. For example, a participant watching a funny film might experience amusement that builds gradually over time. The time course of the psychological process is likely to vary idiosyncratically from participant to participant, and without moment-by-moment reports, the progression of amusement over time will be difficult to specify. The need for obtaining a valid and accurate measure of psychological activity to use as a predictor for brain activity is a limitation as valid psychological indices are not always available. Self-reported emotion, for example, may not give an accurate picture of emotional experience in many situations. In addition, reporting emotions might change the underlying experience in important ways

(Taylor, Phan, Decker, & Liberzon, 2003). Thus, our ability to localize emotional activity in the brain is only as good as our ability to accurately tell what someone is feeling through other means. Brain activity may provide a *better* measure of some aspects of emotional processing, but this information is difficult to uncover in the linear modeling system because, to the degree that brain activity departs from a priori predictions based on behavioral measures, it will tend to go undetected.

Much of the literature on emotion has attempted to partially circumvent the problem raised by the uncertain time course corresponding to emotion by presenting brief emotionally evocative events of different types and looking for activity increases that follow a specified canonical model (Hariri, Mattay, Tessitore, Fera, & Weinberger, 2003; Lang et al., 1998; Ochsner et al., 2004; Wager, Phan, Liberzon, & Taylor, 2003). The cost of this approach is that these studies cannot investigate strong, naturalistic emotions. Many other processes are similarly difficult to assess psychologically, including anticipatory processes, shifts in strategy or performance, and changes in states of arousal.

A related problem is that even in tasks with a psychological profile that is relatively easy to specify, the specification relies on logical task analysis and may not map precisely onto brain function. For example, an attention-switching task might require participants to switch attention between two objects on some trials but not others (Wager, Jonides, Smith, & Nichols, 2005; Yantis et al., 2002). The knowledge of which trials are "switch trials" is used to build the GLM model, but the model cannot capture spontaneous shifts in attention that are not proscribed by the task instructions. Thus, there is a need to develop analyses appropriate for modeling activity with a psychological time course that is uncertain.

An alternative analysis strategy that may be appropriate in such situations is the data-driven approach. Rather than taking psychological activity as given and testing for brain changes that fit the psychological model, data-driven approaches attempt to characterize reliable patterns in the data and relate those patterns to psychological activity post hoc. One particularly popular data-driven approach in the fMRI community is independent components analysis (ICA), a variant on a family of analyses that also includes principal components and factor analyses (Beckmann & Smith, 2004; Calhoun, Adali, & Pekar, 2004; McKeown & Sejnowski, 1998). Recent extensions of these methods can identify brain activity patterns (components) that are systematic across participants (Beckmann & Smith, 2005; Calhoun et al., 2004) and can identify state-related changes in activity that can subsequently be related to psychological processes. However, these methods do not provide statistics for inferences about whether a component varies over time and when changes occur in the time series. In addition, because they do not contain any model information, they capture regularities whatever the source; thus, they are highly susceptible to noise, and components can be dominated by artifacts.

The development of hybrid data and model-driven approaches has the potential to mitigate some of the worst problems of each approach (Calhoun, Adali, Stevens, Kiehl, & Pekar, 2005; McIntosh, Chau, & Protzner, 2004). In this chapter, we discuss a hybrid approach for identifying changes in fMRI time series in individual and group data that allows for valid population inference. The approach uses ideas from statistical control theory and change point (CP) theory to model slowly varying processes with uncertain onset times and durations of underlying psychological activity. The main benefits of the methods presented here are that they are semi-model-free methods of detecting activation and are therefore insensitive to the phase lag of the hemodynamic response. In this sense, they share some of the attractive features of data-driven analysis methods. However, on the other hand, they retain the inferential nature of the more rigid modeling approach.

The change point analysis that we develop is a multisubject extension of the exponentially weighted moving average (EWMA) change point analysis (also called statistical quality control charts; Neubauer, 1997; Roberts, 1959; Shehab & Schlegel, 2000). Activity during a baseline period is used to estimate noise characteristics in the fMRI signal response. This activity is used to make inferences on whether, when, and for how long subsequent activity deviates from the baseline level. We extend existing EWMA models for individual subjects (a single time series) then develop a group analysis using a hierarchical model, which we term HEWMA (hierarchical EWMA). Group-level changes are of primary interest in the neurosciences because group analyses can be used to make inferences about how a population of participants perform a task (often referred to as second-level or "random effects" analyses in the fMRI literature; Wager et al., 2007). Finally, we apply the method to the detection of differences between groups (e.g., patients vs. controls) or conditions within a group.

Once a systematic deviation from baseline has been detected in the group, we estimate the time of change and recovery time (if any). Variations across the brain in the onset and number of CPs and in the duration of a shift away from baseline activity can be used to constrain inferences about the functions of brain regions underlying changes in psychological state. CPs are of potential interest for a number of reasons. First, they may provide a basis for discriminating anticipatory activity from responses to a challenge (e.g., activity that begins in anticipation of pain from that elicited by painful stimuli; Koyama, McHaffie, Laurienti, & Coghill, 2005; Wager, 2005). Second, CPs may be used to identify brain regions that become active

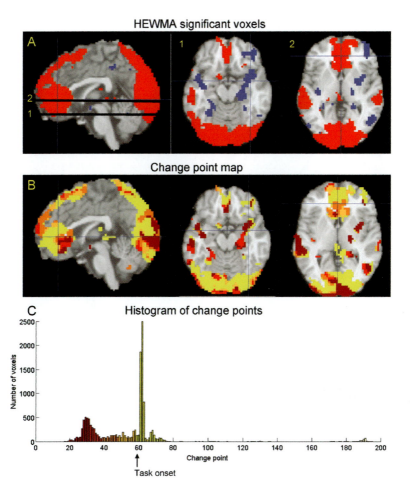

Color Figure 8.5

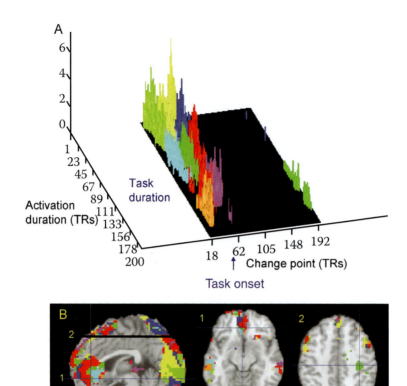

Color Figure 8.6

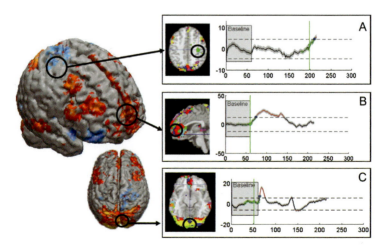

Color Figure 8.7

at different times during a challenge (e.g., the early, mid-, or late phases of a tonic painful stimulus). Third, CPs may provide meaningful characterizations of differences among individuals. In clinical studies, the onset time of brain responses to anxiety may provide clinically relevant markers of anxiety disorders. In studies of emotion, the speed of recovery from adverse events is thought to be an important predictor of emotional resilience (Fredrickson, Tugade, Waugh, & Larkin, 2003; Tugade & Fredrickson, 2004), and CPs could provide direct brain measures of recovery time. In cognitive psychology, brain CPs in problem solving and insight tasks may provide a direct neural correlate of traditional time-to-solution measures in cognitive studies (Cheng & Holyoak, 1985; Christoff et al., 2001).

The HEWMA method could be used to analyze fMRI data voxelwise throughout the brain, data from regions of interest (ROIs), or temporal components extracted using ICA or similar methods. Here, we provide power and false-positive rate (FPR) analyses based on simulations, and we apply HEWMA to voxelwise analysis of an anxiety-producing speech preparation task. We demonstrate how the method detects deviations from a pretask instruction baseline and can be used to characterize differences between groups in both evoked fMRI activity and CPs.

Methods

There is a large variety of CP detection problems that present themselves in the analysis of time series and dynamical systems. In this chapter, we apply ideas from statistical control theory and CP theory to model slowly varying brain processes (i.e., periods of enhanced neural activity detectable with fMRI) with uncertain onset times and durations. We first develop the method for detecting CPs in a single time series using EWMAs and then develop a hierarchical extensioń (HEWMA) appropriate for multisubject fMRI studies.

Exponentially weighted moving averages

Given a process that produces a sequence of observations $X = (x_1, x_2, \ldots x_n)$. (i.e., an fMRI time series), we first consider a two-state model in which the data are modeled as the combination of two normal distributions, one with mean θ_0 and (co)variance Σ, and the second with mean θ_1 and covariance Σ. During a baseline acquisition period, the process generates a distribution of data with mean θ_0, and while in this state the process is considered to be *in control*. The observations follow this distribution up

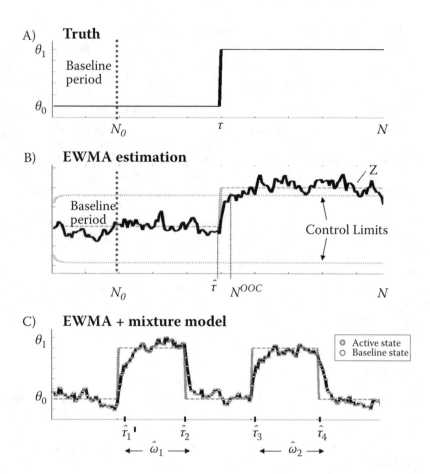

Figure 8.1 A schematic overview of: (A) the model of true activation, (B) the EWMA statistic and its control bounds, and (C) the Gaussian mixture model.

to some unknown time τ, the CP, when the process changes (i.e., a new psychological state results in increased or decreased neural activity), resulting in the generation of fMRI observations from the second distribution with mean θ_1 (see Figure 8.1A). While in this second state, the process is deemed to be *out of control* or in the out-of-control (OOC) state. The statistical model for this framework can be written as follows:

$$x_t = s_t + \varepsilon_t \quad \text{for} \quad t = 1, \ldots n \qquad (8.1)$$

where s_t denotes the signal, and ε_t is the error at time t. s_t is specified by

$$s_t = \begin{cases} \theta_0 & \text{for } t = 1, \ldots \tau \\ \theta_1 & \text{for } t = \tau + 1, \ldots n \end{cases} \tag{8.2}$$

and ε_t is specified by a mean-zero normal distribution with covariance matrix Σ, that is,

$$\varepsilon_t \sim N(0, \Sigma) \tag{8.3}$$

The diagonals of the $n \times n$ matrix Σ are the error variance estimates for each observation, and the off diagonals are the covariance among observations induced by autocorrelation in the fMRI time series. At a later stage, we relax the constraint of a single CP.

The EWMA control chart is based on the EWMA statistic z_t. The statistic is a temporally smoothed version of the data, which provides some regularization of the data and increases the power of the ensuing statistical test. It is defined as follows:

$$z_t = \lambda x_t + (1 - \lambda) z_{t-1} \qquad \text{for} \quad t = 1, \ldots n \tag{8.4}$$

or, equivalently,

$$z_t = \lambda \sum_{j=0}^{t-1} (1 - \lambda)^j x_{t-j} + (1 - \lambda)^t \theta_0 \qquad \text{for} \quad t = 1, \ldots n \tag{8.5}$$

where $0 < \lambda < 1$ is a constant smoothing parameter chosen by the analyst, and the starting value z_0 is set equal to an estimate of the process target (e.g., the baseline mean θ_0). Thus, each value of z_t is a weighted average of the current observation x_t and the previous value of the EWMA statistic. Notably, since the EWMA statistic is a weighted average of the current and all past observations, it is relatively insensitive to violations to the normality assumption.

Smoothing the data can increase power to detect deviations from the null model by regularizing the data; however, the optimal choice of smoothing parameter depends on the nature of the deviations. A general rule of thumb is to choose λ to be small (more smoothing) if one is interested in detecting small but sustained shifts in the process and larger (less smoothing) if the shifts are expected to be large but brief. Optimal values of λ are given by Lucas and Saccucci (1990).

In general, we are interested in making inferences on two features of the model. First, we seek to develop statistical tests to determine *whether* a change in distribution has indeed taken place (i.e., whether we can reject the null hypothesis $\theta_0 = \theta_1$). If a change is detected, we would also like to estimate *when* exactly the change took place, that is, estimate the unknown parameter τ.

For detecting activation, the null hypothesis is that there is a single, baseline state. The alternative is that there are two or more states with different mean activity levels, although here we consider only the simplest two-state (baseline and activation) alternative. Thus,

$$H_0 : \mu = \theta_0 \quad \text{for} \quad t = 1, \ldots n$$

$$H_a : \mu = \theta_0 \quad \text{for} \quad t = 1, \ldots \tau \quad \text{and} \quad \mu = \theta_1 \quad t = \tau + 1, \ldots n$$

Our aim is to assess the probability of observing the data under the null hypothesis $X \sim N(\theta_0, \Sigma)$. Inferences about EWMA statistic deviations from baseline can be made using a classical hypothesis testing framework, with a few adjustments described below. For each time point following the baseline period, we compute a test statistic T_t:

$$T_t = \frac{|z_t - \theta_0|}{\sqrt{Var(z_t)}} \tag{8.6}$$

where $Var(z_t)$ is the variance of the EWMA statistic at time t, the calculation of which is described below. Under the null hypothesis, this statistic follows a t distribution with df (degrees of freedom), which are based on the number of observations in the baseline period and corrected for autocorrelation using the Satterthwaite approximation. Thus, classical p values for the magnitude of each deviation from baseline may be obtained. If the p value is smaller than the desired Type I error level (e.g., .05), then the single-state null hypothesis is rejected. Confidence bands, or control limits, for EWMA statistic deviations can be calculated as follows:

$$|z_t - \theta_0| > c\sqrt{Var(z_t)} \tag{8.7}$$

where c is a critical value from the t distribution corresponding to the desired FPR control, and $Var(z_t)$ is the variance of the EWMA statistic at time t (see Figure 8.1B). Two problems must be solved to implement this test: First, $Var(z_t)$ must be formulated, and second, a value of c must be chosen that provides appropriate correction for search across n observations. We describe solutions to these problems below.

EWMA statistic variance

Using classical inference to test for deviations in the vector of EWMA statistics Z requires that we know the variance of Z. In most statistical control problems, the errors in the original data X are considered to be independent and identically distributed (*iid*), that is, $\Sigma = I\sigma^2$, where I denotes the identity matrix and σ^2 the error variance. In this case, it can be shown (Montgomery, 2000) that

$$Var(z_t) = \sigma^2 \frac{\lambda}{2-\lambda}(1-(1-\lambda)^{2t})$$

(8.8)

and as $t \to \infty$, the asymptotic variance approaches

$$Var(z_t) = \sigma^2 \frac{\lambda}{2-\lambda}$$

(8.9)

However, noise in fMRI data is autocorrelated (Aguirre, Zarahn, & D'Esposito, 1997; Wager et al., 2007), so the application to fMRI analysis requires extension of the noise model to allow for nonwhite noise (WN). When the process error follows an AR(1) model, the form of $Var(z_t)$ has previously been derived (Schmid, 1997). In appendix A, we derive similar results for both the general AR(p) and ARMA(1,1) noise models. Knowledge of the exact form of the variance of the EWMA statistic allows for better and more accurate tests and simplifies the hierarchical weighting later in the group analysis. The ARMA(1,1) model is, with proper choice of constants, equivalent to the AR(1) model often used in fMRI analysis (e.g., in SPM2 software; Friston et al., 2002).

Correction for search across time

The procedure outlined above provides p values for the null hypothesis test that the process is in control at each time point. However, because the test is repeated over n observations, correction for searching over time is warranted unless there is a strong a priori prediction of which observations should be out of control. A simple correction may be obtained using Bonferroni correction for the number of observations, but this correction will be conservative (and thus not very powerful) because fMRI data are typically positively correlated across time.

A more accurate result is given by performing Monte Carlo integration to get corrected p values (searching over time). To do so, we use the fact that under the null hypothesis, T follows a multivariate t distribution with covariance matrix Σ^* and df degrees of freedom, where Σ^* is the covariance matrix of the time series of EWMA statistics Z.

Once $Var(z_i)$ is known, Σ^* can be calculated using the fact (Schmid & Schöne, 1997) that if $\{X_t\}$ is a weakly stationary process with mean θ_0 and autocovariance $\gamma(h)$ and $\gamma \in (0,1)$, then the off-diagonal terms of Σ^* are given by

$$Cov(z_t, z_{t-i}) = \frac{1}{2}\left((1+\lambda)^i Var(z_{t-i}) + \frac{1}{(1+\lambda)^i}(Var(z_t) - Var(z_i)) \right) \quad (8.10)$$

Knowing Σ^* allows us to accurately account for the temporal dependence (autocorrelation) in the time series in the Monte Carlo simulation.

Familywise error rate (FWER) control across the time series is provided by testing the observed T statistics against the maximum absolute T value obtained across the time series under the null hypothesis (Nichols & Holmes, 2002). We thus need to assess what are the distribution of maximum T values, where

$$T_{max} = \max_{k \in [0,T]}\{|T_k|\} \quad (8.11)$$

The Monte Carlo integration proceeds by generating a large number (we used 10,000 in all results presented here) n-length time series of multivariate random T values with covariance Σ^*. We use the multivariate T random number generator provided in Matlab (Mathworks, Natick, MA). T_{max} is saved from each time series, and the 95th percentile of the distribution of maxima provides a critical t value T^* for two-tailed FWER control.

Estimating change points

In the preceding section, we outlined a procedure for detecting *whether* a change in distribution has taken place at some point in the time series. In this section, we deal with the situation of estimating *when* exactly the change took place; that is, we want to estimate the unknown CP parameter τ. When a significant EWMA statistic indicates that a process is OOC (i.e., the state of activation has changed), it is fair to assume that the CP has occurred at an earlier time as changes are likely to continue for some time before the critical threshold for significance is reached.

Nishina (1992) proposed an approach for estimating the CP using the EWMA statistics directly. The last time point at which the process crosses θ_0 before exceeding the upper or lower control limit (and becoming significant) is the last *zero crossing*, and it is the estimate of τ. More formally, let us assume that N^{OOC} is the first time the EWMA statistic exceeds the predefined threshold $c\sqrt{Var(z_t)}$, that is,

$$N^{OOC} = \min\{t \mid z_t - \theta_0 \mid > c\sqrt{Var(z_t)}\} \tag{8.12}$$

The CP estimator of τ for an *increase* in the process mean is given by the closest time point prior to N^{OOC}, which lies below θ_0. That is, we define

$$\hat{\tau} = \max\{t \mid t \leq N^{OOC}, \mid z_t \mid \leq \theta_0\} \tag{8.13}$$

The CP estimator of τ for a *decrease* is defined in an analogous manner. This is the zero-crossing method, and its main advantages are that it is conceptually straightforward and is computationally efficient. A drawback is that it does not allow us to construct confidence intervals for τ. If we want these, we instead need to use a maximum likelihood estimate (MLE; see appendix B). In practice, we will be most interested in calculating the confidence set on the group level, and we discuss an approach toward obtaining such intervals using the zero-crossing method when discussing the group analysis.

Dealing with multiple change points

A limitation of the zero-crossing method is that only a single, initial CP is assessed, and there is no clear provision for assessing return to the baseline state or the presence of multiple CPs. One possible approach would be to assume a return to baseline once the EWMA statistic crosses back across the control limit. Hence, the total number of OOC points can give a rough indication of the activation duration, although durations are likely to be biased toward zero. Alternatively, we can use a Gaussian mixture model to classify each observation as either belonging to the baseline (in control) or activated (OOC) distribution. This procedure also allows us to estimate the length of time spent in the activated state.

In the mixture model approach, we model the fMRI time course as a mixture of two normal distributions, with different means, as follows: $X_0 \sim N(\theta_0, \sigma^2)$ for the baseline state, and $X_1 \sim N(\theta_1, \sigma^2)$ for the activated state (see Figure 8.1C for an example). We can write this mixture as

$$X = (1 - \Delta)X_0 + \Delta X_1 \tag{8.14}$$

where the random variable Δ is equal to one with probability p and equal to zero with probability $1 - p$. The density function of X can be written as

$$f_X(x) = (1 - p)f_{X_0}(x) + pf_{X_1}(x) \tag{8.15}$$

where $f_{X_i}(x)$ is the normal probability density function with mean θ_i and variance σ^2.

We can fit this model to the data using maximum likelihood methods. The unknown parameters of the model are $(\theta_0, \theta_0, \sigma^2, p)$ and the log likelihood can be written:

$$l(\theta_0, \theta_1, \sigma^2, p \mid \mathbf{x}) = \sum_{i=1}^{n} \log(f_X(x_i)) \tag{8.16}$$

The parameters that maximize this term can be found using the Expectation-Maximization (EM) algorithm (see appendix C).

Once we have determined the MLEs of the parameters in this model, we need to classify each data point according to which state they belong. This can be done using Bayes' formula. The probability that a data point belongs in the active (OOC) state is given by

$$P(active \mid x_i) = \frac{p f_{X_1}(x_i)}{f_X(x_i)} \tag{8.17}$$

If $P(active \mid x_i) > 0.5$, then the time point is classified as belonging to the active state; otherwise, it is classified as belonging to the original baseline state.

HEWMA: A hierarchical extension of EWMA

The EWMA procedure outlined is suitable for studying a single time series for an individual subject. In fMRI analysis, we are typically most interested in detecting whether an effect is present over an entire group of subjects. Group changes are of primary interest in the neurosciences for making population inferences. For this reason, we developed a group analysis using a hierarchical (i.e., mixed-effects) model. Here, we introduce the HEWMA model that allows us to perform a mixed-effects analysis on fMRI group data using the same type of analysis that the EWMA method allowed for single-subject data. We use the EWMA statistic and covariance matrix defined previously to obtain the population average and its corresponding covariance matrix. Thereafter, the Monte Carlo procedure used in the EWMA framework is applied to get p values and test the hypothesis of consistent activation within the group.

Again, we are studying one voxel of the brain at a time (i.e., the massive univariate approach). We begin with the standard assumption that each subject's data have been warped to a standard brain atlas, or individual ROIs have been chosen, so that the time series from a brain area of interest can be studied in a group. Suppose our study consists of m subjects. Let $\{x^i_t\}$ denote the data for subject i, where $i = 1, \ldots m$. Our hierarchical mixed-effects model takes the following form:

$$x^i_t = s^i_t + \varepsilon^i_t \qquad (8.18)$$

$$s^i_t = s^{pop}_t + \eta_t \qquad (8.19)$$

where η_t is a subject-level error term at time t, and s^i, the underlying signal for subject i, is either in a baseline or activated state at each time t according to

$$s^i_t = \begin{cases} \theta^i_0 & for \quad t = 1, \ldots \tau \\ \theta^i_1 & for \quad t = \tau + 1, \ldots N \end{cases} \qquad (8.20)$$

Finally, the population signal

$$s^{pop}_t = \begin{cases} \theta_0 & for \quad t = 1, \ldots \tau \\ \theta_1 & for \quad t = \tau + 1, \ldots N \end{cases} \qquad (8.21)$$

shows how the subject mean state values are drawn from a larger population. In matrix format, we can write Equation 8.18 as

$$X^i = S^i + E^i = I * S^i + E^i \qquad (8.22)$$

where $X^i = (x^i_1, x^i_2, \ldots x^i_n)^T$, $S^i = (s^i_1, s^i_2, \ldots s^i_n)^T$, and $E^i = (\varepsilon^i_1, \varepsilon^i_2, \ldots \varepsilon^i_n)^T$. Here, $E^i \sim N(0, \Sigma_i)$, I is the $n \times n$ identity matrix, and the vector S^i can be considered the equivalent of beta weights — one weight for each time point. Similarly, we can write Equation 8.19 as

$$S^i = S_{pop} + U \qquad (8.23)$$

where $S_{pop} = (s^{pop}_1, s^{pop}_2, \ldots s^{pop}_n)^T$ and U is $N(0, \Sigma_B)$.

In the hierarchical setting, we can treat the between-subject variance in either of two ways. First, we could treat the vector S^i as beta weights and let U be an $n \times 1$ vector of iid $N(0, \sigma_B)$ random variables. Thus, the subject-level effect is allowed to vary over time. In this scenario, $S_B = I\sigma_B$, where σ_B is the variance of η_t. Alternatively, we could assume that S^i has an error term that is constant over time and let U be an $n \times 1$ vector of ones times a univariate $N(0, \sigma_B)$ random variable. We can write this as $U = 1 * u$, where $\mathbf{1}$ is the vector of ones, and u is a univariate random variable. In this situation, $\Sigma_B = \mathbf{1}^T \mathbf{1} \sigma_B$.

However, in our implementation we use the first form of the covariance matrix.

Regardless, the model can be written in single-level format as

$$X^i = S_{pop} + U + E^i = S_{pop} + V^i \tag{8.24}$$

where $V^i \sim N(0, \Sigma_i + \Sigma_B)$; that is, the overall error term is distributed with a variance equal to the sum of between-subject and within-subject variances. Thus, in the HEWMA model the unknown parameters are, $\theta_0, \theta_1,$ τ, and the variance components Σ_i and Σ_B. Note that if we have first performed a single-level analysis (EWMA) on each subject, we can use the results in the second level. In this case, we can assume that the within-subject variance components Σ_i are known, and brought forward, from the first level of analysis.

The EWMA statistic at time t for subject i, which we denote Z_t^i, is defined as in Equation 8.4. The HEWMA statistic, defined more formally below, is the weighted sum of the individual subjects' EWMA statistics. The subjects are weighted by the inverse of their respective variances, which are calculated as described in the EWMA section. However, in the group analysis, we will also need to take into consideration the between-subject variation. The total variation in an individual subject's EWMA statistic is written $V_i^* = \Sigma_{i_*}^* + \Sigma_B^*$, where Σ_i^* is the variance from the single-subject analysis, and Σ_B^* can be estimated using Equations 8.8 and 8.10 in combination with the fact that $\Sigma_i = I\sigma_B$. The only unknown term that needs to be estimated within the HEWMA framework is therefore the parameter σ_B. Hence, we can write $\Sigma_B^* = \alpha Q$, where Q denotes the known portion and α the unknown portion of the covariance matrix.

The HEWMA statistic and the parameter α are found iteratively in a manner outlined below.

Using an initial estimate of the entire relevant variance component, we can perform the weighted (hierarchical) regression. The HEWMA statistic is a weighted average of the individual EWMA statistics, with the weights inversely proportional to the total variance for each subject, that is,

$$Z_{pop} = \left[\sum_{i=1}^{m} W^i \right]^{-1} \sum_{i=1}^{m} W^i Z^i \tag{8.25}$$

where $W^i = V_i^{*-1}$, and the covariance matrix for Z_{pop} is given by

$$\left[\sum_{i=1}^{m} W^i \right]^{-1} \tag{8.26}$$

The estimation of the parameter α can be performed using a restricted maximum likelihood (ReML) approach (see appendix D), and the whole process of estimating Z_{pop} and its variance components is performed iteratively. This is equivalent to the variance component estimation procedure performed in SPM2 (Friston et al., 2002).

The final step in the HEWMA framework is performing a Monte Carlo simulation to get a corrected p value (searching over time). This is done as described in the EWMA section, except here we use Z_{pop} and its covariance matrix to calculate the relevant test statistics and define the multivariate t distribution. As a final note, we will often be interested in calculating a confidence interval for the CP on the group level. To do so, we can bootstrap the individual subjects' CP estimates, use this to estimate the distribution of $\hat{\tau}$, and thereby obtain confidence intervals.

Simulations

To test the EWMA and HEWMA methodology and the efficiency of the CP estimation procedure, we performed a set of three simulation studies outlined in detail below. In Simulation 1, we simulated a single-subject data set with four active regions, each with a different activation onset time, and estimated both the likelihood of activation and CPs using EWMA with the zero-crossing method. In Simulation 2, we assessed the FPR and power for the HEWMA method across values of the smoothing parameter λ. Simulation 3 assessed power and FPR across varying durations of baseline period activity.

Simulation 1

As shown in Figure 8.2, we constructed a 64×64 phantom image containing a square region of size 48×48 representing a human brain. The image intensities were assigned values of 1 or 0 for the points inside or outside the square, respectively. Four smaller squares, with dimensions 8×8, were placed inside the larger square to simulate ROIs with static contrast to the larger square. To simulate a dynamic image series, this base image was re-created 250 times according to a boxcar paradigm consisting of a prolonged period of activation of length 50 time points during which the signal within the four squares increased to 2. The onset time of activation varied between the four regions and took values of 60, 80, 100, and 120 time points. Hence, each region had activation of similar length and intensity, but with varying onset times. Noise simulated using an autoregressive process of order 2 (AR(2)) model with standard deviation equal to 1 was added to each voxel's time course. We analyzed the simulated data set using EWMA with $\lambda = 0.2$ and an AR(2) noise model. We further estimated onset times (CPs) and p values for all active voxels.

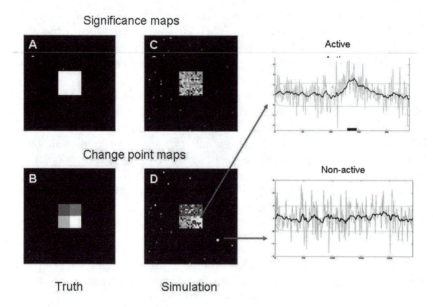

Figure 8.2 Results from a simulated single run experiment (Simulation 1) using an effect size equal to 1 and an AR(2) noise model. (A-B). The true significance and change point maps, (C) the significance map obtained from the EWMA analysis of the data (using $\lambda = 0.2$ and the AR(2) control bounds), and (D) the change point map estimated using the zero-crossing method. To the right are examples of both active and non-active time courses plotted together with their control limits. The data is represented by the light gray line and the EWMA statistic by the dark black line.

Simulation 2

The next simulation sought to study the FPR and perform power calculations for the HEWMA method. Actual fMRI noise was extracted from nonsignificant voxels of the brain (HEWMA detection $p > .95$), obtained from the experimental data described in the next section. In total, 50,350 noise time courses of length 215 time points were included in the study. The simulation mimicked a group analysis consisting of 20 subjects. For the FPR study, null hypothesis data with no activation were created by randomly sampling time series from the collection of noise time courses. This was done for each of 20 "subjects," and a random between-subject variation with a standard deviation of size one third of the within-subject variation was added to each subject's time course. A significance level of $\alpha = 0.05$ was used to determine "active" voxels. For the power calculations, the same procedure was repeated, with the difference that an active period of length 50 time points was added to the noise data, with intensity equivalent to a Cohen's *d* of 0.5. This coincides with values observed in experimental data (Wager, Vazquez, Hernandez, & Noll, 2005).

The HEWMA method was performed on 5,000 replications of each of these two data types for λ values set equal to 0.1, 0.3, 0.5, 0.7, and 0.9. The analysis was further performed using error models in the HEWMA framework corresponding to WN and AR(1), AR(2), and ARMA(1,1) noise. For each simulation, the first 60 time points were used as a baseline period.

Simulation 3

The procedure was identical to that for Simulation 2, except that in this simulation, the baseline length was 20, 40, 60, or 80 time points. The analysis was again performed using error models in the HEWMA framework corresponding to WN and AR(1), AR(2), and ARMA(1,1) noise. For each simulation, λ was set equal to 0.2, and a significance level of α = 0.05 was used.

Experimental fMRI data collection and analysis

Participants

We applied the HEWMA method to data from 30 participants scanned with BOLD fMRI at 3 T (GE, Milwaukee, WI). The experiment was conducted in accordance with the Declaration of Helsinki and was approved by the University of Michigan institutional review board. Six participants were excluded because of motion or nonlinear normalization artifacts, leaving 24 participants.

Task design

The task used was a variant of a well-studied laboratory paradigm for eliciting anxiety (Dickerson & Kemeny, 2004; Gruenewald, Kemeny, Aziz, & Fahey, 2004; Roy, Kirschbaum, & Steptoe, 2001), shown in Figure 8.3.

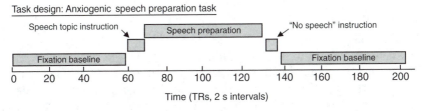

Figure 8.3 Task Design: Anxiogenic speech preparation task. Here TR denotes the time resolution of the study.

The design was an off-on-off design, with an anxiety-provoking speech preparation task occurring between lower-anxiety resting periods. Participants were informed that they were to be given 2 min to prepare a 7-min speech, and that the topic would be revealed to them during scanning. They were told that after the scanning session, they would deliver the speech to a panel of expert judges, although there was "a small chance" that they would be randomly selected not to give the speech.

After the start of fMRI acquisition, participants viewed a fixation cross for 2 min (resting baseline). At the end of this period, participants viewed an instruction slide for 15 sec that described the speech topic, which was to speak about "why you are a good friend." The slide instructed participants to be sure to prepare enough for the entire 7-min period. After 2 min of silent preparation, another instruction screen appeared (a "relief" instruction, 15-sec duration) that informed participants that they would not have to give the speech. An additional 2-min period of resting baseline followed, which completed the functional run.

Heart rate was monitored continuously, and heart rate increased after the topic presentation, remained high during preparation, and decreased after the relief instruction (data are presented elsewhere). Because this task involved a single change in state, as in some previous fMRI experiments (Breiter & Rosen, 1999; Eisenberger, Lieberman, & Williams, 2003), and the precise onset time and time course of subjective anxiety were unknown, this design was a good candidate for the HEWMA analysis.

Image acquisition

A series of 215 images was acquired using a T2*-weighted, single-shot reverse spiral acquisition (gradient echo, TR = 2000, TE = 30, flip angle = 90°) with 40 sequential axial slices (FOV = 20, 3.12 × 3.12 × 3 mm, skip 0, 64 × 64 matrix). This sequence was designed to enable good signal recovery in areas of high susceptibility artifact (e.g., orbitofrontal cortex, OFC). High-resolution T1 spoiled gradient recall (SPGR) images were acquired for anatomical localization and warping to standard space.

Image analysis

Offline image reconstruction included correction for distortions caused by magnetic field inhomogeneity. Images were corrected for slice acquisition timing differences using a custom four-point sync interpolation and realigned (motion corrected) to the first image using automated image registration (AIR; Woods, Grafton, Holmes, Cherry, & Mazziotta, 1998). SPGR images were coregistered to the first functional image using a mutual information metric (SPM2). When necessary, the starting point for the automated registration was manually adjusted and rerun until a satisfactory result was obtained. The SPGR images were normalized to the Montreal Neurological Institute (MNI) single-subject T1 template using SPM2 (with the default basis set). The warping parameters were applied to functional images, which were then smoothed with a 9-mm isotropic Gaussian kernel.

Individual-subject data were subjected to linear detrending across the entire session (215 images) and analyzed with EWMA. An AR(2) model was used to calculate the EWMA statistic (Z) and its variance, and Z and variance estimates were carried forward to the group-level HEWMA analysis. We used custom software (see acknowledgment section for download information and appendices) to calculate statistical maps throughout the brain, including HEWMA (group) t and p values for activations (increases from baseline) and deactivations (decreases from baseline); individual and group CPs (calculated on the group HEWMA t time series) using the zero-crossing method, activation duration as estimated by the number of OOC points, and CP and run-length estimates using the Gaussian mixture model described above.

Significant voxels were classified into sets of voxels showing similar behavior using k-means clustering. We considered activations and deactivations separately, and used k-means clustering on the group CP and longest activated run length (from the mixture model) to assign voxels into classes with similar behavior. To do this, we used the k-means algorithm implemented in Matlab 7.4 with the $v \times 2$ matrix of values for the v significant activated (or deactivated) voxels as input. The number of classes was determined by visual inspection of the joint histogram of CP and duration values. Twelve classes were used for the analyses reported here. Sets of contiguous suprathreshold voxels (*regions*) of the same class were the unit of analysis for interpretation.

Examining the systematic features in the time courses of ROIs permitted us to make inferences about the role the region played in the speech preparation task. Rather than testing whether a voxel is activated during the preparation interval on average compared with baseline periods, the HEWMA method can detect a number of different types of interesting systematic features, including sustained activation during the preparation task, transient activation during instruction presentation, fluctuations in baseline activity that may be related to the start of scanning, and others. Of particular interest are voxels with activation onset that is near the time of task onset (at 60 TRs or 120 sec) and with activity that is sustained throughout the task (at least 60 TRs/120 sec), which may reflect sustained anxiety.

Results

Simulation results

Simulation 1

We used EWMA to create a significance map and a CP map (CPM) that accurately depict the difference in onset time between regions. Setting the smoothing parameter $\lambda = 0.2$ and the significance level $\alpha = 0.05$, we analyzed each voxel using the EWMA procedure outlined in the Methods section. Figure 8.2A depicts the theoretical significance map, with equal amount of activation present within each of the four active regions. Figure 8.2C depicts the actual significance map obtained using EWMA. This indicates that we were able to accurately detect a large number of active voxels within the region of activity, with a minimal number of false positives outside the region. Figure 8.2B depicts the theoretical CPM, in which the intensity varies depending on the onset time. Figure 8.2D depicts the actual CPM obtained by calculating the zero-crossing CP estimate for each voxel deemed active in the prior analysis. The CPM provided accurate estimates of the onset times for the four regions, as indicated by the similar intensity values for the true values (Figure 8.2C) and estimates (Figure 8.2D). Examination of the error in CP estimation showed a distribution that was centered at zero with a slight left skew (mean = -2.0, $SD = 6.3$, median = 0, and IQR (interquartile range) = 5).

Simulation 2

Figure 8.4A and 8.4B shows the FPR and power calculations for each noise type as a function of the smoothing parameter λ. Figure 8.4A shows that the number of false positives increased for each noise type as a function of λ (i.e., with less smoothing). This is natural as low values of λ entail a greater amount of smoothing and minimize the risk of the null hypothesis data venturing too far from the baseline mean. The nominal α level of .05 is shown by the horizontal dashed line. As λ increased, the amount of smoothing decreased, and the FPR exceeded $\alpha = 0.05$. The ARMA model performed worse than the other models in FPR and power, although the other models appeared to behave in a similar manner (but they are somewhat conservative, with FPRs near 0.01 with low λ). All models controlled the FPR appropriately with $\lambda \leq .4$.

Studying Figure 8.4B, it appears that although the power increased slightly for each noise type as a function of λ, it did not vary in a significant manner. All noise models gave roughly equivalent results. In summary, our simulation studies indicated that a low value of λ will give a test with high power and low FPRs. Increasing the value of λ will lead

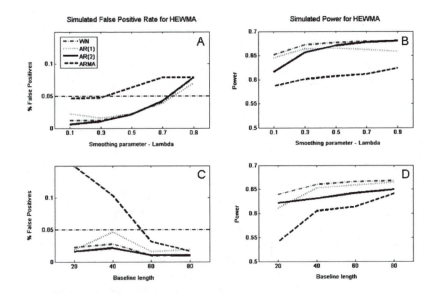

Figure 8.4 (A-B) Simulation 2. Simulated power and false positive rates for HEWMA with varying smoothness parameter λ, and fixed baseline length of 60 TRs. (C-D) Simulation 3. Same plots with fixed λ = 0.2 and varying baseline length.

to a slight increase in power, but at the cost of an increase in FPR. In the continuation, we used λ = 0.2.

Simulation 3

Figure 8.4C and 8.4D shows the FPR and power calculations for each noise type as a function of the baseline period length. Studying Figure 8.4C, it is clear that the number of false positives decreased for each noise type as the baseline period increased. This is natural as a long baseline period allows for more data to accurately estimate the parameters of the model. The ARMA model performed significantly worse than the other models and gave rise to a dramatically inflated FPR for baseline lengths less than 60 time points. This performance may be due to the fact that the baseline period was too short to get an accurate estimate of the variance components for this model type as the ARMA parameter estimation was more complex than for the other models (i.e., MLE vs. method of moments). Studying Figure 8.4D, it appears that although the power increased slightly for each noise type as a function of baseline length, it did not vary substantially across baseline durations. Again, the ARMA model performed worse than the other models.

In summary, our simulation studies indicated that an increased baseline leads to increased power as well as decreased FPR, which is advantageous. However, it is interesting to note that the WN, AR(1), and AR(2) models were all robust enough to handle a baseline period as short as 20 time points. Naturally, these values may depend to some degree on the noise characteristics. The ARMA model, on the other hand, required a baseline of at least 60 time points.

fMRI results

As expected, compared with baseline, the task elicited both significant activity increases (red in Figure 8.5A) and decreases (blue in Figure 8.5A) in a number of brain regions. Increases in visual cortex, superior parietal cortex, temporal cortex, and lateral and medial prefrontal cortices are shown in red. The activation was consistent with what might be expected in a cognitively complex task, which involved visual cues at two periods during the task, the mental effort and subvocal rehearsal required to prepare a speech, and the anxiety elicited by the task context. In particular, the rostral PFC has been strongly implicated in processing of self-relevant information and the representation and regulation of aversive emotional states (Ochsner et al., 2004; Phan, Wager, Taylor, & Liberzon, 2002; Quirk & Gehlert, 2003; Quirk, Russo, Barron, & Lebron, 2000; Ray et al., 2005; Wager et al., 2003). Information about the onset and duration of activation provided by the HEWMA analysis can constrain interpretation of the roles of these regions in task performance.

Figure 8.5B shows CPMs of the time of onset of activity (indicated by color) for activated regions. Figure 8.5C shows a histogram of CP values, with onsets color-coded according to onset time in Figure 8.5B. The range of estimated onset times, from around 15 TRs (30 sec) to around 180 TRs from the start of scanning indicates that different regions were activated at very different times during scanning. Most significant voxels showed activation onsets around the time of task onset (60 TRs), when the visual cue to begin speech preparation was presented. These include rostral medial prefrontal cortex (rMPFC), lateral OFC, occipital and parietal cortices (yellow in Figure 8.5B). However, other regions became active before the instructional cue, signaling that they may play a role in anticipation or preparation to begin the task. These regions include some visual areas, superior temporal cortex, and subgenual anterior cingulate. Another set of regions appeared to be activated before task onset but showed decreases during speech preparation; these include the amygdala and extended amygdala, ventral anterior insula, and striatum.

Likewise, activation duration estimates from the Gaussian mixture model ranged from transient increases (approximately 13 TRs or 26 sec) to

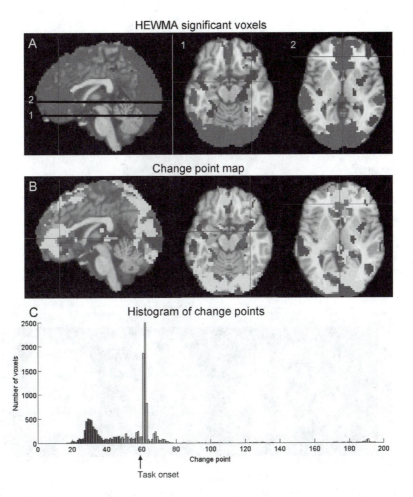

Figure 8.5 (**See color insert following page 152**)(A) A saggital slice (left) and axial slices (center and right) showing significantly activated voxels in red and deactivated voxels in blue in the speech preparation task. The threshold used was $p < 0.05$, corrected for search over time (but not space). (B) Group change-point (CP) estimates using the zero-crossing method. Earlier CPs are shown in red, and later ones in yellow. (C) A histogram of CPs for significant voxels, colored as in (B). Most voxels responded around the time of task onset (yellow), although another set of voxels showed systematic activation before the task onset (red).

sustained increases (~170 TRs, 340 sec). The two-dimensional histogram of significant voxels by CP and estimated duration is shown in Figure 8.6A. The diversity of onset times and durations suggests that a variety of different GLM models would be required to detect these activations.

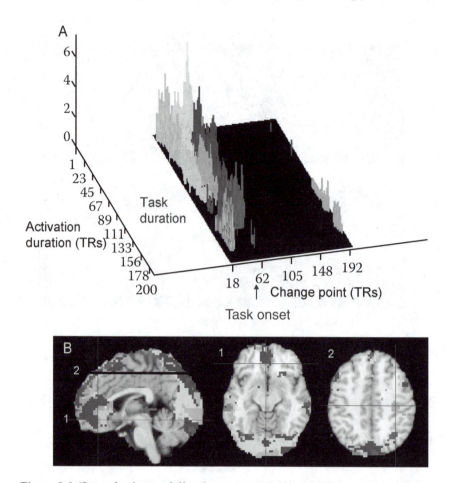

Figure 8.6 **(See color insert following page 152)** (A) A 2-D histogram of significant voxels by CP (x-axis) and activation duration (y-axis) estimated using the mixture model. Log frequency is shown on the z-axis. Bars are color-coded according
to class based on k-means classification, voxels of the same color thus have similar
CP and duration profiles. (B) A saggital slice (left) and axial slices (right) showing significant voxels, color-coded according to class as in (A). The slices show
adjacent regions of rostral medial prefrontal cortex that are active throughout the
task and begin to respond upon task presentation (red) or in anticipation (cyan).
A sensorimotor region (green) has a much later onset of activity.

The *k*-means classification provides a way to identify classes of activated voxels with similar onset and duration estimates. Class membership is indicated by color in the histogram in Figure 8.6A, and Table 8.1
lists the number of voxels in each of the 12 classes specified, along with
means for CPs and duration estimates and their standard deviations across

Table 8.1 Classes of Significant Voxels from K-Means Clustering

Num. Voxels	CP	Std	Duration	Std	Color
2778	61.3	1.5	13.1	4.48	yellow
1368	61.1	1.8	81.5	10.74	red
1290	29.5	4.3	23.1	13.21	light green
1237	61.3	2.2	43.2	7.86	blue
818	59.9	4.3	142.4	14.37	magenta
773	35.7	6.2	151.6	8.99	orange
614	31.6	3.9	79.4	14.74	cyan
613	49.7	3.6	79.0	13.26	green
594	29.6	2.0	173.8	8.17	red
482	46.5	3.3	22.4	12.61	cyan
208	189.6	5.1	149.8	21.9	green
30	170.2	23.9	42.4	25.26	blue

Note: Classification of significant voxels by change point (CP) and maximum-likelihood duration of the longest activated period using k-means clustering. A twelve-class solution was chosen based on visual inspection of the histogram (Fig. 8.6A). Colors correspond to those in Fig. 8.6.

voxels within the class. The largest class of activated voxels showed both onset times around the start of the task and durations lasting as long (60 TRs) or slightly longer than the task. The red and blue classes (Table 8.1, Figures 8.6 and 8.7), for example, became active at task onset. Activity in the red class, which includes rMPFC, persisted for 80 TRs (Figure 8.6B, 40 sec past the onset of the relief cue), whereas activity in the blue class, which includes precuneus, diminished before the relief cue (43 TRs/86-sec duration on average, compared to 120 sec of speech preparation). These regions may be related to the anxiety inherent in task performance.

Other classes seem clearly related to visual processing of the cues. The yellow and light green classes were activated at task onset or before (ramping up before the instruction) and persisted for only approximately 25 to 45 sec after the onset of the 15-sec visual instruction. Yet other classes, such as the green class that began to be active around 150 TRs (300 sec), after the relief cue, have more ambiguous interpretations. These regions may be related to relief, or they may show a drift in signal at the end of the session due to fatigue or increased movement.

Examining the group time courses of voxels in these regions corroborates this view and provides additional evidence. The sensorimotor region that comprises most of the late-onset green class is shown in Figure 8.7A, and it appears to drift upward at the end of scanning. Notably, the deviation is in the same direction for all participants, so is unlikely to be related to head movement unless participants moved in a systematic way at the end

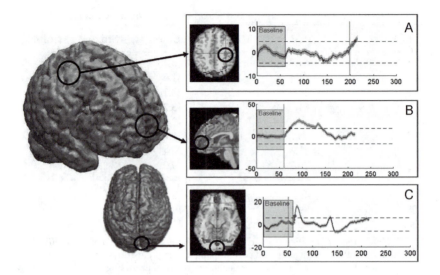

Figure 8.7 (**See color insert following page 152**) The brain surface is shown in lateral oblique and axial views. Significant voxels are colored according to significance. Increases are shown in red-yellow, and decreases are shown in light-dark blue. (A) A time course from a region showing late-onset responses (green class in Figure 8.6). The time course was extracted from a single representative voxel in the region. The baseline period is indicated by the shaded gray box, and the HEWMA-statistic is shown by the thick black line (+/− one standard error across participants, shown by gray shading). The control limits are shown by dashed lines. This activation is unlikely to be anxiety-related. (B) A similar plot for the rMPFC (red class). The time course parallels the structure of the task in that activation begins around the onset of speech instructions and is sustained throughout the duration of the preparation interval. (C) HEWMA time series plot for a representative region in the primary/secondary visual cortex (yellow class). Activity peaks twice during each presentation of visual instructions.

of scanning, but may be related to other nuisance variables. rMPFC voxels, shown in Figure 8.7B, closely parallel the time course of subjective anxiety and heart rate increases in the task. Occipital voxels, such as the one shown in Figure 8.7C (yellow class), became active when the instruction cue was presented and again when the relief cue was presented, consistent with a large literature implicating these regions in visual processing. The baseline period in Figure 8.7 is indicated by the shaded gray box in each panel, and the HEWMA statistic time course is shown by the thick black line (± one standard error across participants, shown by gray shading). Control limits are shown by dashed lines; thus, the region is significantly activated if the HEWMA statistic exceeds the control limit at any time point.

Importantly, the time course of activation in rMPFC parallels the structure of the task in that activation began around the onset of speech instructions (CP estimate 122 sec, actual task onset 120 sec) and was sustained throughout the duration of the preparation interval. This region has been related in many neuroimaging studies to subjective anxiety and self-referential processing (Breiter & Rosen, 1999; Dougherty et al., 2004; Eisenberger et al., 2003; Ray et al., 2005; Wang et al., 2005) and is thus a neurophysiologically plausible candidate to show sustained activation related to the anxiogenic task.

Discussion

Typically, statistical methods in fMRI can be categorized into two broad categories: hypothesis and data-driven approaches. Hypothesis-driven approaches test whether activity in a brain region is systematically related to some known input function. In this approach, typically the GLM is used to test for differences in activity among psychological conditions or groups of participants. However, for many psychological processes, the precise timing and duration of psychological activity can be difficult to specify in advance. In this situation, the GLM approach becomes impractical as the psychological activity cannot be specified a priori. Data-driven methods, such as ICA, give an account of the data using few a priori assumptions. Instead, they attempt to characterize reliable patterns in the data and relate those patterns to psychological activity post hoc. The main drawback of these methods is that they do not provide statistics for making inferences about whether a component varies over time and when changes occur in the time series.

The purpose of the HEWMA method is to allow for the detection of systematic changes in activity with a variety of onset times and activation durations. The differences in onset and duration are likely to reflect differences in functional anatomy, that is, the way in which each activated region participates in the task. Both the EWMA and HEWMA methods for fMRI data analysis are designed to detect regions of the brain where the signal deviates reliably from a baseline state. The methods make no a priori assumption about the behavior of these changes, and the method will detect activation and deactivation as well as regions with both short and prolonged activation duration. In this sense, both EWMA and HEWMA can be thought of as searches for activity differences across time, correcting for the multiple comparisons tested and accounting for the correlation among observations.

Once a systematic deviation from baseline has been detected, the second step in the analysis entails estimating *when* exactly the change took place as well as the recovery time (if any). This estimation procedure can be performed using the zero-crossing method, the MLE, or a Gaussian mixture model. Once these estimates are obtained, we can cluster the active voxels into groups with estimates that behave in a similar manner. This allows us to classify regions and even discard regions for which the activation was triggered by effects such as drift or movement. As a final step, after estimating the CP for each active voxel in the brain, we summarize the results in a CPM. A CPM is an image of the brain with a color-coded CP mask superimposed, with its intensity varying depending on the estimated onset time of activation.

The main decisions that need to be made before applying these methods to experimental data are the choice of the smoothing parameter λ and the length of the baseline period. According to our power and FPR analyses, a relatively low value of λ gives high power, with a strong control of the FPR. In our analysis of experimental data, we typically choose a value of 0.2 as this appears to give rise to an adequate amount of smoothing for the analysis of fMRI data. The optimal value of λ will vary depending on whether brief or sustained changes are of greater interest, with lower values more appropriate for more sustained activity. The length of the baseline period is another issue. The data within this period are used to estimate the baseline mean as well as the within-subject variation, and our simulations showed that, unsurprisingly, longer baseline periods produced more accurate estimates. However, our analysis indicated that the method is relatively stable for even very short baseline periods for WN, AR(1), and AR(2) models. The ARMA model showed increased sensitivity to short baseline periods with drastically increased FPR and decreased power, and a longer baseline period (>60 time points) is recommended. The AR(2) model may be most appropriate for fMRI data as it has the flexibility to model periodic noise oscillations that are often produced in fMRI as a result of physiological changes (e.g., pulsatile motion of the brain due to breathing and cardiac activity).

HEWMA appears to be an appropriate analysis for group fMRI data, particularly when it is not possible to replicate experimental manipulations within subjects (e.g., a state anxiety induction that cannot be repeated without changing the psychological nature of the state). Emotional responses are one prime candidate for applications of the method. But, there are a number of other domains in which it may be useful as well, and the method applies to any longitudinal data with enough observations so that repeated-measures analysis of variance (ANOVA) (for example) is impractical. HEWMA may be particularly useful for arterial spin labeling and perfusion MRI studies, which measure brain activity over time without the complicating factors of signal drift and highly colored noise in fMRI (Liu, Wong, Frank, & Buxton, 2002; Wang et al., 2005).

Another potential use is in identifying voxels of interest and characterizing brain responses in "ecologically valid" tasks, such as free viewing of films. For example, according to one article, participants watched a 60-min segment of an action movie (Hasson, Nir, Levy, Fuhrmann, & Malach, 2004). The investigators examined the time course of activity throughout the brain and assessed whether increases in particular regions were systematically related to features of the film (e.g., presentation of scenes, hands, faces). HEWMA could be used in this situation to identify voxels that responded consistently across participants during viewing, which would reduce false positives by providing a reduced set of voxels of interest and providing some quantitative tools for characterizing the duration and number of activated periods.

HEWMA could also be applied to changes in state-related activity evoked by learning (e.g., tonic increases brain activity as a function of expertise) or to studies of tonic increases following solutions to "insight" problem-solving tasks. Expertise results in functional and structural reorganization of cortex (Kilgard & Merzenich, 1998; Kourtzi, Betts, Sarkheil, & Welchman, 2005), and HEWMA could be used to more precisely characterize the time course of both types of changes (i.e., do shifts occur gradually or suddenly?). In an insight task, participants are presented with a problem that requires a novel combination of elements (Bowden, Jung-Beeman, Fleck, & Kounios, 2005; MacGregor, Ormerod, & Chronicle, 2001). Once participants solve the task, there is a qualitative shift in their understanding of how the elements of the problem relate that cannot be reversed (the solution is "obvious" once one knows it). This profound shift is poorly understood, in part because appropriate methods have not been devised to study its brain mechanisms in healthy participants.

Another potential use is in longitudinal studies of brain function or structure, and how they change with development or with the progression of a neurological or psychiatric disorder. For example, Mayberg and colleagues conducted several longitudinal studies of resting fluorodeoxyglucose (FDG) PET activity in depressed patients over the course of treatment (Goldapple et al., 2004; Mayberg et al., 2002). The time course of brain activity changes throughout the treatment process are unknown, and HEWMA could be used to locate regions that respond to treatment and identify the time at which they do so.

Conclusion

In this chapter, we developed a hybrid data and model-driven approach, HEWMA, that can be used to make inferences about individual or group fMRI activity, even when conditions are not replicated (e.g., a single experimental induction of emotion). This approach can complement GLM-based and purely data-driven methods (such as ICA) by providing inferences about whether, when, and for how long systematic state-related activation occurs in a particular brain region. Although it is developed here for fMRI data analysis, the method could be useful in detection of deviation from a baseline state in any type of time series data, including arterial spin labeling (ASL), longitudinal studies of brain structure, or positron emission tomographic (PET) activity, and others.

The HEWMA method is an extension of EWMA, a time series analysis method in statistical process control theory and CP theory, to multisubject data. It permits population inference and can be used to analyze fMRI data voxelwise throughout the brain, data from ROIs, or temporal components extracted using ICA or similar methods. Simulations showed that the method has acceptable FPR control, and application to an fMRI study of anxiety showed that it produces reasonable and novel results with empirical data. A toolbox implementing all functions in Matlab is freely available from the authors (see next section).

Acknowledgment

We would like to thank Christian Waugh, Doug Noll, and Luis Hernandez for providing data with which to develop the model. Software implementing the EWMA and HEWMA analyses is available for download from http://www.columbia.edu/cu/psychology/tor/ or by contacting the authors.

References

Aguirre, G. K., Zarahn, E., & D'Esposito, M. (1997). Empirical analyses of BOLD fMRI statistics. II. Spatially smoothed data collected under null-hypothesis and experimental conditions. *Neuroimage, 5,* 199–212.

Beckmann, C. F., & Smith, S. M. (2004). Probabilistic independent component analysis for functional magnetic resonance imaging. *IEEE Transactions on Medical Imaging, 23,* 137–152.

Beckmann, C. F., & Smith, S. M. (2005). Tensorial extensions of independent component analysis for multisubject FMRI analysis. *Neuroimage, 25,* 294–311.

Bowden, E. M., Jung-Beeman, M., Fleck, J., & Kounios, J. (2005). New approaches to demystifying insight. *Trends in Cognitive Sciences, 9,* 322–328.

Breiter, H. C., & Rosen, B. R. (1999). Functional magnetic resonance imaging of brain reward circuitry in the human. *Annals of the New York Academy of Sciences, 877,* 523–547.

Brockwell, P. J., & Davis, R. A. (2002). *Introduction to time series and forecasting* (2nd ed.). New York: Springer-Verlag.

Calhoun, V. D., Adali, T., & Pekar, J. J. (2004). A method for comparing group fMRI data using independent component analysis: Application to visual, motor and visuomotor tasks. *Magnetic Resonance Imaging, 22,* 1181–1191.

Calhoun, V. D., Adali, T., Stevens, M. C., Kiehl, K. A., & Pekar, J. J. (2005). Semi-blind ICA of fMRI: A method for utilizing hypothesis-derived time courses in a spatial ICA analysis. *Neuroimage, 25,* 527–538.

Cheng, P. W., & Holyoak, K. J. (1985). Pragmatic reasoning schemas. *Cognitive Psychology, 17,* 391–416.

Christoff, K., Prabhakaran, V., Dorfman, J., Zhao, Z., Kroger, J. K., Holyoak, K. J., et al. (2001). Rostrolateral prefrontal cortex involvement in relational integration during reasoning. *Neuroimage, 14,* 1136–1149.

Dickerson, S. S., & Kemeny, M. E. (2004). Acute stressors and cortisol responses: A theoretical integration and synthesis of laboratory research. *Psychological Bulletin, 130,* 355–391.

Dougherty, D. D., Rauch, S. L., Deckersbach, T., Marci, C., Loh, R., Shin, L. M., et al. (2004). Ventromedial prefrontal cortex and amygdala dysfunction during an anger induction positron emission tomography study in patients with major depressive disorder with anger attacks. *Archives of General Psychiatry, 61,* 795–804.

Eisenberger, N. I., Lieberman, M. D., & Williams, K. D. (2003). Does rejection hurt? An FMRI study of social exclusion. *Science, 302,* 290–292.

Fredrickson, B. L., Tugade, M. M., Waugh, C. E., & Larkin, G. R. (2003). What good are positive emotions in crises? A prospective study of resilience and emotions following the terrorist attacks on the United States on September 11th, 2001. *Journal of Personality and Social Psychology, 84,* 365–376.

Friston, K. J., Glaser, D. E., Henson, R. N., Kiebel, S., Phillips, C., & Ashburner, J. (2002). Classical and Bayesian inference in neuroimaging: Applications. *Neuroimage, 16,* 484–512.

Goldapple, K., Segal, Z., Garson, C., Lau, M., Bieling, P., Kennedy, S., et al. (2004). Modulation of cortical-limbic pathways in major depression: Treatment-specific effects of cognitive behavior therapy. *Archives of General Psychiatry, 61,* 34–41.

Gruenewald, T. L., Kemeny, M. E., Aziz, N., & Fahey, J. L. (2004). Acute threat to the social self: shame, social self-esteem, and cortisol activity. *Psychosomatic Medicine, 66,* 915–924.

Hariri, A. R., Mattay, V. S., Tessitore, A., Fera, F., & Weinberger, D. R. (2003). Neocortical modulation of the amygdala response to fearful stimuli. *Biological Psychiatry, 53,* 494–501.

Hasson, U., Nir, Y., Levy, I., Fuhrmann, G., & Malach, R. (2004). Intersubject synchronization of cortical activity during natural vision. *Science, 303,* 1634–1640.

Hinkley, D. V. (1970). Inference about the change-point in a sequence of random variables. *Biometrika, 57,* 1–17.

Kilgard, M. P., & Merzenich, M. M. (1998). Cortical map reorganization enabled by nucleus basalis activity. *Science, 279,* 1714–1718.

Kourtzi, Z., Betts, L. R., Sarkheil, P., & Welchman, A. E. (2005). Distributed neural plasticity for shape learning in the human visual cortex. *PLoS Biology, 3,* e204.

Koyama, T., McHaffie, J. G., Laurienti, P. J., & Coghill, R. C. (2005). The subjective experience of pain: Where expectations become reality. *Proceedings of the National Academy of Sciences, 102*, 12950–12955.

Lang, P. J., Bradley, M. M., Fitzsimmons, J. R., Cuthbert, B. N., Scott, J. D., Moulder, B., et al. (1998). Emotional arousal and activation of the visual cortex: an fMRI analysis. *Psychophysiology, 35*, 199–210.

Liu, T. T., Wong, E. C., Frank, L. R., & Buxton, R. B. (2002). Analysis and design of perfusion-based event-related fMRI experiments. *Neuroimage, 16*, 269–282.

Lucas, J. M., & Saccucci, M. S. (1990). Exponentially weighted moving average control schemes: Properties and enhancements. *Technometrics, 32*, 1–29.

MacGregor, J. N., Ormerod, T. C., & Chronicle, E. P. (2001). Information processing and insight: a process model of performance on the nine-dot and related problems. *Journal of Experimental Psychology: Learning, Memory, and Cognition, 27*, 176–201.

Mayberg, H. S., Silva, J. A., Brannan, S. K., Tekell, J. L., Mahurin, R. K., McGinnis, S., et al. (2002). The functional neuroanatomy of the placebo effect. *American Journal of Psychiatry, 159*, 728–737.

McIntosh, A. R., Chau, W. K., & Protzner, A. B. (2004). Spatiotemporal analysis of event-related fMRI data using partial least squares. *Neuroimage, 23*, 764–775.

McKeown, M. J., & Sejnowski, T. J. (1998). Independent component analysis of fMRI data: examining the assumptions. *Human Brain Mapping, 6*, 368–372.

Montgomery, D. C. (2000). *Introduction to statistical quality control* (4rth ed.). New York: Wiley.

Neubauer, A. S. (1997). The EWMA control chart: properties and comparison with other quality-control procedures by computer simulation. *Clinical Chemistry, 43*, 594–601.

Nichols, T. E., & Holmes, A. P. (2002). Nonparametric permutation tests for functional neuroimaging: a primer with examples. *Human Brain Mapping, 15*, 1–25.

Nishina, K. (1992). A comparison of control charts from the viewpoint of change-point estimation. Quality and reliability. *Engineering International, 8*, 537–541.

Ochsner, K. N., Ray, R. D., Cooper, J. C., Robertson, E. R., Chopra, S., Gabrieli, J. D., et al. (2004). For better or for worse: neural systems supporting the cognitive down- and up-regulation of negative emotion. *Neuroimage, 23*, 483–499.

Phan, K. L., Wager, T., Taylor, S. F., & Liberzon, I. (2002). Functional neuroanatomy of emotion: a meta-analysis of emotion activation studies in PET and fMRI. *Neuroimage, 16*, 331–348.

Pignatiello, J. J., & Samuel, T. R. (2001). Estimation of the change point of a normal process mean in SPC applications. *Journal of Quality Technology, 33*, 82–95.

Quirk, G. J., & Gehlert, D. R. (2003). Inhibition of the amygdala: Key to pathological states? *Annals of the New York Academy of Science, 985*, 263–272.

Quirk, G. J., Russo, G. K., Barron, J. L., & Lebron, K. (2000). The role of ventro-medial prefrontal cortex in the recovery of extinguished fear. *Journal of Neuroscience, 20,* 6225–6231.

Ray, R. D., Ochsner, K. N., Cooper, J. C., Robertson, E. R., Gabrieli, J. D., & Gross, J. J. (2005). Individual differences in trait rumination and the neural systems supporting cognitive reappraisal. *Cognitive, Affective, and Behavioral Neuroscience, 5,* 156–168.

Roberts, S. W. (1959). Control chart tests based on geometric moving averages. *Technometrics, 1,* 239–250.

Roy, M. P., Kirschbaum, C., & Steptoe, A. (2001). Psychological, cardiovascular, and metabolic correlates of individual differences in cortisol stress recovery in young men. *Psychoneuroendocrinology, 26,* 375–391.

Schmid, W. (1997). *On EWMA charts for time series* (Vol. 5). Heidelberg: Physica-Verlag.

Schmid, W., & Schöne, A. (1997). Some properties of the EWMA control chart in the presence of autocorrelation. *Annals of Statistics, 25,* 1277–1283.

Shehab, R. L., & Schlegel, R. E. (2000). Applying quality control charts to the analysis of single-subject data sequences. *Human Factors, 42,* 604–616.

Siegmund, D. (1986). Boundary crossing probabilities and statistical applications. *Annals of Statistics, 14,* 361–404.

Taylor, S. F., Phan, K. L., Decker, L. R., & Liberzon, I. (2003). Subjective rating of emotionally salient stimuli modulates neural activity. *Neuroimage, 18,* 650–659.

Tugade, M. M., & Fredrickson, B. L. (2004). Resilient individuals use positive emotions to bounce back from negative emotional experiences. *Journal of Personality and Social Psychology, 86,* 320–333.

Wager, T. D. (2005). The neural bases of placebo effects in pain. *Current Directions in Psychological Science, 14,* 175–179.

Wager, T. D., Hernandez, L., Jonides, J., & Lindquist, M. (2007). Elements of functional neuroimaging. In J. Cacioppo, L. Tassinary, & G. Berntson (Eds.), *The handook of psychophysiology (3rd ed.).* New York: Cambridge University Press 1, 19–55.

Wager, T. D., Jonides, J., Smith, E. E., & Nichols, T. E. (2005). Towards a taxonomy of attention-shifting: Individual differences in fMRI during multiple shift types. *Cognitive, Affective, and Behavioral Neuroscience, 5,* 127–143.

Wager, T.D., Phan, K. L., Liberzon, I., & Taylor, S. F. (2003). Valence, gender, and lateralization of functional brain anatomy in emotion: A meta-analysis of findings from neuroimaging. *Neuroimage, 19,* 513–531.

Wager, T. D., Vazquez, A., Hernandez, L., & Noll, D. C. (2005). Accounting for non-linear BOLD effects in fMRI: parameter estimates and a model for prediction in rapid event-related studies. *Neuroimage, 25,* 206–218.

Wang, J., Rao, H., Wetmore, G. S., Furlan, P. M., Korczykowski, M., Dinges, D. F., et al. (2005). Perfusion functional MRI reveals cerebral blood flow pattern under psychological stress. *Proceedings of the National Academy of Science of the United States of America, 102,* 17804–17809.

Woods, R. P., Grafton, S. T., Holmes, C. J., Cherry, S. R., & Mazziotta, J. C. (1998). Automated image registration: I. General methods and intrasubject, intramodality validation. *Journal of Computer Assisted Tomography, 22,* 139–152.

Worsley, K. J., & Friston, K. J. (1995). Analysis of fMRI time-series revisited — again. *Neuroimage, 2,* 173–181.

Yantis, S., Schwarzbach, J., Serences, J. T., Carlson, R. L., Steinmetz, M. A., Pekar, J. J., et al. (2002). Transient neural activity in human parietal cortex during spatial attention shifts. *Nature Neurosci, 5,* 995–1002.

chapter nine

Using an econometric model of change points to locate turning points in individual time series

Henian Chen
New York State Psychiatric Institute and Columbia University

Patricia Cohen
New York State Psychiatric Institute and Columbia University

Kathy Gordon
New York State Psychiatric Institute

Contents

Introduction 184
Change in time series data 184
Study questions 185
    Study participants 186
Narrative interviews.. 186
Monthly narration-based ratings... 187
Change point in financial difficulty.. 187
Predictors of sustained financial difficulties 188
Financial turning points and onset or persistence
of psychiatric disorder... 190
Conclusion... 191
References 192

Introduction

There are cases when the investigator's goal in analyses of time series data is to identify units that can be said to have experienced a turning point or to relate the timing of normative turning points to some other predictor or event. Such an investigation might often be preliminary to identifying the cause of such changes. In the initial analyses reported here, we employed a model developed and used in the econometric field to identify change in a time series model (Bai, 1994; Bai & Perron, 2003; Zeileis, Leisch, Hornik, & Kleiber, 2002). In distinction from more common use of this model to identify points in aggregate-based time series indicators, we applied this model to individual developmental data.

The Children in the Community (CIC) Transition data are based on narrative descriptions of behavior and experiences covering monthly changes between the 17th and 27th birthdays (Cohen, Chen, Hamigami, Gordon, & McArdle, 2000; Cohen, Kasen, Chen, Hartmark, & Gordon, 2003). Previous reports have shown that developmental courses vary dramatically from person to person, and that individual development generally proceeds by spurts and occasional decline despite the apparent steady and smooth increase of developmental averages across persons (Cohen et al., 2003).

The analyses reported here employed this model, described as structural change analyses in econometrics, to identify a turning point at which the developmental course of an individual or demographic subgroup took a decided, relatively lasting turn.

Change in time series data

The most familiar time-series model is a simple first-order autoregressive model in which the value of the dependent variable Y at the previous time point $(t - 1)$ is used to predict each Y_t value over the n observed time points. The assumption of stationarity indicates that these autoregressive coefficients (the regression constant and β_t) are constant over time. Bai's (1994) definition of structural change tests this null hypothesis against the alternative of a significant change in autoregression. Bai's work was based on earlier tests designed for a previously identified possible single structural change point (Chow, 1960). The Chow test splits the time series into two subperiods before and after a possible break date, estimates the parameters for each subperiod, and then tests the equality of the two sets of parameters using a classic F statistic (Chow's statistic). For an unknown single structural change, Quandt (1960) extended the Chow test and proposed taking the largest Chow statistic (Quandt's statistic) over all possible break dates. Starting with unknown change points, F statistics can be calculated for a set of potential change points, and their supremum can be used as the test statistic, rejecting the null if a computed F statistic is larger than a critical value. The Quandt's statistic had no practical application for many years because there were no critical values for determining probabilities. In the early 1990s, the problem was solved simultaneously by several sets of authors, with the most elegant and general statements given by Andrews (1993) and Andrews and Ploberger (1994). These authors provided tables of critical values, and Hansen (1997) provided a method by which to calculate p values.

Bai and Perron (1998, 2003) developed tests for multiple structural change points by using a supF test. Their method is successive, starting by testing for a single structural change. If the test rejects the null hypothesis, the sample is split in two at the identified point, and the test is reapplied to each subsample. This sequence continues until each subsample test fails to find evidence of a structural change. They provided a method based on a sequential application of the supF test.

In general, the goal is knowledge of the timing of significant change. In linear regression models, a theory of least squares estimation was developed by Bai (1994) and Chong (2001) for the case of a single structural change point. Bai derived the asymptotic distribution of the break point estimator allowing the construction of confidence intervals that indicate the degree of estimation accuracy. Chong developed a comprehensive asymptotic theory for an autoregressive process of order one with an unknown single structural break. Bai and Perron (2003) extended the analysis to multiple structural change models. They established the limiting distribution of the break date estimators for shifts with shrinking magnitudes. The key insight is that when there are multiple structural changes, the sum of squared residuals, as a function of break date, can have a local minimum near each break date. The global minimum can be used as a break date estimator, and the other local minima can be viewed as candidate break date estimators. The sample is then split at the break date estimate, and analysis continues on the subsamples. The number of least squares regressions required to compute all the break dates is of order T, the number of time points.

Study questions

A minority of young people may experience significant and sustained financial difficulties during the transition into adulthood. Among those who experience such financial problems we hypothesized an increase in psychiatric disorder, viewing the persistent financial problem here as a turning point indicator or even causal factor.

Study participants

The sample consisted of 240 members from the CIC study, a cohort of 800 young adults, from an ongoing investigation of a random sample of children born between 1964 and 1974 and residing in 100 randomly selected areas in two upstate New York counties in 1975 (see www.nyspi. cpmc.columbia.edu/childcom for more details on sampling, sample characteristics, and retention). Families were generally representative of the northeastern United States in terms of demographic characteristics and socioeconomic status (SES; Cohen & Cohen, 1996). The cohort, 50% female and primarily white (91% vs. 8% black and 1% other), ranged in age from 9 to 18 years old in 1983. Mothers and cohort offspring were interviewed twice while the cohort was adolescent with extensive protocols that included psychiatric diagnostic assessment of the child. Cohort offspring were also interviewed at mean age 33. At all interviews, consent was obtained from all participants according to institutional review board standards. A National Institutes of Health Certificate of Confidentiality exists for these data.

Narrative interviews

The transition study conducted telephone-based narrative interviews, typically taking 3 to 5 h to complete. Interviewers were intensively trained and supervised, employing a manual that provided many illustrations of the match of concrete behavioral examples to scale points. The data collection in this study began by establishing a framework for that 10-year period by asking the respondents to complete a "Life Chart" (Lyketsos, Nestadt, Cwi, Helthoff, & Eaton, 1994). This document, completed in advance of the interview, charts the changes over these years in where the subject lived, worked, and studied as well as dates of significant experiences that help the respondent to reconstruct the period covered by the interview. The narrative in this study covers six domains of the person's life: residence, finance, school, employment, romance, and parenting. Changes in study variables were dated to the month in which they occurred. Thus, coding of the structured narrative method generated 120 consecutive monthly records on each of the defined variables, with the value of each code retained until the month when a new code was entered. To ensure reliability of measures, all interviewer-coded interviews were recorded and blindly recoded by another interviewer, and the scores were averaged across coders (for more about this narrative interview and its generally excellent interrater reliability, see Cohen, Kasen, Bifulco, Andrews, & Gordon, 2005).

Monthly narration-based ratings

A central construct of the study was the extent to which, at each point in time, the respondent's role behavior was more like that of a child or approximated that of a *full adult*, defined as an individual having independence from parental control, expressing own goals and preferences, and assuming responsibilities. These ratings of "transition level" were quantified in each of five domains: residence, career (combining advanced training or education and employment), financial support, romantic partnership, and family formation. Role behavior was rated on a 100-point scale, where 0 represents a young childlike role and 99 represents a wholly adult role. In addition, difficulties encountered in carrying out each role were also described by the narrator and rated. The midpoint (50) was indicative of a degree of difficulty that would be considered normative for that age group or setting (e.g., some difficulty in educational projects or minor problems with a college roommate were considered normative). A value lower than 50 would indicate the extent to which external circumstances facilitated the adopted role, for example, when generous family financial support made possible a highly desirable independent residence. A very high difficulty rating on financial role would indicate severe problems, such as a health problem causing inability to work or high medical expenses; unexpected loss of financial assets; loss of income from, or need to supply income to, a former spouse or other person; problems with expenses connected with offspring; and so on.

Change point in financial difficulty

Our goal was to identify, using the first order autoregressive model to detect a single structural change point, participants who experienced a serious increase in financial role difficulty. All applications were carried out using the statistical software package R (http://www.R-project.org/), and all methods introduced are available in the package Strucchange (Zeileis, 2006; Zeileis et al., 2002). Of 240 narrators, this model detected a significant increase in 116 young people, about half of the sample. These change points occurred nearly throughout the data range (19.97 to 25.65), on average about a year later than the average age covered (22.98, standard deviation [SD] =1.62). On average, the increase in financial difficulty lasted 30 months (SD = 19.55, range 5 to 87); however, the duration was limited in some cases by the age coverage, which ended at the 27th birthday. The positive changes averaged an increase of 18 points (SD = 9.66, range 4 to 60).

Financial Difficulty

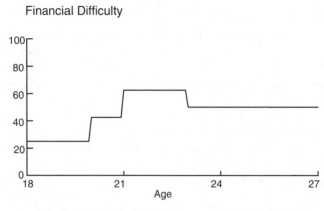

Sup F=80.24, P<0.01, change point at age=20.92

Figure 9.1 A trajectory indicating large stable increase in financial difficulty. Preadult predictors of serious financial difficulty in the transition years.

We also note that in these narratives it was assumed that monthly values of variables were stable until the time point at which the narrator could identify a change. As a consequence, the variance in autocorrelation across the months was often quite small, around a mean close to 1.0. This small variance dramatically increased the method's sensitivity to relatively small changes. For this reason, we further examined the trajectories to identify those individuals who may be said to have experienced a financial turning point by virtue of its extended duration as well as magnitude. Examination of the difficulty curves for those with the larger magnitude increases yielded 46 participants with substantial financial difficulties, defined as a large increase (more than 18 points) lasting more than 12 months. In this group, the mean increase was 25 points over 31 months on average. The remaining identified changes involved either short duration ($N = 26$) (mean change = 19, mean months = 6), thus not meeting our definition of a turning point as involving sustained change, or relatively small increases of long-lasting duration ($N = 44$) (mean change = 9, mean months = 40), again not meeting our definition of a significant turning point. Figure 9.1 shows an example of such a turning point in one narrator's history.

Predictors of sustained financial difficulties

Potential sex, race, and family of origin SES differences between the financial turning point sample and the remaining narrators were examined (see Table 9.1). As can be seen, there was no significant association with sex or

Table 9.1 Prior Differences between the Narrators with and without Sustained Financial Difficulties during the Transition to Adulthood

	Financial difficulty turning point	
	Yes (N = 46)	No (N = 193)
Female, number (%)	21 (45.7)	93 (48.2)
White, number (%)	45 (97.8)	177 (91.7)
Post-high school training, number (%)	29 (63.0)	133 (68.6)
Verbal IQ, mean (SD)	98.62 (12.70)	101.59 (13.17)
Family socioeconomic status, mean (SD)	0.22 (0.96)	(0.10 (0.98)
Truancy, mean (SD)	8.40 (3.31)	7.43 (3.05)

Note: SD, standard deviation.

race. Those with such a turning point were a little less likely to have entered post-high school training programs: Post-high school training was entered by 29 (63%) of those with later financial difficulty and 133 (68.6%) of those without such a period within the transition decade ($p > .10$). We investigated as potential risks both school attendance regularity in the prenarrative period and the potential impact of (average) intelligence as measured by picture-vocabulary tests twice during the pretransition assessments.

We investigated potential risks for subsequent serious financial difficulty using a Cox regression model. Potential predictors included sex, race, and family of origin SES as well as two personal history variables examined here as likely risks: intelligence, measured by picture vocabulary tests on two adolescent occasions and averaged, and irregularity of high school attendance reported in earlier interviews. Family SES is a standardized mean of standardized parental educational level, standardized occupational level, and standardized family income category. There are likely reciprocal relationships among financing source, financial problems, and ultimate level of post-high school education; for these reasons we did not include educational level in the multivariable analyses.

The combined effects of prior demographic and personal history variables in these analyses are reflected in the hazard of serious financial difficulty associated with each predictor. In these analyses, the hazard ratio is the likelihood of onset of such a turning point at any given time expressed as a ratio in comparison with the likelihood of such onset in those without such risk, controlling the effects of all other variables in the model.

We use age 27 as the "censored age," after which we have no further information on such onset for the 194 subjects without financial difficulty and the exact age of onset of the turning point associated with financial difficulties for the 46 subjects with such an onset. Table 9.2 provides the

Table 9.2 Hazard of Sustained Financial Difficulty in the Transition to Adulthood
Associated with Sex, Family Socioeconomic Status (SES), and Prior Risk

Variable	Estimate	Standard error	χ^2	*p* value	Hazard ratio	95% confidence limits
Sex	−0.226	0.312	0.525	.47	0.798	0.433–1.470
Family SES	0.538	0.172	9.806	<.01	1.712	1.223–2.397
Verbal IQ	−0.027	0.013	4.037	<.05	0.974	0.949–0.998
Truancy	0.094	0.047	3.939	<.05	1.099	1.001–1.206

hazard ratios (the increased odds of onset of financial difficulty at any given time point) estimated in the SAS Cox regression model.

Each *SD* unit of higher family SES was associated with elevated hazard of new serious financial problems by 71.2%, perhaps because youth from lower SES families tended to have financial problems consistently over the post-high school decade. Each unit of higher IQ was associated with a 2.6% decrease (1.000 − 0.974) in the hazard of serious persistent financial problem. A history of school truancy during public school significantly increased the hazard of a serious financial problem in young adulthood.

Financial turning points and onset or persistence of psychiatric disorder

Much previous research has shown that serious financial problems may be associated with depression or depressive symptoms (Catalano, 1991; Dooley, Catalano, & Wilson, 1994; Hammarstrom & Janlert, 1997; Mendes, Rapp, & Kasl, 1994; Vinokur, Price, & Caplan, 1996). Associations with heavy alcohol use, alcohol abuse, and alcohol-related diseases have also been shown (Brenner, 1987; Conger, Ge, Elder, Lorenz, & Simons, 1994; Humphreys, Moos, & Finney, 1996; Moos, Fenn, Billings, & Moos, 1989; Peirce, Frone, & Cooper, 1996). Investigations of financial difficulty preceding onset or exacerbation of personality disorder have not been carried out.

The CIC study assessed psychiatric disorders both prior to and after the transition period, at about age 17 and again at about age 30 for this portion of the cohort. The earlier Axis I disorders (mood, anxiety, disruptive, and substance use disorders) were assessed by combined parent and youth report using the Diagnostic Interview Schedule for Children — 1 (Costello et al., 1984). Adolescent personality disorders were assessed by adaptation of adult questionnaires for suitability for child and parent report (Johnson, Cohen, Kasen, Skodol, & Brook, 1999). Post-transition

Table 9.3 Psychiatric Disorder Following Serious Sustained Financial
Difficulties between Ages 17 and 27

Psychiatric disorder	Financial difficulty turning point, number (%)		Adjusted odds ratio (95% CI)
	Yes (N = 46)	No (N = 193)	
Axis I disorder	16 (34.8)	39 (20.1)	2.25 (1.09–4.66)
Personality disorder	9 (19.6)	19 (9.8)	2.58 (1.05–6.36)
Mood disorder	7 (15.2)	20 (10.3)	1.52 (0.59–3.90)
Anxiety disorder	8 (17.4)	20 (10.3)	1.67 (0.67–4.14)
Substance abuse disorder	5 (10.9)	2 (1.0)	12.72 (2.31–70.05)

Note: CI, confidence interval.

diagnostic assessments were carried out by the Structured Clinical Interviews for DSM-IV Axis I Disorders and Axis II Personality Disorders (Skodol, Johnson, Cohen, & Crawford, 2007). In testing the relationship of persistent financial problem with the onset or persistence of psychiatric disorder, we compared this group with narrative data from the remainder of the transition sample. Prior disorder, IQ, and demographic variables (age at prior assessment, sex, race, and SES of family of origin) were included as control variables.

As shown in Table 9.3, in these logistic regression analyses, the association between a financial difficulty turning point and any subsequent psychiatric disorder reflected in the odds ratio (OR) was statistically significant net of the prior risks (OR = 2.25, confidence interval [CI] = 1.09 to 4.66). Whereas neither depressive nor anxiety disorders were elevated in association with a turning point in financial difficulty, the association with subsequent substance abuse disorder was extremely large (OR = 12.72, CI = 2.31 to 70.05). The association with personality disorder (OR = 2.58, CI = 1.05 to 6.36), although smaller, was also statistically significant. In additional analyses not detailed here, we showed that a particular risk of new onset of avoidant or dependent personality disorder during the fourth decade of life followed such financial difficulty.

Conclusion

Do these sustained financial difficulties with onset during the transition to adulthood reflect a risk or cause of subsequent disorder, or is this turning point indicator a sign of approaching or currently exacerbated psychiatric disorder? In this study, we could not unambiguously discriminate between these two possibilities. This is a common problem in the determination of factors associated with onset of disorder: Prior problems may be an early sign of functional decline associated with later frank symptoms, or potentially they may be causally related to such later disorder.

We were unable to make such a discrimination in our narrative interviews. Although our original intent in defining "difficulties" was to reflect problems not attributable to the narrator's behavior, we found that such a discrimination was difficult and counterproductive. For example, when a narrator or a narrator's partner ran up large credit card balances that they could not repay, even if this was potentially preventable, this caused serious and sometimes long-lasting problems. Thus, the turning point-associated subsequent disorders we identified here may reflect both effects of the difficulties encountered and earlier signs of the emergence of emotional and behavioral problems (presaging subsequent frank disorders). Such emergence may have weakened avoidance of difficulties but also may have been exacerbated by the extended effort to cope with these difficulties. Nevertheless, the identification of such turning points has been a useful exercise in the location of danger signals for subsequent disorder and strengthened our understanding of family and adolescent risks for experiencing such trials in the transition to adulthood.

References

Andrews, D. W. K. (1993). Tests for parameter instability and structural change with unknown change point. *Econometrica, 61,* 821–856.

Andrews, D. W. K., & Ploberger, W. (1994). Optimal tests when a nuisance parameter is present only under the alternative. *Econometrica, 62,* 1383–1414.

Bai, J. (1994). Least squares estimation of a shift in linear processes. *Journal of Time Series Analysis, 15,* 453–472.

Bai, J., & Perron, P. (1998). Estimating and testing linear models with multiple structural changes. *Econometrica, 66,* 47–78.

Bai, J., & Perron, P. (2003). Computation and analysis of multiple structural change models. *Journal of Applied Econometrics, 18,* 1–22.

Brenner, M. (1987). Economic change, alcohol consumption and heart disease mortality in nine industrialized countries. *Social Science and Medicine, 25,* 119–132.

Catalano, R. (1991). The health effects of economic insecurity. *American Journal of Public Health, 81,* 1148–1152.

Chong, T. T. L. (2001). Structural change in AR(1) models. *Econometric Theory, 17,* 87–155.

Chow, G. C. (1960). Tests of equality between sets of coefficients in two linear regressions. *Econometrica, 28,* 591–605.

Cohen, P., Chen, H., Hamigami, F., Gordon, K., & McArdle, J. J. (2000). Multilevel analyses for predicting sequence effects of financial and employment problems on the probability of arrest. *Journal of Quantitative Criminology, 16,* 223–235.

Cohen, P., & Cohen, J. (1996). *Life values and adolescent mental health.* Mahwah, NJ: Erlbaum.

Cohen, P., Cohen, J., Aiken, L. K., & West, S. G. (1999). The problem of units and the circumstance for POMP. *Multivariate Behavioral Research, 34,* 315–346.

Cohen, P., Kasen, S., Bifulco, A., Andrews, H., & Gordon K. (2005). The accuracy of adult narrative reports of developmental trajectories. *International Journal of Behavioral Development, 29,* 345–355.

Cohen, P., Kasen, S., Chen, H., Hartmark, C., & Gordon K. (2003). Variations in patterns of developmental transitions in the emerging adulthood period. *Developmental Psychology, 39,* 657–669.

Conger, R. D., Ge, X., Elder, G. H., Lorenz, F. O., & Simons, R. L. (1994). Financial problems, coercive family process, and developmental problems of adolescents. *Child Development, 65,* 541–561.

Costello, A. J., Edelbrock, C.S., Dulcan, M. K., Kalas, R., & Klaric, S. H. (1984). Testing of the NIMH diagnostic interview schedule for children (DISC) in a clinical population: Final report to the Center for Epidemiological Studies, National Institute for Mental Health. Pittsburgh, University of Pittsburgh.

Dooley, D., Catalano, R., & Wilson, G. (1994). Depression and unemployment. *American Journal of Community Psychology, 22,* 745–765.

Hammarstrom, A., & Janlert, U. (1997). Nervous and depressive symptoms in a longitudinal study of youth unemployment. *Journal of Adolescence, 20,* 293–305.

Hansen, B. E. (1997). Approximate asymptotic p-values for structural change tests. *Journal of Business and Economic Statistics, 15,* 60–67.

Humphreys, K., Moos, R. H., & Finney, J. W. (1996). Life domains, alcoholics anonymous, and role incumbency in the 3 year course of problem drinking. *Journal of Nervous and Mental Disease, 184,* 475–481.

Johnson, J. G., Cohen, P., Kasen, S., Skodol, A., & Brook, J. (2000). Age-related change in personality disorder trait levels between early adolescence and adulthood: A community-based longitudinal investigation. *Acta Psychiatrica Scandinavica, 102,* 265–275.

Lyketsos, C. G., Nestadt, G., Cwi, J., Helthoff, K., & Eaton, W. W. (1994). The Life Chart Interview: A standardized method to describe the course of psychopathology. *International Journal of Methods in Psychiatric Research, 4,* 143–155.

Mendes, C. F., Rapp, S. S., & Kasl, S. V. (1994). Financial strain and depression in a community sample of elderly men and women: A longitudinal study. *Journal of Aging and Health, 6,* 448–468.

Moos, R. H., Fenn, C. B., Billings, A. G., & Moos, B. S. (1989). Assessing life stressors and social resources: Applications to alcoholic patients. *Journal of Substance Abuse, 1,* 135–152.

Peirce, R. S., Frone, M. R., & Cooper, M. L. (1996). Financial stress, social support, and alcohol involvement: A longitudinal test of the buffering hypothesis in a general population survey. *Health Psychology, 15,* 38–47.

Quandt, R. E. (1960). Tests of the hypothesis that a linear regression obeys two separate regimes. *Journal of the American Statistical Association, 55,* 324–330.

Skodol, A. E., Johnson, J. G., Cohen, P., Sneed, J. R., & Crawford, T. N. (2007). Personality disorder and impaired functioning from adolescence to adulthood. *British Journal of Psychiatry, 190,* 415–420.

Vinokur, A. D., Price, R. H., & Caplan, R. D. (1996). Hard times and hurtful partners: How financial strain affects depression and relationship satisfaction of unemployed persons and their spouses. *Journal of Personality and Social Psychology, 71,* 166–179.

Zeileis, A. (2006). Implementing a class of structural change tests: An econometric computing approach. *Computational Statistics and Data Analysis, 50,* 2987–3008.

Zeileis, A., Leisch, F., Hornik, K., & Kleiber, C. (2002). Strucchange: An R package for testing for structural change in linear regression models. *Journal of Statistical Software, 7,* 1–38.

chapter ten

Developmental structural change in the maturity of role assumption

Patricia Cohen
New York State Psychiatric Institute and Columbia University

Kathy Gordon
New York State Psychiatric Institute

Stephanie Kasen
New York State Psychiatric Institute and Columbia University

Henian Chen
New York State Psychiatric Institute and Columbia University

Contents

Introduction 196
Narrative interviews 197
Monthly role function measures 197
Hypothesized differences in subgroups of this population-based
study 199
Analyses 200
    Women from above-average SES families 200
    Women from below-average SES families 203
Turning points in the relationship between two or more variables 208
    Narrator A 210
    Narrator B 211
    Narrator C 212
Conclusion 213
References 213

Introduction

Structural change over time is a "turning point" construct that crosses many disciplinary borders. Often, it is used to reflect a change in an organizational structure that is followed by other changes or even created to facilitate these changes. Historical studies may examine how change in some central variable or variables such as population size, density, or composition may promote a whole series of subsequent changes in the relationships among other variables. Structural change is a central construct in psychoanalysis in which therapeutic efficacy is often viewed as essentially involving changes in the connections among different constructs and affects (e.g. Huber, Henrich &, Klug, 2005; Sugarman, 2006). Developmental studies often focus on how a change in one or two variables may influence a change in a number of other variables, as for example puberty effects or effects of age-related decline or increase in cognitive function.

Here, we define *structural change* as a change in the relationships among two or more measured variables (Nesselroade, 2001; Nesselroade & Schmidt McCollam, 2000). This may be reflected in correlated changes in values of multiple variables over time for a single sampled unit, such as an individual, couple, or a group (Cattell's P or within-person factor analysis; Cattell, 1978). More commonly, empirical studies of structural change examine changes in the across-unit multivariate factor structure assessed on two or more occasions (Cattell's O factor analysis, 1978), such as before and after some significant event or as a consequence of therapeutic intervention. A major proponent of investigation of these phenomena has been John Nesselroade (Kim and Nesselroade 2003). Nevertheless, at a conference on factor analysis in the 21st century, both Nesselroade and Michael Browne introduced a number of cautions about the likely future of empirical efforts in this domain (Nesselroade, 2004).

On the whole, we found that structural change is seldom considered in developmental theory and related empirical investigations, but it is implicitly accepted when theoreticians agree that the meaning of some behaviors or even traits changes over developmental stages. In the analyses reported here, we employed ratings of narrative descriptions of behavior covering the 120 months of the decade between the 17th and 27th birthdays as described in Chapters 1, 4, and 9. These data were collected as part of the Children in the Community longitudinal study of a randomly sampled cohort. The study hypotheses involved tests of changes in the relationships among assumed roles that reflect maturational change over the decade, the central topic of this investigation. These first analyses examined differential age-related structural change in role behaviors for subgroups of these participants.

Narrative interviews

The transition study of the transition from adolescence to adulthood was carried out by telephone-based narrative interviews of a random sample of 400 young adults, typically taking 3 to 5 h to complete. Interviewers were intensively trained and supervised, employing a manual that provided many illustrations of the match of concrete behavioral examples to scale points. The data collection in this study began by establishing a framework for that 10-year period by asking the respondents to complete a Life Chart (Lyketsos, Nestadt, Cwi, Helthoff, & Eaton, 1994). This document, completed in advance of the interview, charts the changes over these years in where the subject lived, worked, and studied as well as dates of significant experiences that occurred then, such as graduations, special vacations or trips, engagements, marriage, births, major illness or victimization, special achievement or honors, or any other experiences that help the respondent to reconstruct the period covered by the interview.

Monthly role function measures

A central construct of the study was the extent to which, at each point in time, the respondent's role behavior was more like that of a child or approximated that of a *full adult*, defined as an individual having independence from parental control, expressing own goals and preferences, and assuming responsibilities. The narrative in this study covered six domains of the person's life: residence, finance, school, employment, romantic relationships, and parenting. Narrators were asked to describe their behaviors in each of these roles and settings, including responsibilities usually associated with greater maturity (called here *role level*) and the extent to which role-relevant decisions and choices were made by themselves or others (*role agency*). These narratives went most smoothly when each domain was addressed for the entire period, focusing on where they were on these issues and behaviors at the time of their 17th birthday and continuing to note changes as dated to the month in which they occurred over the decade. Thus, coding of the structured narrative method generated 120 consecutive monthly records on each of the defined variables, with the value of each code retained until the month when a new code was entered. To ensure reliability of measures, all interviewer-coded interviews were recorded and blindly recoded by another interviewer, and the scores were averaged across coders (For more about this narrative interview and its generally excellent interrater reliability, see Cohen, Kasen, Bifulco, Andrews, & Gordon (2005).

Role level was rated on a 100-point scale, where 0 represents a fully child-like role and 99 represents a wholly adult role. Behaviors or other indicators of a given level were provided in the detailed interviewer manual. Four transition role quality variables (agency, identification/satisfaction with current role, difficulty, and mastery) were also assessed in each transition domain. These were also rated on 100-point scales whenever a relevant change occurred in this decade. The lowest agency point (0) indicated that the current role was achieved entirely by external forces such as parental persuasion despite or against own preferences rather than by one's own design. The highest values (near 100), on the other hand, denoted that considerable personal effort and planning had preceded attainment of the current role. Identification scored near zero would indicate that even at that time the role was perceived to be highly incompatible with the narrator's needs, goals, and interests. For example, a participant might indicate being overwhelmed by full-time parenthood with regret that it had not been delayed, whereas a high rating would indicate that the newly assumed role was highly compatible with then-current goals and personal convictions. For example, dropping out of college might have been viewed as a very positive development at the time regardless of potential later reconsiderations.

These role-related variables seem particularly apt for identifying a structural change occurring over this transition period in which relinquishing earlier roles and assuming adult roles is normative. In the 10 years between their 17th and 27th birthdays, we expect young people to have major changes in the structure of their lives. These can be expected to be reflected in structural changes in how various aspects of their lives relate to each other. In an exploratory manner, we used factor analysis to find these changes.

Two tasks preceded our analyses: selection of the role variables most likely to show this turning point in the structural relationships among variables and consideration of demographic differences in how this turning point may be manifest. For the first task, we selected the two variables that indexed the move toward adult roles in four of our five domains: residence, career (combining employment and advanced education/training), financial support, and romantic partnering. For each of the domains, we included both role level and the role agency indicating how instrumental they were in achieving the role status that they were in at the time. We did not use the family formation role variables for two reasons: First, in the early post-high school years most men and women were not at all interested in assuming such a role in the near future. This lack of variance

made it more appropriate to view this variable as a potential explanation of turning points in the structural relationships among other role
variables. Second, the agency variable in the family formation domain is
problematic because its meaning was conditional on the level of family
formation: Sometimes it assessed how instrumental they were in avoiding
pregnancy and at other times how instrumental they were in becoming
pregnant or caring for existing children.

Hypothesized differences in subgroups of this population-based study

We hypothesized that the most powerful demographic influences on the
timing and nature of the changes in the structure of role behaviors would
be gender and socioeconomic status (SES) of the family of origin. Despite a
"loosening" of cultural norms for sex-specific roles, the traditional differences in the nature and timing of such role assumptions remain influential, probably influenced both by biological sex differences related to child
bearing and rearing and by residual cultural differences. In addition to
sex differences, a powerful influence on life trajectories and role assumption is socioeconomic class of family of origin. These differences come
partly from the constraints on offspring role assumption attributable to
(1) lack of family resources, (2) limits on the option-facilitating social con-
tacts of lower SES families, and (3) subcultural differences in expectations
and lifestyles that tend to characterize families from different SES backgrounds. Therefore, we examined turning points in the structural relationships among role variables in four groups: males and females from
families who were above and below the average level on an SES index that
combined standardized measures of family income, parental education
level, and occupational status of parents.

Combining these observations, we examined two basic hypotheses.
First, because youth from lower SES families tend to assume more adult
roles at a younger age, we hypothesized that age changes in the structure of role assumption variables from these individuals' 18th to their 26th
years would be less. Second, there is, nevertheless, a still strong influence of
gender-specific expectations regarding roles. Therefore, we hypothesized
that sex differences in the structure of role assumption at both ages would
be similar for youth from lower and higher socioeconomic class families.

We selected 2 years to represent the "pre" and "post" periods with
regard to a turning point in the structure of roles that represented the
transition from adolescence to adulthood. For each group, we examined
the factor structure in the year beginning with their 18th birthday and
compared it to the year beginning with 26th year, averaging for each

Table 10.1 Means (Standard Deviation, SD) for Each of the Study Variables
for Women from Higher (N = 71) and Lower (N = 55) Socioeconomic
Status (SES) Families at Ages 18 and 25

Domain	Variable	High SES Mean (SD)		Low SES Mean (SD)	
		18 years	25 years	18 years	25 years
Career	Level	23.6(21.9)	58.2(28.1)	28.4(23.8)	48.8(27.8)
	Agency	51.6(11.4)	62.8(11.7)	51.9(12.5)	59.4(15.4)
Finance	Level	32.2(19.2)	58.1(21.8)	28.5(19.8)	49.8(23.4)
	Agency	40.5(13.7)	61.6(12.9)	43.8(15.0)	56.6(15.3)
Residence	Level	33.2(11.9)	66.5(16.2)	34.3(15.8)	65.6(17.8)
	Agency	35.0(14.6)	62.7(13.3)	33.7(13.3)	60.5(14.8)
Partner	Level	33.2(23.2)	66.1(29.4)	40.9(26.0)	65.2(28.1)
	Agency	46.7(14.0)	55.0(12.1)	48.8(12.1)	52.0(11.4)
Parenting	Level	1.4(6.2)	21.5(33.2)	11.8(23.8)	41.0(35.8)

participant the values of each variable over the 12 months in the year. We
report findings here for women from high and low SES families, a more
complete report is examined all four groups.

Table 10.1 provides the means and standard deviations of each of the
study variables for each of the two groups of women at each of the two
selected ages.

Analyses

For each group we carried out a factor analysis of the set of eight variables
at each age, using a promax rotation of principal components with values
exceeding 1.0.

Women from above-average SES families

As noted, the factored variables included level of adult role assumption
and level of agency in achieving that role with regard to residence, career
(combining employment and advanced education/training), financial
support, and romantic partnering. Table 10.2 shows the correlation matrix
and three-factor structure at age 18 for this group of women. Here, we see
a factor that combines role level and agency in obtaining that role for both
financial support and career. A second factor includes the role and agency

Table 10.2 Role Variable Correlations and Factor Loadings at Ages 18 and 25 for 71 Women from Higher Socioeconomic Status Families

Age 18 domain	Variable	Career	Finance		Residence		Partner		Factor Loadings		
		Agency	Level	Agency	Level	Agency	Level	Agency	I	II	III
Career	Level$_{18}$	.34	.49	.45	.08	0.0	.32	.04	.90		
	Agency$_{18}$		.15	.25	.01	.18	.09	.10	.54		
Finance	Level$_{18}$			.58	.29	.18	.02	-.04	.74		
	Agency$_{18}$				.38	.34	.12	.08	.65		
Residence	Level$_{18}$					.54	-.03	-.04		.87	
	Agency$_{18}$						.22	.17		.87	
Partner	Level$_{18}$							.50			.84
	Agency$_{18}$										.84

(Continued)

Table 10.2 Role Variable Correlations and Factor Loadings at Ages 18 and 25 for 71 Women from Higher Socioeconomic Status Families (Continued)

Age 25 domain	Variable	Career	Finance		Residence		Partner		Factor Loadings		
		Agency	Level	Agency	Level	Agency	Level	Agency	I	II	III
Career	$Level_{25}$	.25	.68	.20	-.22	-.16	-.10	-.14	.56		
	$Agency_{25}$		.23	.42	.15	.20	.09	-.06	.75		
Finance	$Level_{25}$			.50	-.15	-.14	-.28	-.25	.69		
	$Agency_{25}$				.06	.13	-.01	-.01	.85		
Residence	$Level_{25}$					.63	.42	-.16		.92	
	$Agency_{25}$						.31	.07		.81	
Partner	$Level_{25}$							.49		.68	
	$Agency_{25}$										.99

Note: $r > \pm .22$, $p < .05$.

Factor correlations: Age 18, Factors 1, 2 = .30, Factors 1, 3 = .07, Factors 2, 3 = .00; Age 25, Factors 1, 2 = -.15, Factors 1, 3 = -.29, Factors 2, 3 = .25.

variables for residence, and the third factor includes the role and agency variables for romantic partnership. The correlation between the first two factors was .30, and neither was significantly correlated with the romantic partnership factor.

The factor analysis in Table 10.2 of roles for this same group of women at age 25 also yielded three factors. The first included the same variables as in the first in the analyses of age 18 roles: both level and agency for the career and financial support domains. However, at this age, the agency loadings were larger than the level variables, whereas at the earlier age they were approximately equal. The second factor again included the two residential variables; however, at this age romantic partnership also loaded on this factor. The third factor included only the romantic agency variable.

Perhaps the most striking difference in this factor structure was the change from a positive correlation between the first two factors at the younger age to a negative correlation at the older age. This finding along with romantic partnership's new relationship with residential level and agency suggest a new interpretation of the second factor. Graphic presentations of these factors and correlated variables make the differences in the structure of these variables at these two ages apparent (Figure 10.1). At the earlier age, the positive correlation between the career/finance and residence factors may be taken as primarily a reflection of the relationship between beginning maturity and independence in these young women in these three domains (career, financial support, and residence), which in this above-average SES group was *not* related to romantic involvement level. In the age 25 data, in contrast, the second factor may be better interpreted as a measure of the development of a home rather than as an expression of independence. And, to some degree this development is in conflict with a focus on career development and financial independence, as demonstrated by the now-negative correlation between these two factors.

This interpretation was further supported when we added the family formation (parenting) role-level variable as a correlate of these factors. As noted, this variable had virtually no variance at age 18. However, it was related to each of the factors at age 25: negatively with the career/finance factor, positively with the residence-partner commitment factor, and positively with the partner agency factor (see Figure 10.1). Thus, this third "factor" of partner agency may be most critical when the young woman is desiring offspring, is pregnant, or has offspring but no current partner, perhaps as a consequence of divorce.

Women from below-average SES families

As noted, we anticipated that the factor structure of role-related variables would differ by SES of the family of origin. In Table 10.3 we provide the

High SES females

At 18-years old

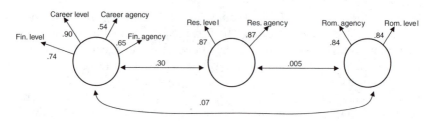

At 25-years old

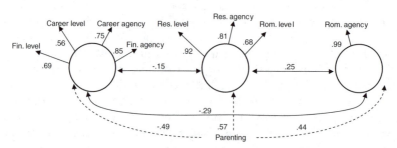

Figure 10.1 Structure of factors and related variables at ages 18 and 25 for women from higher SES families.

Abbreviations are: Fin = Finance, Res = Residence, Rom = Romance

correlations and factor structure of the same variables as shown above at age 18 and 25. Again, the set of eight variables at each age was factored using a promax rotation of principal components with values exceeding 1.0.

At age 18, we see that financial level of self-support and agency in getting to that level were on a factor by themselves, although this factor was correlated (+0.30) with the third factor that included career level and agency. In this population, career level and agency combined with partner agency for these young women, suggesting a potential "look ahead" for a segment of this population. Residence level and agency combined with level of partner commitment, showing a pattern that was apparent in the older girls from the higher SES families. On the whole, an outstanding characteristic of the structure of these role variables at this age is the impact of level of romantic commitment and agency on residential, career, and financial roles. This is in contrast to the independence of romantic role in the 18-year-old women from above-average SES families. The correlation

Table 10.3 Role Variable Correlations and Factor Loadings at Ages 18 and 25 for 55 Women from Lower Socioeconomic Status Families of Origin

Age 18 domain	Variable	Career	Finance		Residence		Partner		Factor Loadings		
		Agency	Level	Agency	Level	Agency	Level	Agency	I	II	III
Career	Level$_{18}$	.48	.45	.46	-.18	-.16	-.23	.27			.58
	Agency$_{18}$		.18	.35	.01	-.04	.05	.36			.85
Finance	Level$_{18}$			.72	-.24	.06	-.35	.06	.97		
	Agency$_{18}$				-.03	.04	-.20	.24	.85		
Residence	Level$_{18}$					.62	.52	.17		.86	
	Agency$_{18}$						.41	.19		.92	
Partner	Level$_{18}$							.10		.63	
	Agency$_{18}$										.73

(Continued)

Table 10.3 Role Variable Correlations and Factor Loadings at Ages 18 and 25 for 55 Women from Lower Socioeconomic Status Families of Origin (Continued)

Age 25 domain	Variable	Career	Finance		Residence		Partner		Factor Loading		
		Agency	Level	Agency	Level	Agency	Level	Agency	I	II	III
Career	Level25	.71	.68	.63	.00	.16	-.23	.18	.88		
	Agency25		.51	.55	.15	.31	-.02	.15	.77		
Finance	Level25			.78	.02	.23	-.21	.10	.87		
	Agency25				.09	.33	-.20	.14	.87		
Residence	Level25					.71	.54	.14		.92	
	Agency25						.22	.11		.76	
Partner	Level25							.17		.73	
	Agency25										(.29)

Note: r > ± .22, p < .05

Factor correlations   Age 18: Factors 1, 2 = −.23, Factors 1, 3 = .30, Factors 2, 3 = .02 Age 25: Factors 1, 2 = .07.

Low SES females

At 18-years old

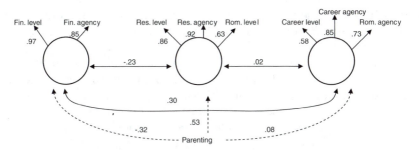

At 25-years old

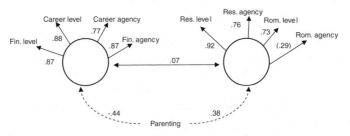

Figure 10.2 Structure of factors and related variables at ages 18 and 25 for women from lower SES families.

Abbreviations are as above: Fin = Finance, Res = Residence, Rom = Romance

between the first two factors was −.23, showing that financial independence/maturity did not go with residential independence/maturity for these 18-year-olds, unlike the positive correlation found for the higher SES family offspring. Again, the pattern of the higher SES women at age 25 was more like that of the lower SES women at age 18, with evidence of alternative role focus, home building versus financial independence.

In the graphic presentation of these factors (Figure 10.2), we add parenting and again show that the variable relationship pattern of these younger women from lower SES families was more like that of the 25-year-old women from higher SES families. Parenting was highly correlated (*r* = .53) with the residential/romantic commitment level factor and negatively correlated with the financial factor, although not with the career/romantic agency factor.

At age 25, the factor structure has consolidated to two factors, much more similar to that of the same-age women from higher SES families. However, the clear conflict between career/financial independence and homemaking/parenting shown in the latter group did not characterize these women: The two factors were uncorrelated, and the only trace of such an effect remained in the correlations of opposite sign of parenting with these two factors.

Thus, both groups may be seen to have experienced a turning point in this period of transition to adulthood when this point is defined as a structural change in the relationships among the different roles assumed, or not assumed, by these young women. To some extent, the larger differences in the structure of these roles in women from higher as compared to lower SES families of origin in the immediate post-high school years were lessened as they approached full adulthood. Nevertheless, a "conflict" between home and career that developed in the young women from higher SES backgrounds was not distinct in those from lower SES families.

Turning points in the relationship between two or more variables

In the next analyses, we attempted to identify structural change defined as change in the relationships between changes over time in two variables. These analyses began with an entire study sample and continued with identification of individuals within the sample who may have had such a turning point experience. Again using the narrative data from the transition study, we explored the utility of examining time-related change in the relationship between two aggregate variables as reported by individual narrators.

Again, the rationale was based on theory regarding role development. These analyses examined the relationship between two characteristics of role function averaged across the different role domains. The basic hypothesis motivating this investigation was that "choices" in early adulthood as reflected in our agency variables may be poorly or even negatively related to satisfaction with the role once it is assumed (reflected in our "identification" variable). Thus, in the initial post-high school years a young person may elect to move out of the family home and try to maintain an independent residence. Having done so, this young person may find that residence maintenance tasks are a time-consuming nuisance. Similar discrepancies between having made and worked toward choices in education/training programs, financial independence, or romantic partner selection and the subsequent evaluation of the consequent assumed roles may be more likely at this early age. With increasing maturity and experience, we hypothesized that, on average, the relationship between the effort expended to secure a given role and the satisfaction or identification with

Table 10.4 Multilevel Model of Prediction of Role Satisfaction over the Months from the 17th to the 27th Birthday from Age and Role Agency in a Sample of 239 Narrators

	Mean (*SE*)	Linear trajectory (*SE*)	Agency(*SE*)	Year × Agency (*SE*)
Variance across narrators	28.20 (2.60)**	1.235 (.116)**		
Fixed effects	54.99 (0.35)**	−0.148 (0.073)*	0.435 (0.005)**	0.042 (0.001)**

Note: SE, standard error.

*p < .05. **p < .001.

that role when attained will become increasingly positive. Initial analyses tested this hypothesis for the group as a whole.

These analyses consisted of multilevel regressions of means and linear trajectories of role satisfaction of 239 narrators over the 120 months from the 17th to the 27th birthdays. Predictors at the "fixed" or average-level analysis were age (centered at 22 with units representing annual change), role agency (centered), and the role agency × age interaction. Table 10.4 provides the results of these analyses in which we can see the significance of the hypothesized relationship, on average, with the *B* for agency increasing from (0.435 − 5 years*0.042) = .225 at age 17 to (0.435 + 5 years*0.042) = 0.645 at age 27. We also note that there remained significant individual-level variance in the annual changes in role satisfaction over the decade (1.235, *SE* [standard error] = 116, *p* < .001).

But, of course, such an average effect does not necessarily indicate that there may be a more abrupt turning point for some individuals or a longer-term significance of this changing relationship. On the other hand, should we find some participants who are less satisfied with increasing agency as they age, might they be moving toward future emotional or other life problems?

To investigate these issues, we carried out parallel analyses on each of the 239 narrators, seeking to identify those with a potential turning point. From these analyses, we then focused on those with a sizable age-by-agency interaction. Because of the possibility that this change in some narrators may reflect sparse variance in either satisfaction or agency rather than a strong overall influence, we also examined means and standard deviations of both agency and satisfaction. Our effort to select those with the most dramatic structural change proceeded by examination of those narrators with the most extreme age-by-agency interactions. In addition to high values on the interaction, we added a further criterion on inspection

Table 10.5 Prediction of Role Satisfaction over the Months from
the 17th to the 27th Birthday from Age and Role Agency in 3
Narrators with Extreme Age × Agency Interactions

Narrator	Age × Agency	SD agency	SD satisfaction
A	−.309	5.72	8.22
B	.291	7.25	5.43
C	.447	5.51	11.41

Note: SD, standard deviation.

of the data on these participants, namely, that they also showed substantial variance over time in both satisfaction and agency. In the absence of this criterion, some extreme values of the interaction were produced by high stability in one or both variables followed by relatively brief instability. Table 10.5 provides these estimates for three narrators with extreme positive and narrative age-by-agency interactions and relatively high variable in agency and satisfaction. In Figure 10.3, we present the raw and smoothed data on three of the study narrators selected in this manner.

We present here information on these narrators (Figure 10.3) who showed relatively clear turning points in the relationship between agency and satisfaction. The lines represent a Lowess smoother (tension = .50), which allows for easier pattern recognition than the original data points.

Narrator A

In the teen years we probed, both agency and satisfaction with roles were extremely stable. Then, agency began a slow rise, although somewhat less than is normative for these years, but satisfaction fell rapidly. This pattern continued to his 27th birthday. This narrator lived with his parents for several years after high school and continued to receive financial support from them. He had a serious romantic partner, but when he was almost 22, she initiated a breakup. In the data points in the figure, his satisfaction remained above 60 up to this point (although the smoothing line anticipates the change in trajectory). Then, following a series of events not shown here, his satisfaction continued downhill. After age 23, he moved out of his parental home and became financially independent. Whereas he was satisfied with his resulting living arrangements, he was unhappy with his financial situation. For a few years, he initiated a business of his own; following discontinuation of this effort, he was dissatisfied with his employment situation. A new romantic relationship began in which he was never very happy. This narrator also nominated the apparent

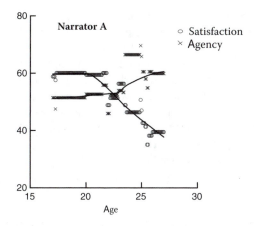

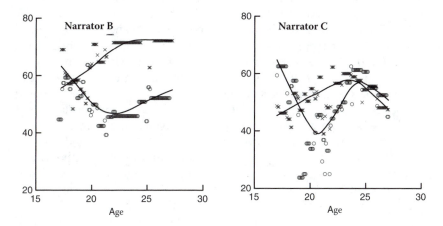

Figure 10.3 Raw and smoothed data on role agency and role satisfaction based on three narrators from the transitions study.

precipitating event that led to this negative relationship between agency and satisfaction. When asked if he had ever experienced a failure that hurt him deeply, he nominated the breakup of his relationship at age 22. He also reported treatment for depression about a year later.

Narrator B

For Narrator B, agency and satisfaction had a negative correlation for the first 4 years of the reported period. As with many late adolescents, her life appears somewhat chaotic in the record. Her residence changed several times, including a return to the parental home. She attended college for several months and then quit. Before her 20th birthday, she had a baby and became a single head of household. Over this whole period, her role agency increased, but her role satisfaction decreased. When she reached 21, this relationship changed. Her agency slowed its increase and eventually leveled off. But, her satisfaction reached a low point at age 21 and then rose steadily to age 27. In the record, the only specific event we could suggest as a "precipitator" of this change was a very brief period when she was on welfare. After this, her life was quite stable.

Narrator C

Narrator C is another for whom agency and satisfaction had a negative correlation in the early years of the period covered. Like many young people, her independence emerged in fits and starts, with "relapses" into dependence on her parents. Between high school graduation and age 23, she had five periods when she lived with her parents and otherwise lived by herself, with friends, or with a partner. She also had periods when she turned to her parents for financial support. When she first moved out and lived on her own, she was quite instrumental in making this move (agency = 62.5) but not well satisfied with the situation that eventuated (satisfaction = 25). She was not eager to move back to her parents (agency = 47.5), but when she got there it was an improvement (satisfaction = 60). This illustrates the negative correlation between her agency and satisfaction that was not uncommon in young people first trying out their independence but who were not so happy with the results. Romantically, this young woman had a steady partner from age 17 to nearly 21. The level of commitment in this relationship was never high, and it declined toward its end, when they mutually agreed to a breakup. She tried a new relationship but broke up at age 22. Then, at age 23 she began another romantic relationship that became a serious commitment within a year and continued to age 27. She had a baby when nearly 25 and another soon after. In this case, no single event seems to mark the turning point, but a period of experimenting with independence seemed to gradually give way to building an independent life. Subsequently, agency and satisfaction increased in tandem. The downturn in agency at around age 24 probably represents the mutual decision making necessary in a relationship with a commitment to a shared future.

On the whole, for those narrators who represent relative extremes in the changing relationship between agency and satisfaction, most unambiguous turning points involved romantic role commitment (connecting with or disconnecting from a romantic partner). As we predicted, a structural change in the relationship between agency and satisfaction (averaged over residential, financial, career, romantic, and family formation domains) did identify some narrators who had a significant turning point in the relationship between role agency and role satisfaction.

Conclusion

What have we learned about identifying turning points in individuals from these data? These illustrations confirmed two of our conclusions from our several efforts to identify individuals with turning points in individual variables. The first is that there needs to be an appropriate match between the level of detail and frequency of potential "points" manifest in the data and the level of change that is implied in the study's turning point definition. Whereas a sufficient number of time points and amount of detail is necessary, it is also possible to have a number that may be too great to yield an unambiguous answer to the turning point issue in question. When there are a large number of assessed points, use of a smoother may make the overall trend much easier to see.

The second conclusion comes from our review of Dr. Rutter's wise paper on turning points in human development (Rutter, 1996). There may be many nontrivial changes in an individual's behavior, perspective, or trajectory in life. Those that may be identified at a given point may nevertheless have a substantial history of "germination." Thus, when asked, an individual may identify an important long-term change in goals, feelings about others, self-concept, understood options, or even constraints. Yet, these may not be readily observed even by those who are close to the individual and may take an extended period to actually come to fruition, if ever. By the time such turning points have been accomplished, those close to the individual may have gradually accepted the new directions as part of the person without reflection on the change itself.

References

Cattell, R.B. (1978) *The scientific use of factor analysis in behavioral and life sciences.* New York: Plenum Press.

Cohen, P., Kasen, S., Bifulco, A., Andrews, H., & Gordon, K. (2005). The accuracy of adult narrative reports of developmental trajectories. *International Journal of Behavioral Development, Narrative-Based, 29,* 345–355.Huber, D., Henrich, G., & Klug, G. (2005) The scales of psychological capacities: Measuring change in psychic structure. *Psychotherapy Research, 15,* 445–456.

Kim, J. E., & Nesselroade, J. R. (2003). Relationships among social support, self-concept, and wellbeing of older adults: A study of process using dynamic factor models. *International Journal of Behavioral Development. 27,* 49–65.

Lyketsos, C. G., Nestadt, G., Cwi, J., Helthoff, K., & Eaton, W. W. (1994). The Life Chart Interview: A standardized method to describe the course of psychopathology. *International Journal of Methods in Psychiatric Research, 4,* 143–155.

Nesselroade, J. R. (2001). Intraindividual variability in development within and between individuals. *European Psychologist, 6,* 187–193.

Nesselroade, J. R. (2004, May 14). *Factoring at the individual level: Some matters for the second century of factor analysis.* Paper presented at the conference Factor Analysis at 100: Historical Developments and Future Directions. Retrieved August 6, 2007, from http://www.fa100.info/nesselroade.pdf.

Nesselroade, J. R., & Schmidt McCollam, K. M. (2000). Putting the process in developmental processes. *International Journal of Behavioral Development, 24,* 295–300.

Rutter, M. (1996). Transitions and turning points in developmental psychopathology as applied to the age span between childhood and mid-adulthood. *International Journal of Behavioral Development, 19,* 603–626.

Sugarman, A.(2006). Mentalization, insightfulness, and therapeutic action: The importance of mental organization. *International Journal of Psychoanalysis, 87,* 965–987.

appendix one

Computer programs for change-point analysis

The SAS profile likelihood script for estimating quadratic-linear mixed-effects model

```
%macro changepoint;
data temp&count;
set temp;
if tage GE &count then tage1=0;
if tage LT &count then tage1=(tage-&count)*(tage-&count);
run;
%mend changepoint;
%macro mixed;
ods output fitstatistics=fit&count ;
proc mixed data=temp&count method=ml;
class person;
model gc=tage tage1/solution chisq;
random intercept tage tage1/type=un subject=person G GCORR;
run;
%mend mixed;
%macro output;
data fit&count;
set fit&count;
value&count=value;
drop value;
run;
data fit;
merge fit fit&count;
run;
%mend output;
%MACRO ALLJOB;
        %LOCAL count;
        %LOCAL stop;
        %LET stop = 30;
        %LET count= 10;
```

```
      %DO %WHILE (&count <= &stop);
            %changepoint;
            %mixed;
            %output;
%LET count = %EVAL(&count+1); *Increment count by 1;
            %END;
%MEND ALLJOB;
%ALLJOB;
proc print data=fit;
run;
```

The NLMIXED script for estimating quadratic-linear mixed-effects model

```
/*Starting values were chosen from the results of
profile likelihood estimates*/
PROC NLMIXED data=temp method=firo;
PARMS ml=81 ms1=0.1 ms2=-0.2 mtau=21
ve=12.3 v0=73.9 v1=0.012 v2=0.0006 v3=1 to 10 by 1
c01=-0.65 c02=-0.17 c03=-5 to 5 by 1
c12=0.0015 c13=-1 to 1 by 0.5 c23=-1 to 1 by 0.5;
 l = ml + d0 ;
 s1 = ms1 + d1 ;
 s2 = ms2 + d2 ;
       tau = mtau + d3 ;
 yt = l + s1 * tage + s2 *
max(0,tau-tage)*max(0,tau-tage);
       MODEL gc ~ NORMAL(yt, ve);
 RANDOM d0 d1 d2 d3 ~ NORMAL([0,0,0,0],
       [v0,
       c01, v1,
       c02, c12, v2,
       c03, c13, c23, v3]) SUBJECT=person;
  RUN;
```

The winBUGS script for estimating bivariate quadratic-linear mixed-effects model

```
model;
{
# likelihood for gc and gf
 for( i in 1 : nsubj ) {
 for( j in 1 : ntime ) {
 gc[i , j] ~ dnorm(mugc[i , j],taugc)
```

```
  mugc[i , j] <- b[i,1] + b[i,2] * age[i , j] + b[i,3] *
(max(0,b[i,4]-age[i , j] ))*(max(0,b[i,4]-age[i , j] ))
  gf[i , j] ~ dnorm(mugf[i , j],taugf)
  mugf[i , j] <- b[i,5] + b[i,6] * age[i , j] + b[i,7] *
(max(0,b[i,8]-age[i , j] ))*(max(0,b[i,8]-age[i , j] ))
  } }
# prior distribution for the inverse of the intra-
individual variability of gc and gf
  taugc ~ dgamma(0.001,0.001)
  taugf ~ dgamma(0.001,0.001)
# hyperprior distribution for the random-effects
parameters
  for( i in 1 : nsubj ) {
  b[i,1:8]~dmnorm(mub[1:8], taub[1:8,1:8])
  }
#hyperprior distribution of the fixed parameters
  mub[1:8]~dmnorm(mean[1:8],prec[1:8,1:8])
  taub[1:8, 1:8] ~ dwish(R[1:8, 1:8], 8)
  sigma2[1:8, 1:8] <- inverse(taub[1:8, 1:8])
  for (i in 1 : 8) {sigmab[i] <- sqrt(sigma2[i, i]) }
  sigmagc <- 1 / sqrt(taugc)
  sigmagf <- 1 / sqrt(taugf)
}
# known matrix loading
mean = c(0, 0, 0,0,0,0,0,0)
R = structure(.Data = c(0.1, 0, 0,0,0,0,0,0,
                  0, 0.1, 0,0,0,0,0,0,
                  0, 0, 0.1,0,0,0,0,0,
                  0,0,0,0.1,0,0,0,0,
                  0,0,0,0,0,0,0.1,0,
                  0,0,0,0,0,0,0,0.1
                  0,0,0,0,0,0,0.1,0
                  0,0,0,0,0,0,0,0.1
                  ), .Dim = c(8, 8))
prec = structure(.Data = c(1.0E-6, 0, 0,0,0,0,0,0,
                  0, 1.0E-6, 0,0,0,0,0,0,
                  0, 0, 1.0E-6,0,0,0,0,0,
                  0,0,0,1.0E-6,0,0,0,0,
                  0,0,0,0,1.0E-6,0,0,0,
                  0,0,0,0,0,1.0E-6,0,0,
                  0,0,0,0,0,0,1.0E-6,0,
                  0,0,0,0,0,0,0,1.0E-6
                  ), .Dim = c(8, 8))
```

appendix two

Equivalent forms of the Level 1 equation for the bereavement model in Chapter 7

$$Y_{ij} = d_{ij} \cdot B_i + (1 - d_{ij}) \cdot \left[B_i + \Delta_{BL,i} + \Delta_{LF,i} - \Delta_{LF,i} \cdot e^{-S \cdot t_{ij}} \right] + \varepsilon_{ij} \qquad \text{(A2.1)}$$

$$Y_{ij} = d_{ij} \cdot B_i + (1 - d_{ij}) \cdot \left[F_i + (B_i + \Delta_{BL,i} - F_i) \cdot e^{-S \cdot t_{ij}} \right] + \varepsilon_{ij} \qquad \text{(A2.2)}$$

$$Y_{ij} = d_{ij} \cdot B_i + (1 - d_{ij}) \cdot \left[B_i + \Delta_{BF,i} + (\Delta_{BL,i} - \Delta_{BF,i}) \cdot e^{-S \cdot t_{ij}} \right] + \varepsilon_{ij} \qquad \text{(A2.3)}$$

$$Y_{ij} = d_{ij} \cdot B_i + (1 - d_{ij}) \cdot \left[L_i + \Delta_{LF,i} - \Delta_{LF,i} \cdot e^{-S \cdot t_{ij}} \right] + \varepsilon_{ij} \qquad \text{(A2.4)}$$

$$Y_{ij} = d_{ij} \cdot B_i + (1 - d_{ij}) \cdot \left[F_i + (L_i - F_i) \cdot e^{-S \cdot t_{ij}} \right] + \varepsilon_{ij} \qquad \text{(A2.5)}$$

$$Y_{ij} = d_{ij} \cdot B_i + (1 - d_{ij}) \cdot \left[B_i + \Delta_{BF,i} + (L_i - B_i - \Delta_{BF,i}) \cdot e^{-S \cdot t_{ij}} \right] + \varepsilon_{ij} \qquad \text{(A2.6)}$$

$$Y_{ij} = d_{ij} \cdot B_i + (1 - d_{ij}) \cdot \left[F_i - \Delta_{LF,i} \cdot e^{-S \cdot t_{ij}} \right] + \varepsilon_{ij} \qquad \text{(A2.7)}$$

$$Y_{ij} = d_{ij} \cdot B_i + (1 - d_{ij}) \cdot \left[B_i + \Delta_{BF,i} - \Delta_{LF,i} \cdot e^{-S \cdot t_{ij}} \right] + \varepsilon_{ij} \qquad \text{(A2.8)}$$

$$Y_{ij} = d_{ij} \cdot (L_i - \Delta_{BL,i}) + (1 - d_{ij}) \cdot \left[L_i + \Delta_{LF,i} - \Delta_{LF,i} \cdot e^{-S \cdot t_{ij}} \right] + \varepsilon_{ij} \qquad \text{(A2.9)}$$

$$Y_{ij} = d_{ij} \cdot (L_i - \Delta_{BL,i}) + (1 - d_{ij}) \cdot \left[F_i + (L_i - F_i) \cdot e^{-S \cdot t_{ij}} \right] + \varepsilon_{ij} \qquad \text{(A2.10)}$$

$$Y_{ij} = d_{ij} \cdot (L_i - \Delta_{BL,i}) + (1 - d_{ij}) \cdot \left[L_i - \Delta_{BL,i} + \Delta_{BF,i} \right.$$

$$\left. + (\Delta_{BL,i} - \Delta_{BF,i}) \cdot e^{-S \cdot t_{ij}} \right] + \varepsilon_{ij} \tag{A2.11}$$

$$Y_{ij} = d_{ij} \cdot (F_i - \Delta_{LF,i} - \Delta_{BL,i}) + (1 - d_{ij}) \cdot [F_i - \Delta_{LF,i} \cdot e^{-S \cdot t_{ij}}] + \varepsilon_{ij} \tag{A2.12}$$

$$Y_{ij} = d_{ij} \cdot (L_i + \Delta_{LF,i} - \Delta_{BF,i}) + (1 - d_{ij}) \cdot \left[L_i + \Delta_{LF,i} - \Delta_{LF,i} \cdot e^{-S \cdot t_{ij}} \right] + \varepsilon_{ij} \tag{A2.13}$$

$$Y_{ij} = d_{ij} \cdot (F_i - \Delta_{BF,i}) + (1 - d_{ij}) \cdot \left[F_i + (L_i - F_i) \cdot e^{-S \cdot t_{ij}} \right] + \varepsilon_{ij} \tag{A2.14}$$

$$Y_{ij} = d_{ij} \cdot (F_i - \Delta_{BF,i}) + (1 - d_{ij}) \cdot \left[F_i - \Delta_{LF,i} \cdot e^{-S \cdot t_{ij}} \right] + \varepsilon_{ij} \tag{A2.15}$$

appendix three A

The variance of the EWMA statistic assuming ARMA (1,1) noise

The ARMA(1,1) process is defined as

$$X_t - \phi X_{t-1} = W_t + \theta W_{t-1} \tag{A1}$$

where ϕ .and θ are constants, and W_t is a normally distributed white noise process with mean 0 and variance σ^2. The autocorrelation function for an ARMA(1,1) process can be calculated (Brockwell & Davis, 2002) as follows:

$$\gamma(h) = \begin{cases} \dfrac{1+\theta^2+2\phi\theta}{1-\phi^2}\sigma^2 & \text{if } h = 0 \\[2ex] \dfrac{(1-\phi\theta)(\phi-\theta)}{1-\phi^2}\sigma^2\phi^{h-1} & \text{if } h \geq 1 \end{cases} \tag{A2}$$

In deriving the variance of the EWMA statistic we assume throughout that $\theta_0 = 0$, and thus $E(Z_t) = 0$. Also, it is beneficial to use the second form of the statistic given in Equation A5, that is,

$$Z_t = \lambda \sum_{i=0}^{t-1}(1-\lambda)^i Z_{t-i}. \tag{A3}$$

In this format, we see that

$$Var(Z_t) = E\left(Z_t^2\right) = \lambda^2 \sum_{i=0}^{t-1}\sum_{j=0}^{t-1}(1-\lambda)^i(1-\lambda)^j \gamma(i-j)$$

$$= \lambda^2 \sum_{i=0}^{t-1}(1-\lambda)^{2i}\gamma(0) + 2\lambda^2 \sum_{i=0}^{t-2}\sum_{j=i+1}^{t-1}(1-\lambda)^j \phi^{j-i-1}\gamma(1)$$

$$= \frac{\lambda^2\gamma(0)}{\lambda(2-\lambda)}(1-(1-\lambda)^{2t}) + \frac{2\lambda^2\gamma(1)}{\phi}\sum_{i=0}^{t-2}\left(\frac{1-\lambda}{\phi}\right)^i\sum_{j=i+1}^{t-1}(\phi(1-\lambda))^j \tag{A4}$$

The variance of Z_t can be simplified further under the additional assumption that $|\phi(1-\lambda)| < 1$. In this situation, the second sum can be written:

$$\sum_{i=0}^{t-2}\left(\frac{1-\lambda}{\phi}\right)^i \sum_{j=i+2}^{t-1}(\phi(1-\lambda))^j = \sum_{i=0}^{t-2}\left(\frac{1-\lambda}{\phi}\right)^i \left(\frac{(\phi(1-\lambda))^{i+1} - (\phi(1-\lambda))^t}{1-\phi(1-\lambda)}\right)$$

$$= \frac{1}{1-\phi(1-\lambda)}\left\{\phi(1-\lambda)\sum_{i=0}^{t-2}(1-\lambda)^{2i} - (\phi(1-\lambda))^t \sum_{i=0}^{t-2}\left(\frac{1-\lambda}{\phi}\right)^i\right\}$$

$$= \frac{1}{1-\phi(1-\lambda)}\left\{\phi(1-\lambda)\left(\frac{1-(1-\lambda)^{2(t-1)}}{\lambda(2-\lambda)}\right) - (\phi(1-\lambda))^t \sum_{i=0}^{t-2}\left(\frac{1-\lambda}{\phi}\right)^i\right\}$$

$$= \frac{1}{(1-\phi(1-\lambda))}\left\{\frac{\phi(1-\lambda)}{\lambda(2-\lambda)}(1-(1-\lambda)^{2(t-1)}) - (\phi(1-\lambda))^t \sum_{i=0}^{t-2}\left(\frac{1-\lambda}{\phi}\right)^i\right\}$$

$$(A5)$$

Inserting the expanded sum back into the variance calculation we obtain

$$Var(Z_t) = \frac{\lambda\gamma(0)}{(2-\lambda)}(1-(1-\lambda)^{2t}) + \frac{\lambda}{(2-\lambda)}\frac{2(1-\lambda)\gamma(1)}{(1-\phi(1-\lambda))}(1-(1-\lambda)^{2(t-1)})$$

$$- \frac{2\lambda^2\gamma(1)(\phi(1-\lambda))^t}{\phi(1-\phi(1-\lambda))}\sum_{i=0}^{t-2}\left(\frac{1-\lambda}{\phi}\right)^i$$

$$(A6)$$

If we let $t \to \infty$, we obtain, the last term goes to zero, and the asymptotic variance is equal to

$$Var(Z_t) = \frac{\lambda\gamma(0)}{(2-\lambda)} + \frac{\lambda}{(2-\lambda)}\frac{2(1-\lambda)\gamma(1)}{(1-\phi(1-\lambda))} = \frac{\lambda}{(2-\lambda)}\left\{\gamma(0) + \frac{2(1-\lambda)}{(1-\phi(1-\lambda))}\gamma(1)\right\}$$

$$= \frac{\lambda\sigma^2}{(2-\lambda)(1-\phi^2)}\left\{1+\theta^2 + 2\phi\theta + \frac{2(1-\lambda)(1-\phi\theta)(\phi-\theta)}{(1-\phi(1-\lambda))}\right\}.$$

$$(A7)$$

Note that if ϕ and θ are both set equal to zero, the variance terms are, as expected, equivalent to those of the white noise (WN) case given in Equations A8 and A9.

The variance of EWMA statistic assuming AR(p) noise

The autoregressive process of order p, AR(p), is defined as

$$X_t = \phi_1 X_{t-1} + \phi_2 X_{t-2} + \quad + \phi_p X_{t-p} + Z_t \tag{A8}$$

where $\{Z_t\} \sim$ WN(0, σ^2), and $\theta_1, \ldots \theta_p$ are constants. The autocorrelation function for an AR(p) process is given by

$$\gamma(k) = \sum_{m=1}^{p} A_m G_m^{-h} \tag{A9}$$

where $G_m, m = 1, \ldots p$, are the roots of

$$1 - \phi_1 z - \phi_2 z^2 + \quad - \phi_p z^p = 0 \tag{A10}$$

and A_m are constants (Brockwell & Davis, 2002).

In a similar manner as outlined in the ARMA(1,1) case, the variance for the EWMA statistic under AR(p) noise can be expressed as

$$Var(Z_t) = \lambda^2 \sum_{i=0}^{t-1} \sum_{j=0}^{t-2} (1-\lambda)^i (1-\lambda)^j \gamma(i-j)$$

$$= \lambda^2 \sum_{i=0}^{t-1} (1-\lambda)^{2i} \gamma(0) + 2\lambda^2 \sum_{i=0}^{t-2} \sum_{j=i+1}^{t-1} (1-\lambda)^i (1-\lambda)^j \left(\sum_{m=1}^{p} A_m G_m^{-(j-i)} \right)$$

$$= \frac{\lambda^2 \gamma(0)}{\lambda(2-\lambda)} (1-(1-\lambda)^{2t}) + 2\lambda^2 \sum_{m=1}^{p} A_m \left(\sum_{i=0}^{t-2} [(1-\lambda)G_m]^i \sum_{j=i+1}^{t-1} \left(\frac{1-\lambda}{G_m} \right)^j \right)$$

$$\tag{A11}$$

Under the additional assumption that $|(1-\lambda)G_m^{-1}|<1$, the last sum can be written

$$\sum_{i=0}^{t-2}[(1-\lambda)G_m]^i\sum_{j=i+1}^{t-2}((1-\lambda)G_m^{-1})^j+\sum_{i=0}^{t-2}[(1-\lambda)G_m]^i\left[\frac{((1-\lambda)G_m^{-1})^{i+1}((1-\lambda)G_m^{-1})^t}{1-((1-\lambda)G_m^{-1})}\right]$$

$$=\left[\frac{G_m}{G_m-(1-\lambda)}\right]\left[((1-\lambda)G_m^{-1})\sum_{i=0}^{t-2}(1-\lambda)^{2i}-((1-\lambda)G_m^{-1})^t\sum_{i=0}^{t-2}[(1-\lambda)G_m]^i\right]$$

$$=\left[\frac{G_m}{G_m-(1-\lambda)}\right]\left[((1-\lambda)G_m^{-1})\frac{1}{\lambda(2-\lambda)}(1-(1-\lambda)^{2(t-1)})\right.$$

$$\left.-((1-\lambda)G_m^{-1})^t\sum_{i=0}^{t-2}[(1-\lambda)G_m]^i\right] \tag{A12}$$

Inserting the expanded sum back into the variance calculation, we obtain

$$Var(Z_t)=\frac{\lambda\gamma(0)}{(2-\lambda)}(1-(1-\lambda)^{2t})+2\lambda^2$$

$$\times\sum_{m=1}^{p}\frac{A_mG_m}{G_m-(1-\lambda)}\left[\frac{(1-\lambda)}{G_m\lambda(2-\lambda)}(1-(1-\lambda)^{2(t-1)})-\left(\frac{1-\lambda}{G_m}\right)^t\sum_{i=0}^{t-2}[(1-\lambda)G_m]^i\right] \tag{A13}$$

For the special case $p=1$, we have an AR(1) process, and we can write $A_1=\frac{\sigma^2}{1-\phi^2},G_1=\frac{1}{\phi}$, and $\gamma(0)=A_1$. Using these parameters, if $|\phi(1-\lambda)|<1$, we can write

$$Var(Z_t)=\frac{\lambda}{(2-\lambda)}\frac{\sigma^2}{(1-\phi^2)}(1-(1-\lambda)^{2t})+2\lambda^2\frac{\sigma^2}{(1-\phi^2)}\frac{1}{(1-\phi(1-\lambda))}$$

$$\times\left[\frac{(1-\lambda)\phi}{\lambda(2-\lambda)}(1-(1-\lambda)^{2(t-1)})-(\phi(1-\lambda))^t\sum_{i=0}^{t-2}\left[\frac{(1-\lambda)}{\phi}\right]^i\right]$$

$$=\frac{\sigma^2}{(1-\phi^2)}\lambda^2\left\{\frac{(1-(1-\lambda)^{2t}}{\lambda(2-\lambda)}+\frac{2\phi(1-\lambda)(1-(1-\lambda)^{2(t-1)}}{\lambda(2-\lambda)(1-\phi(1-\lambda))}\right.$$

$$\left.-\frac{2(\phi(1-\lambda))^t}{(1-\phi(1-\lambda))}\sum_{i=0}^{t-2}\left[\frac{(1-\lambda)}{\phi}\right]^i\right\} \tag{A14}$$

If we let $t \to \infty$, we obtain the asymptotic variance:

$$Var(Z_t) = \frac{\sigma^2}{(1-\phi^2)} \lambda^2 \left\{ \frac{1}{\lambda(2-\lambda)} + \frac{2\phi(1-\lambda)}{\lambda(2-\lambda)(1-\phi(1-\lambda))} - 0 \right\}$$

$$= \frac{\sigma^2}{(1-\phi^2)} \frac{\lambda}{(2-\lambda)} \left\{ 1 + \frac{2\phi(1-\lambda)}{(1-\phi(1-\lambda))} \right\}$$

$$= \frac{\sigma^2}{(1-\phi^2)} \frac{\lambda}{(2-\lambda)} \left\{ \frac{(1+\phi(1-\lambda))}{(1-\phi(1-\lambda))} \right\}. \tag{A15}$$

This is the result that was given by Schmid (1997).

appendix three B

Maximum likelihood estimation of change point

An alternative approach to estimating the CP is to calculate the maximum likelihood estimator of τ. Let us assume that the parameters θ_0, θ_1, and τ are all unknown and need to be estimated, but that the covariance matrix Σ is known from the EWMA stage of the analysis. Let $\mathbf{S}(\tau)$ be the mean vector, where the τ first elements are equal to θ_0, and the remaining $N - \tau$ are equal to θ_1. The log-likelihood function for the model described in Equations 1 to 3 can be written as

$$l(\theta_0, \theta_1, \tau \mid \mathbf{X}) = -\frac{N}{2} \log |\Sigma| - \frac{1}{2} (\mathbf{X} - \mathbf{S}(\tau))^T \Sigma^{-1} (\mathbf{X} - \mathbf{S}(\tau)) + const \quad \text{(A16)}$$

The maximum likelihood estimators are given by the values that maximize this function. Under the assumption of *iid* noise, the nonconstant terms of the log likelihood can be written

$$l(\theta_0, \theta_1, \tau \mid \mathbf{X}) = -\frac{1}{2\sigma^2} \left[\sum_{i=1}^{\tau} (X_i - \theta_0)^2 + \sum_{i=t+1}^{T} (X_i - \theta_1)^2 \right] \quad \text{(A17)}$$

The maximum likelihood estimators for θ_0 and θ_1 conditional on $\tau = t$ are given by

$$\hat{\theta}_0^t = \frac{1}{t} \sum_{i=1}^{t} X_i \quad \text{(A18)}$$

and

$$\hat{\theta}_1^t = \frac{1}{T-t} \sum_{i=t+1}^{T} X_i. \quad \text{(A19)}$$

The log likelihood maximized over θ_0 and θ_1 conditional on $\tau = t$ becomes

$$l(t|\mathbf{X}) = -\frac{1}{2\sigma^2}\left[\sum_{i=1}^{t}\left(X_i - \hat{\theta}_0^T\right)^2 + \sum_{i=t+1}^{T}\left(X_i - \hat{\theta}_1^t\right)^2\right]$$

(A20)

To simplify the calculation of the MLE of τ, it is beneficial to remove the inclusion of t from the bounds of the sums in Equation A20. To do so, we begin by rewriting the first sum in the equation as

$$\sum_{i=1}^{t}\left(X_i - \hat{\theta}_0^t\right)^2 = \sum_{i=1}^{t}\left(X_i^2 - 2X_i\hat{\theta}_0^t + \hat{\theta}_0^{t2}\right)$$

$$= \sum_{i=1}^{t}X_i^2 - 2t\hat{\theta}_0^{t2} + t\hat{\theta}_0^{t2}$$

$$= \sum_{i=1}^{t}X_i^2 - t\hat{\theta}_0^{t2}$$

$$= \sum_{i=1}^{T}X_i^2 - \sum_{i=t+1}^{T}X_i^2 - t\hat{\theta}_0^{t2}$$

$$= \sum_{i=1}^{T}\left(X_i^2 - 2X_i\hat{\theta}_0^T + \hat{\theta}_0^{T2}\right) + T\hat{\theta}_0^{T2} - \sum_{i=t+1}^{T}X_i^2 - t\hat{\theta}_0^{t2}$$

$$= \sum_{i=1}^{T}\left(X_i - \hat{\theta}_0^T\right)^2 + T\hat{\theta}_0^{T2} - \sum_{i=t+1}^{T}X_i^2 - t\hat{\theta}_0^{t2}$$

(A21)

Similarly, the second sum can be written

$$\sum_{i=t+1}^{T}\left(X_i - \hat{\theta}_1^t\right)^2 = \sum_{i=t+1}^{T}X_i^2 - (T-t)\hat{\theta}_1^{t2}$$

(A22)

Adding these two sums gives

$$\sum_{i=1}^{T}\left(X_i - \hat{\theta}_0^T\right)^2 + T\hat{\theta}_0^{T2} - t\hat{\theta}_0^{t2} + (T-t)\hat{\theta}_1^{t2}$$

(A23)

Now, by noting that

$$T\hat{\theta}_0^{T2} = T\left[\frac{1}{T}\sum_{i=1}^{T}X_i\right]^2 = \frac{1}{T}\left[t\hat{\theta}_0^t + (T-t)\hat{\theta}_1^t\right]^2$$

(A24)

we can write

$$T\hat{\theta}_0^{T2} - t\hat{\theta}_0^{t2} - (T-t)\hat{\theta}_1^{t2}$$

$$= \frac{1}{T}\left[t^2\hat{\theta}_0^{t2} + 2t(T-t)\hat{\theta}_0^t\hat{\theta}_1^t + (T-t)^2\hat{\theta}_1^{t2} - tT\hat{\theta}_0^{t2} - T(T-t)\hat{\theta}_1^{t2}\right]$$

$$= \frac{1}{T}\left[-t(T-t)\hat{\theta}_0^{t2} + 2t(T-t)\hat{\theta}_0^t\hat{\theta}_1^t + (T-t)(T-t-T)\hat{\theta}_1^{t2}\right]$$

$$= \frac{t(T-t)}{T}\left[\hat{\theta}_0^{t2} - 2\hat{\theta}_0^t\hat{\theta}_1^t + \hat{\theta}_1^{t2}\right]$$

$$= \frac{t(T-t)}{T}\left[\hat{\theta}_0^t - \hat{\theta}_1^t\right]^2 \tag{A25}$$

Combining these results, the log likelihood maximized over θ_0 and θ_1 conditional on $\tau = 1$ becomes

$$l(t|\mathbf{X}) = -\frac{1}{2\sigma^2}\left[\sum_{i=1}^{T}\left(X_i - \hat{\theta}_0^T\right)^2 - t(T-t)\left(\hat{\theta}_0^t - \hat{\theta}_1^t\right)^2 / T\right] \tag{A26}$$

The MLE of τ is therefore

$$\hat{\tau} = \underset{1 \le t \le T}{\arg\max}\left\{t(T-t)\left(\hat{\theta}_0^t - \hat{\theta}_1^t\right)^2 / T\right\} \tag{A27}$$

where we can find $\hat{\tau}$ by searching iteratively over all values of t.

Confidence intervals for change points

Once τ is estimated, it is desirable to compute confidence intervals for τ, which provide the basis for tests of differences in CPs among brain regions and among groups of individuals. The asymptotic distribution of the MLE for τ can be calculated (Hinkley, 1970) and theoretically used to obtain confidence intervals for the time of the process change. Once we have obtained the confidence intervals for the CPs, we can use them to test whether regions differ in onset time. Instead of using the exact distribution, it is common to use the log-likelihood function, defined in Equation A14 to obtain a confidence set for the CP. The confidence set we will use is of the form

$$\Omega = \left\{t | l(\hat{\tau}) - l(t) < D\right\} \tag{A28}$$

There are a variety of candidates for the value D. It has been suggested (Siegmund, 1986) that one should use

$$D = -\ln(1 - \sqrt{1 - \alpha})$$
(A29)

to obtain a $100(1 - \alpha)\%$ confidence set for the CP. Simulation studies (Pignatiello & Samuel, 2001) indicated that this value of D gives good results.

appendix three C

EM algorithm for
Gaussian mixture model

E-step: $\hat{\gamma}_i = \dfrac{\hat{p}f_{X_2}(x_i \mid \hat{\theta}_j, \hat{\Sigma}_j)}{(1-\hat{p})f_{X_1}(x_i \mid \hat{\theta}_j, \hat{\Sigma}_j) + \hat{p}f_{X_2}(x_i \mid \hat{\theta}_j, \hat{\Sigma}_j)}$ for $i = 1,\quad T$

M-step: $\hat{p} = \dfrac{1}{T}\displaystyle\sum_{i=1}^{T}\hat{\gamma}_i,$ $\hat{\theta}_j = \dfrac{\Sigma_{i=1}^{T}\hat{\gamma}_i x_i}{\Sigma_{i=1}^{T}\hat{\gamma}_i}$ $\displaystyle\sum_j = \dfrac{\Sigma_{i=1}^{T}\hat{\gamma}_i(x_i - \hat{\theta}_j)^T}{\Sigma_{i=1}^{T}\hat{\gamma}_i}$

for $j = 1, 2.$

appendix three D

Estimating variance components using restricted maximum likelihood

In our approach, we estimate the variance components present in the HEWMA model using restricted maximum likelihood (ReML). Our approach is equivalent to that used in SPM, which uses an EM algorithm to estimate the parameters of interest. To simplify notation, we begin by rewriting the problem in matrix form. Let

$$Z_G = [Z^1 Z^2 \quad Z^m]^T \tag{A30}$$

be the combined vector of EWMA statistics for all m subjects. Recall that in the hierarchical model we can write the covariance matrix for each individual subject as $V_1^* = \Sigma_i^* + \Sigma_B^*$. Hence, it follows that the covariance function for Z_G can be written

$$V_G^* = \begin{bmatrix} V_1^* & & & 0 \\ & V_2^* & & \\ & & \ddots & \\ 0 & & & V_m^* \end{bmatrix} \tag{A31}$$

Further, let $G = [I_T I_T \ldots I_T]^T$ be an $mT \times T$ matrix in which I_T is the indicator matrix of dimension T. Using this notation, the HEWMA statistic Z_{pop} can be expressed as

$$Z_G = GZ_{pop} + D_{pop} \tag{A32}$$

where D_{pop} is $N(0, V_G^*)$. We can estimate the HEWMA statistic using generalized least squares regression:

$$\hat{Z}_{pop} = \left(G^T V_G^{*-1} G\right)^{-1} G^T V_G^{*-1} Z$$

$$= \left[\sum_{i=1}^{m} V_i^{*-1}\right]^{-1} \sum_{i=1}^{m} V_i^{*-1} Z^i.$$

(A33)

The covariance matrix for the HEWMA statistic can be written as

$$V_{pop}^* = G^T V_G^{*-1} G = \sum_{i=1}^{m} V_i^{*-1}$$

(A34)

To estimate the HEWMA statistic and its covariance matrix, we need an estimate of V_i^*. In our approach, the within-subject component Σ_i^* is assumed known from the first level. The general form of Σ_B^* is also assumed known up to a scaling term. Hence, we can write the total variance for subject i as $V_i^* = \alpha Q + \Sigma_i^*$, where α is the unknown and Q the known part of Σ_B^*.

The problem of estimating the parameter α is similar to the variance component estimation procedure performed in SPM2 (Friston et al., 2002). There, they find the so-called hyperparameter using an EM algorithm, and we follow the same general outline here. Let $V_G^* = \alpha Q_G + \Sigma_G$, where

$$Q_G = \begin{bmatrix} Q & & & 0 \\ & Q & & \\ & & \ddots & \\ 0 & & & Q \end{bmatrix} \quad \text{and} \quad \Sigma_G = \begin{bmatrix} \Sigma_1^* & & & 0 \\ & \Sigma_2^* & & \\ & & \ddots & \\ 0 & & & \Sigma_m^* \end{bmatrix}.$$

(A35)

Perform the following two steps until convergence:

E-step: $V_G^* = \alpha Q_G + \Sigma_G$

$$C = \left(G^T V_G^{*-1} G\right)^{-1}$$

M-step: $= P = V_G^{*-1} - V_G^{*-1} G C G^T V_G^{*-1}$

$$g = -\frac{1}{2} tr(P Q_G) + \frac{1}{2} tr\left(P^T Q_G P Z_G Z_G^T\right)$$

$$H = \frac{1}{2} tr\left(P^T Q_G P Q_G\right)$$

$$\alpha = \alpha + H^{-1} g.$$

Author Index

A

Adali, T. 151, 152
Aguirre, G. K. 157
Aiken, L. K. 181
Akaike, H. 137
Alpert, A. 97
American Psychiatric Association 89, 90
Andrews, D. W. K. 185
Andrews, H. 11, 186, 198
Arnett, J. J. 61, 62
Ashburner, J. 157
Aziz, N. 165

B

Bachman, J. G. 6, 86, 87
Bai, J. 184, 185
Baltes, P. B. 106
Barber, J. S. 42
Barker, T. 8
Barron, J. L. 170
Bates, D. M. 109
Bauer, D. J. 83, 94
Beal, S. L. 109, 110, 117
Beckmann, C. F. 151
Bentler, P. M. 92
Bergman, A. 62
Best, N. 109, 116, 145
Betts, L. R. 177
Bieling, P. 177
Bifulco, A. 11, 186, 198
Billings, A. G. 190
Blishen, B. R. 26
Blumstein, A. 49, 83, 93
Boivin, M. 32
Boles, S. A. 62
Bolger, N. 11, 131, 132, 133, 135, 137, 138,
    139, 140, 144, 146
Bollen, K. A. 90, 92, 95, 98

Bonanno, G. A. 132, 146
Borge, A. 30
Boulerice, B. 25
Bowden, E. M. 177
Bowles, R. 110
Bradley, M. M. 151
Bradway, K. P. 110
Brame, R. 26, 83, 85, 93
Brannan, S. K. 177
Brant, L. J. 109
Breiter, H. C. 166, 175
Brenner, M. 190
Breslow, M. J. 133
Broidy, L. 26, 49, 83, 97
Brook, J. 190
Brumback, B. 9, 41, 42
Bryk, A. S. 49, 59, 72, 90, 99, 107, 135
Burke, C. T. 11, 131, 132, 133, 135, 137, 138,
    139, 140, 144, 146
Buschke, H. 6, 108, 109
Bushway, S. 49, 83, 97
Buxton, R. B. 176

C

Calhoun, V. D. 151, 152
Campbell, D. T. 83
Capaldi, D. M. 25
Caplan, R. D. 190
Carlin, B. P. 116
Carlson, R. L. 151
Carnelley, K. B. 131, 132, 133, 144, 146
Carr, D. 136
Carrig, M. M. 82, 93
Carroll, W. K. 26
Carter, H. B. 109
Carver, C. S. 132
Caspi, A. 10, 25, 26, 82, 89, 100
Catalano, R. 190
Cattell, R. B. 106, 121, 124, 196

Cauffman, E. 49, 83, 97
Charlebois, P. 9
Chau, W. K. 152
Chen, H. 2, 11, 62, 78, 184
Cheng, P. W. 153
Cheong, Y. F. 59
Cherry, S. R. 166
Chong, T. T. L. 185
Chopra, S. 151, 170
Chow, G. C. 184
Christoff, K. 153
Chronicle, E. P. 177
Claes, M. 18, 26
Clausen, J. A. 5
Coghill, R. C. 152
Cohen, J. 49, 65, 83, 181, 186
Cohen, P. 2, 11, 62, 65, 78, 181, 184, 186, 190,
    191, 198
Colarusso, C. A. 62
Congdon, P. 109, 117
Congdon, R. 59
Conger, R. D. 190
Cook, D. G. 107
Cook, T. D. 83
Cooper, J. C. 151, 170, 175
Cooper, M. L. 190
Costello, A. J. 190
Cote, S. 30
Cottler, L. 89
Cowles, K. 116
Crawford, T. 2, 62, 78, 191
Crosby, L. 25
Cross, S. E. 63
Cudeck, R. 107, 108, 109, 115, 118, 124, 132,
    136, 146
Cumsille, P. 97, 98
Curran, P. J. 10, 82, 83, 90, 93, 94, 95, 98
Cuthbert, B. N. 151
Cwi, J. 186, 197

D

Davidian, M. 106, 109
Davis, R. A.
Deci, E. L. 62
Decker, L. R. 151
Deckersbach, T. 175
Derzon, J. H. 26
Desmarais-Gervais, L. 9
D'Esposito, M. 157
Dickerson, S. S. 165

Dickson, N. 25, 26
Diggle, P. J. 106, 107
Dinges, D. F. 175, 176
Dishion, T. J. 25, 26
Dodge, K. 26
Donaldson, G. A. 63
Donovan, J. E. 87
Dooley, D. 190
Dorfman, J. 153
Dougherty, D. D. 175
Du Toit, S. H. C. 107, 109, 124
Dulcan, M. K. 190
Duncan, S. C. 97
Duncan, T. E. 97

E

Eaton, W. W. 186, 197
Edelbrock, C. S. 190
Eisenberger, N. I. 166, 175
Elder, G. H. 5, 33, 130, 190
Elliott, D. S. 87
Eron, L. D. 29

F

Fagot, B. I. 25
Fahey, J. L. 165
Farrington, D. P. 18, 25, 26, 83
Fenn, C. B. 190
Fera, F. 151
Fergusson, D. M. 26
Ferrer, E. 124
Ferrer-Caja, E. 106
Finney, J. W. 190
Fitzsimmons, J. R. 151
Fleck, J. 177
Forgatch, M. S. 25
Frank, L. R. 176
Fredrickson, B. L. 153
Freeman-Gallant, A. 25
Friston, K. J. 150, 157
Frone, M. R. 190
Fuhrmann, G. 177
Fuller, W. A. 107
Furlan, P. M. 175, 176

G

Gabrieli, J. D. 151, 170, 175
Gagnon, C. 9

Gallant, A. R. 107
Garson, C. 177
Ge, X. 190
Gehlert, D. R. 170
Gilks, W. R. 109
Gilligan, C. 2, 63, 78
Giltinan, D. M. 106, 109
Glaser, D. E. 157
Glueck, E. 9, 39, 43, 45, 46
Glueck, S. 9, 39, 43, 45, 46
Goldapple, K. 177
Goldring, E. 89
Gordon, K. 2, 11, 184, 186, 198
Gotham, H. J. 86
Gottfredson, M. 25, 87, 89
Grafton, S. T. 166
Grant, B. F. 83
Grimm, K. 110
Gross, J. J. 170, 175
Gruenewald, T. L. 165

H

Haapanen, R. 83, 85, 93
Haas, E. 26
Hagan, J. 18
Hall, C. B. 6, 107, 108, 109
Hamagami, F. 2, 106, 110, 114, 184
Hammarstrom, A. 190
Hanna, E. Z. 83
Hansen, B. E. 185
Hansson, R. O. 130
Harding, D. J. 40
Harford, T. C. 90, 95
Haring, M. H. 132, 146
Hariri, A. R. 151
Harring, J. R. 132
Hartmark, C. 2, 184
Hasson, U. 177
Haviland, D. M. 33
Hay, D. 26
Heimer, K. 38
Helthoff, K. 186, 197
Helzer, J. E. 89
Henrich, G. 196
Henry, B. 89
Henson, R. N. 157
Hernán, M. Á. 9, 41, 42
Hernandez, L. 150, 152, 157, 165
Herzog, A. R. 133
Heusmann, L. R. 29

Hirschi, T. 25, 87, 89
Hoffman, J. 63
Hogan, J. W. 43
Holmes, A. P. 158
Holmes, C. J. 166
Holyoak, K. J. 153
Hong, G. 41, 49
Horn, J. L. 124
Horney, J. 85
Horney, J. D. 49, 50
Hornik, K. 184, 187
House, J. S. 133, 136
Huber, D. 196
Huizinga, D. 87
Humphreys, K. 190
Hussong, A. M. 10, 82, 90

J

Janlert, U. 190
Jessor, S. L. 87
Jessor, R. 87
Johnson, J. G. 2, 62, 78, 190, 191
Johnston, L. D. 6, 86, 87
Jonides, J. 150, 151, 152, 157
Jung-Beeman, M. 177

K

Kalas, R. 190
Kasen, S. 2, 11, 62, 78, 186, 190
Kasl, S. V. 190
Katz, M. 6, 108, 109
Kemeny, M. E. 165
Kennedy, S. 177
Kenny, M. E. 63
Kessler, R. C. 133, 136
Kiebel, S. 157
Kiehl, K. A. 152
Kilgard, M. P. 177
Kim, J. E. 196
Kinderman, T. A. 84
Kinney, A. M. 133
Kirschbaum, C. 165
Klaric, S. H. 190
Klebe, K. J. 107, 108, 109, 115, 118, 124, 136, 146
Kleiber, C. 184, 187
Klug, G. 196
Ko, H. 43
Korczykowski, M. 175, 176

Kounios, J. 177
Kourtzi, Z. 177
Koyama, T. 152
Kroger, J. K. 153
Krohn, M. D. 19, 25
Kuo, L. 6, 108, 109

L

Lacourse, E. 8, 18, 26
Lang, P. J. 151
Larkin, G. R. 153
Lau, M. 177
Laub, J. H. 5, 9, 18, 38, 39, 43, 44, 45, 46, 49, 50, 58, 59, 83, 85, 100
Laurienti, P. J. 152
Lebron, K. 170
Lefkowitz, M. M. 29
Lehman, D. R. 132, 146
Leisch, F. 184, 187
Leonard, K. E. 86
Leve, C. S. 25
Levy, I. 177
Li, F. 97
Liang, K.-Y. 106, 107
Liberzon, I. 151, 170
Lieberman, M. D. 166, 175
Linde, A. 116
Lindquist, M. 11, 150, 152, 157
Lindstrom, M. J. 109
Lipsey, M. W. 26
Lipton, R. 6, 107, 109
Liu, T. T. 176
Lizotte, A. J. 25
Loeber, R. 26
Loh, R. 175
Lorenz, F. O. 190
Lucas, J. M. 155
Lunn, D. 109, 145
Lyketsos, C. G. 186, 197
Lynam, D. R. 89

M

MacCallum, R. C. 92
MacGregor, J. N. 177
MacKenzie, D. L. 38
MacMillan, R. 18
Madson, L. 63
Mahler, M. 62
Mahurin, R. K. 177

Malach, R. 177
Marci, C. 175
Marshall, I. H. 49, 50, 85
Matsueda, R. L. 38
Mattay, V. S. 151
Maughan, B. 85
Mayberg, H. S. 177
Mayer, K. H. 43
Mazerolle, P. 49, 83, 85, 97
Mazziotta, J. C. 166
McArdle, J. J. 2, 90, 106, 110, 114, 116, 124, 184
McGinnis, S. 177
McHaffie, J. G. 152
McIntosh, A. R. 152
McKeown, M. J. 151
McMahon, R. J. 84
Medici-Skaggs, N. 25
Menard, S. 87
Mendes, C. F. 190
Meredith, W. 90, 110
Mero, R. P. 133
Merzenich, M. M. 177
Moffitt, T. E. 10, 25, 26, 89, 100
Moffitt, R. 40
Molenberghs, G. 106
Montgomery, D. C. 157
Moore, C. 26
Moos, B. S. 190
Moos, R. H. 190
Morgan, S. L. 40
Morrell, C. H. 109
Moulder, B. 151
Mulvey, E. P. 83, 93
Munson, J. A. 84
Murphy, S. A. 42
Muthén, B. O. 19, 90, 95
Muthén, L. K. 90

N

Nagin, D. S. 2, 8, 9, 18, 19, 20, 25, 26, 27, 32, 33, 38, 83, 85, 93
Nesse, R. M. 136
Nesselroade, J. R. 106, 196
Nestadt, G. 186, 197
Neubauer, A. S. 152
Nichols, T. E. 151, 158
Nir, Y. 177
Nishina, K. 158
Noll, D. C. 165

O

O'Malley, P. M. 6, 86, 87
Ochsner, K. N. 151, 170, 175
Olweus, D. 29
Ormerod, T. C. 177
Osgood, D. W. 85, 87, 88
Osgood, W. 49, 50

P

Pagani, L. 9, 18, 25
Patterson, G. R. 25
Pears, K. C. 25
Pearson, J. D. 109
Peirce, R. S. 190
Pekar, J. J. 151, 152
Perron, P. 184, 185
Pettit, B. 38
Phan, K. L. 151, 170
Phillips, C. 157
Pickles, A. 6, 85
Pine, F. 62
Pinheiro, J. C. 109
Piquero, A. 49, 83, 85, 93, 97
Ploberger, W. 185
Plummer, M. 116
Pogarsky, G. 25
Poulin, F. 25
Prabhakaran, V. 153
Price, R. H. 190
Protzner, A. B. 152

Q

Quandt, R. E. 184
Qui, P. 14
Quinton, D. 85
Quirk, G. J. 170

R

Radloff, L. S. 137
Rando, T. A. 145
Rao, H. 175, 176
Rapp, S. S. 190
Rauch, S. L. 175
Raudenbush, S. W. 41, 49, 59, 72, 90, 99, 107, 135
Ray, R. D. 151, 170, 175
Reiger, D. A. 83

Richardson, S. 109
Rindskopf, D. 9, 70
Roberts, S. W. 152
Robertson, E. R. 151, 170, 175
Robins, J. 9, 40, 41, 42, 48
Robins, L. N. 83, 89
Rosen, B. R. 166, 175
Rosenbaum, P. 9, 33, 40, 58
Roth, J. 49
Rothbard, J. C. 86
Rowan, B. 41, 49
Rowe, D. C. 88
Roy, M. P. 165
Rubin, D. 9, 33, 40
Russo, G. K. 170
Rutter, M. 3, 5, 6, 18, 30, 82, 85, 88, 89, 100, 213
Ryan, R. M. 62

S

Saccucci, M. S. 155
Salthouse, T. A. 124
Sampson, R. J. 5, 9, 18, 39, 43, 44, 45, 49, 50, 58, 59, 83, 84, 85, 100
Sarkheil, P. 177
SAS Institute 145
Sayer, A. G. 83, 97, 98
Scarr, S. 6
Scheier, M. F. 132
Schlegel, R. E. 152
Schmid, W. 157, 158
Schmidt McCollam, K. M. 196
Schöne, A. 158
Schulenberg, J. 6, 86
Schut, H. 130
Schwartz, B. S. 124
Schwarzbach, J. 151
Scott, J. D. 151
Segal, Z. 177
Seguin, J. R. 32
Sejnowski, T. J. 151
Serences, J. T. 151
Shadish, W. R. 83
Shehab, R. L. 152
Sheiner, L. B. 109, 110, 117
Sher, K. J. 86
Shin, L. M. 175
Shishkin, S. L. 6
Shrout, P. E. 11, 131, 135, 137, 138, 139, 140, 144, 146
Silva, J. A. 177

Silva, P. A. 10, 25, 26, 88, 89, 100
Silver, R. C. 131
Simons, R. L. 190
Singer, J. D. 72, 136
Skinner, E. A. 84
Skodol, A. 190, 191
Sliwinski, M. 6, 107, 108, 109
Smith, A. F. M. 107
Smith, C. A. 25
Smith, E. E. 151
Smith, R. S. 5
Smith, S. M. 151
Sneed, J. R. 2, 9, 62, 78, 191
Sonnega, J. 132, 136, 146
Spiegelhalter, D. J. 109, 116, 145
Spieker, S. J. 84
Stanton, W. R. 10, 25, 26, 88
Steinmetz, M. A. 151
Steptoe, A. 165
Stevens, M. C. 152
Stewart, W. F. 107, 109, 124
Stoolmiller, M. 25
Stouthamer-Loeber, M. 100
Stroebe, M. S. 130
Stroebe, W. 130
Strycker, L. A. 97
Sugarman, A. 196

T

Taylor, S. F. 151, 170
Tekell, J. L. 177
Tessitore, A. 151
Thomas, A. 109, 145
Thornberry, T. P. 19, 25
Tisak, J. 90
Tobin, K. 25
Tremblay, R. E. 8, 9, 18, 19, 20, 25, 26, 30, 32
Tugade, M. M. 153
Tweed, R. G. 132, 146

V

Vaillant, G. E. 86
Vazquez, A. 165
Verbeke, G. 106
Verbitsky, N. 42
Vines, K. 116
Vinokur, A. D. 190
Visher, C. 49

Vitaro, F. 9, 18, 26
Vonesh, E. F. 109

W

Wadsworth, K. N. 6, 86
Wager, T. D. 11, 150, 151, 152, 153, 157, 165, 170
Walder, L. O. 29
Wang, J. 175, 176
Wang, L. 110, 116, 124
Waugh, C. E. 153
Weinberger, D. R. 151
Weiss, B. 63
Welchman, A. E. 177
Werner, E. E. 5
West, S. G. 181
West, D. J. 18
Western, B. 38
Wetmore, G. S. 175, 176
Wheaton, B. 18
Willett, J. B. 72, 83, 136
Williams, K. D. 166, 175
Willoughby, M. T. 94
Wilson, G. 190
Wimer, C. 9, 38, 44, 49, 59
Winship, C. 40
Wirth, R. J. 93
Wolfinger, R. D. 109
Wong, E. C. 176
Woodcock, R. W. 106
Woods, R. P. 166
Worsley, K. J. 150
Wortman, C. B. 131, 132, 133, 136, 144, 146

Y

Ya, A. 6
Yantis, S. 151
Ying, J. 6, 108, 109
Yoerger, K. L. 25

Z

Zarahn, E. 157
Zeger, S. L. 106, 107
Zeileis, A. 184, 187
Zelazo, P. 32
Zhao, Z. 153
Zoccolillo, M. 32

Subject Index

A

Age-based models, 106
Aggression, *see* Antisocial behavior
AIC, *see* Fit indices
Alcohol abuse, 27, *see also* Snares
    hypothesis
Antisocial behavior, 6, 9, 10, 17–33, 37–56
    desistence, 81–101
    measurement, 26, 45–46, 89–90
Autocorrelation, 116, 155, 156, 158, 188,
    221, 223
Autonomy, 62–63
Autoregression, 163, 184, 185, 187

B

Bayesian,
    information criterion, 27
    models, 109–110, 116–124, 145

C

Centered data, 68, 74, 143, 168, 209
Change point, 188
Confounding factors, 41
Control chart, 154–155
Counterfactual model, 9, 37–56
Crime, 9, 37–56; *see also* Antisocial
    behavior

D

Data analysis sequence, 68
Data sources
    Americans' Changing Lives Survey, 133
    authors, 165, 178
    Bradway–McArdle, 110
    Changing Lives of Older Couples, 136
    Dunedin cohort, 88–89
    Glueck & Glueck study of delinquents
        followed–up, 43–44
    Montreal experimental study of boys,
        26–27
    Transitions narratives (Children in the
        Community study), 64–65, 186–187,
        196–197
Delinquency, *see* Antisocial behavior
Developmental trajectories, 13–16, 18, 20,
    25, 92–94, 130, 131
Deviance hypothesis, 88, 90, 97–99
Distributions, 10, 20, 22, 26, 49, 59, 70, 109,
    123, 133, 135, 153–159, 163, 168, 185
    censored normal, 20
    multivariate normal, 135
Drug abuse, *see* Substance abuse
Drug use, 18; *see also* Substance use
Dual trajectory model, 19–24

E

Econometric model, 11, 184–192
Efficiency, 109, 163
Error variance, 4, 155, 157
EWMA (exponentially weighted moving
    average), 153–159
    estimating change points, 158
    hierarchical extensions, 160–162
    multiple change points, 159
Explanation vs prediction, 79

F

Factor analysis, 151, 196, 198, 200–208
Fit indices
    Akaike information criterion (AIC), 27,
        116–118, 137
    Chi square test of fit improvement, 92

CFI: comparative fit index, 92
DIC: Deviance information criterion, 116–118
IFI, 92
Fixed effect, 40, 74, 75, 118, 119, 120, 124, 135, 136, 138, 142
fMRI
    change points in,
    experimental design, 165–166
    image analysis, 166–167
fMRI studies
    arterial spin labeling, 176
    learning effects, 177
    longitudinal studies, 177
    perfusion, 176
    voxel identification, 177

G

Gang membership, 25, 27, 30–31
Gender difference, *see* Sex difference
General deviance hypothesis, 97–99
General linear model, 175
Goodness of fit, 123, 124; *see also* Fit indices
Growth curve, 62, 83–105, 139

H

Hazard ratio, 190; *see also* Regression, Cox
Heterotypic continuity, 82–83, 87–88
Hierarchical analysis, 4, 13, 49, 54, 55, 59, 73, 83, 152, 153, 157, 160, 161, 162, 233; *see also* Multilevel model

I

Intelligence, 44
Interactional theory, 19
Intraindividual change, 82, 83, 88, 92, 106
Intraindividual variability, 106, 114, 124, 217
IPTW (inverse probability of treatment weighting), 37–56

L

Lagged effects, 7, 40, 41, 42, 47–49, 53, 54, 56, 84, 97, 152
Latent growth curve models, 83, 88
    comparison to HLM, 83

Launch hypothesis, 10, 100, 101
    definition, 84–88
    strategy, 90
    test, 94–95
Level, *see also* Multilevel models
    Level 1 (within person), 72
    Level 2 (fixed effects/ across persons), 73–4, 137
Likelihood function, 22
Logistic regression models, 47, 48, 50–53, 68, 69, 74, 191

M

Maximum likelihood, 19, 90, 116, 117, 119, 145, 159, 160, 163, 173, 227–230
Measurement, 26–27, 44–47, 65, 88–90, 110–113, 136–137, 143, 165–167, 188, 197–198
Mixed effect model, 106–110, 113–122, 160, 215–216
Model selection, 27, 70, 72
Monte Carlo integration, 109, 157, 158, 160, 163
Moving average, *see* EWMA
Mplus statistical program, 90–91
Multilevel model, 11, 71, 72, 77, 79, 83, 139, 209
Multinomial logit functions, 22–24
Multiphase models, 106–108; *see also* Spline models

N

Narratives, 1, 9, 12, 13, 14, 64, 65, 67, 184, 186, 188, 189, 191, 192, 193, 196, 197, 208, 210, 213

O

Ordinary least squares, 4

P

Poisson model, 21, 27, 49
PROC NL MIXED program, 116, 117, 215
Propensity, 9, 33, 35, 38–43, 49, 56, 58, 59, 87
Protective factors, 82, 84, 85, 86
Psychopathology, 3, 14, 82, 190–191

R

Random effect, 49, 50, 73, 90, 109, 135, 136, 137, 139, 140, 142, 145, 146, 217
Rasch–scale scores, 110–112
Regression model, 4, 47, 48, 50, 93, 108, 133, 185, 189, 190
  Cox regression, 78, 189–190
  logistic, 22, 191
  Poisson, 21–22, 27, 49
Risk factor, 30, 44, 65
Role structure
  changes as turning point, 198
  differences by SES, 199–208

S

School retention, 18
SES (socio–ecomonic status), 5, 12, 26, 45, 70, 186, 188–191, 199–213
Sex difference, 63, 64, 68, 70, 72, 73, 77, 78, 79, 83, 100, 188–191, 199
Simulation studies in fMRI, 163–170
Skew, 10, 49, 138, 168; *see also* Distribution
Slope, 92–93
Snares hypothesis
  strategy, 90
  test, 95–97, 100
  vs launch hypothesis, 84–85
Social class, *see* SES
Spline models, 108
  alternative non–linear and spline models, 114–116
  test of alternative models, 117–120
Statistical quality control charts, *see* EWMA, 152
Structural change, 1, 12, 14, 184, 185, 187, 196–213
Substance abuse, 10, 82–101, 190, 191, 193
Substance use, 27
Survival analysis, 78

T

Time series, 7, 151, 152, 153, 155, 157, 158, 160, 164, 167, 174, 175, 178, 183–192
Trajectories, 2, 8–16, 18–34, 82, 84, 86, 88, 90, 92–98, 100, 101, 106, 130–132, 135–138, 141, 142, 146, 188, 193, 199–209
Trajectory groups, 18, 23–28
  joint, 21
  membership probability, 18, 29–33
Transitions, 3, 11, 13, 14, 15, 25, 33, 62, 65, 68, 211
Triggers, 3, 5, 7, 19, 32, 109, 130, 176
Turning points
  age–based/ Life stages, 6, 18, 71–76, 106–110, 123, 199–200, 208–209
  as change from a baseline, 158–159
  as change in autoregression, 184–185
  as change in time-based correlation between variables, 208–213
  as change in variable relationships, 199–208
  as change in weighted moving average, 153–157
  as predictors of subsequent status, 190
  definition, 3–8, 18, 38, 64, 78, 130, 184, 196, 208–209
  equivalent forms, 139–142
  precipitating events, 7, 18, 130–131, 185
  predictors of, 188–189

V

Violence, 18–34; *see also* Antisocial behavior
Vulnerability, 9, 19, 25–33, 82

W

WinBugs, 109, 116–120, 123, 145, 216